The Secret Life

of

God

A JOURNEY THROUGH BRITAIN

Alex Klaushofer

Hermes Books

ISBN 978-0-9933236-0-7
Hermes Books
www.thesecretlifeofgod.net

Cover image: Darren Harmon

Contents

Introduction   1
Back to the future   11
Pioneering nuns   38
The green desert   83
Hidden hermits   117
Into the silence   144
Sufi ways   165
Divine music   186
Back to nature   209
The pagan path   233
Druid days   258
The end of the beginning   289
In the garden   311

Notes   324
Acknowledgements   332
Bibliography   334

INTRODUCTION

Show me the place where you were born, they say, and I'll show you who you are. You could add: show me your early surroundings, and I'll show you your spiritual temperament. My first memories of place in the hills of north London: the blank faces of the backs of houses, streets edged by woods full of dripping trees. The voice of a bird cutting through the winter evening, bringing news of the terrible grey world into our suburban home; an all-consuming feeling of bleakness.

Deliverance came in the form of my grandmother, who lived next door. A junior school teacher all her life, she had a gift with small children, instinctively bridging the gap between their world and the adult one with storytelling and nature study. Together, we examined the strange formations that grew in the surrounding gardens, stroking the soft grey buds of pussy willow, fondling drooping catkins and extracting 'money' from honesty's silver purse. The excursions into the wider world with my mother were less idyllic: toiling up and down hills, inhaling the sweet, fusty smell of the Northern line and being pulled along Oxford Street by a hurried, cross hand.

When I was seven we moved to the country. Suddenly my world consisted of huge skies and fields bathed in golden light. My parents had bought, for the price of their London semi, a Victorian country house set in almost three acres. Overlooking the River Severn, it was one of a handful of big houses in a north Gloucestershire village that sprawled away from the main road into

1

a back-country of farmland. Before long, I'd negotiated permission to venture several fields away with a new playmate: I might be only eight, but he was ten and therefore responsible, I informed my mother. Soon, I had the run of the village.

The village was full of children and the places we claimed as our own. In the copse we called Bluebell Woods, the boys blocked the stream with dams of sticks and mud which the girls, feeling sorry for the water – so sparkly and yet so trapped – would then dismantle. Then there was The Swing, a rope which hung like a gallows over the stream running into the river, and the centre of a rough, competitive world full of airborne challenges set by the older boys: you could do a straightforward vault to the opposite bank or risk cracking your skull on the base of the tree with the three hundred and sixty-degree 'round-the-world' swing. I usually went to these hangouts with one of my two local friends: S, who lived in a wooden chalet down the road with her noisy family, and R, who lived in a big pink house on the top of the hill at the edge of the village.

My parents threw themselves into village life, and on Sundays the family went to the square-towered church on the higher ground next to the farm. My mother took her place on the flower rota, and my father walked across the fields to join the bell-ringers on Mondays. I spent Friday evenings in the choir stalls, giggling at the boys opposite and the off-key trilling of the old ladies behind. Soon, my solitary garden play started to include the building of little altars, using fallen slates from the roof, and pads of moss from under the laurel hedge for the sanctuary carpet. I decked the altars with fabric from my collection of material scraps, changing them according to the colours I saw in church, where rich damasks of green, purple and white signalled whether it was Advent, Lent or Easter. When S, who was a couple of years older than me, asked if I would get confirmed with her, I immediately agreed. 'Are you sure?' my mother asked, looking at me carefully. There followed confirmation classes, a shopping expedition to Cheltenham for a special dress, and the gift of a gold cross.

The village school, a two-roomed Victorian building in a back lane, was ruled over by the steely Miss Price, whose wooden leg and sudden fits of temper earned her the name Peg Leg. We didn't have lessons as such; a bit of writing and sums interspersed storytelling, singing, drawing or listening to Miss Price read us the Norse myths. Cardboard boxes lined the classroom wall, and at her command we were allowed to choose a box and play with its contents; I favoured the one marked 'Broken Clocks'. A lot of time was spent rehearsing the nativity play or acting out scenes from the Bible for performance in church. After a couple of years, my parents packed me off to the girls' school that was sister to the cathedral school attended by my brother, and I realised there were subjects such as Maths and Geography.

The same undemanding Anglicanism that pervaded the village infused life at my new school. Every day began with an assembly; the days unfolded against a soundtrack of 'Dear Lord and Father of Mankind' and tales of Jesus and his disciples, which I received with the same mix of interest and inattention as the sermons in church. My new schoolfriends were rooted in church life: B's parents both taught at the cathedral school; A's father was the archdeacon of the diocese, a post which came with a large Georgian townhouse in the cathedral close. He and his wife ran an open house, receiving a stream of callers all day long; it was quite usual to find a tramp sitting on the kitchen sofa, having a cup of tea.

As we moved into our teens, our girl-gang began to explore city life. Gloucestershire in the late 1970s and early 1980s was dominated by a biker culture rooted in heavy-metal and progressive rock, a tribal identity badged by motorbikes, leather and long hair. Punk made a brief appearance at The Swing via the Sex Pistols on a portable cassette recorder, but in Gloucester, Rock Ruled. When the pubs closed on Saturday afternoons, about two hundred bikers filled the city square, smoking and exchanging banter. Shoppers on their way to Debenhams could be overcome by the smell of patchouli, and blue-rinsed ladies having a cup of tea in British Home Stores would find hairy young men squeezing themselves into the plastic chairs at the next table. Occasionally a lone mod would loiter by the cinema in his parka, attracting no animosity whatsoever. If they were going to fight, the hardest bikers took their chains to the Cheltenham Gang.

The rock tribe was nothing if not ecumenical. If you didn't have the means for a 750cc or a taste for amplified distortion, you joined the hippy end, a cheaper option requiring only velvet jackets and Genesis albums. My wardrobe filled with Indian tops, my bedroom wall with dreamy landscapes by Roger Dean, and my weekends with a long-locked boyfriend with a 250cc and a reverence for Peter Gabriel. The archdeaconry became the base for our new lives as hippy rock chicks in town. On Friday evenings we'd gather in A's room to don our gear, putting our heads on our way out into the sitting room where her mother was ironing surplices. On Saturdays, we'd repair to the archdeaconry for some downtime between lunchtime drinking in the bikers' pub and the heavy-metal disco in Stroud. My sense of place had shifted, and the view of the cathedral from my bedroom window now represented Life, the perennial problem being how to cross the distance between rural nothingness and lights, people, music.

Partly thanks to this unofficial support from the Church of England, our social life continued even after we'd scattered to different parts of the country. A went to art college and B, having survived a near-fatal car crash, decided to train as a nurse. I went to Oxford, having done a stint as the archdeacon's secretary while his real one was in hospital, bashing out sermons and letters on a 1950's typewriter and then sneaking upstairs for a fag with A. Between terms, like the amoebae we'd studied in biology lessons, the organism re-formed, sometimes incorporating a more kempt group of male friends, including a handsome young cellist called Rich. There were always reasons to have parties: back-for-the-holidays-celebrations, end-of-the-holidays-goodbye gatherings, birthdays and once, for reasons I don't recall, a drunken gathering in my garage, with table lamps imported from the house. Sad about the fact that one party was over, the next day we'd have another to cheer ourselves up. A's twenty-first birthday party in the Chapter House was followed by a picnic in the middle of the cathedral green, getting the blessing of the archdeacon on his way to take evensong. 'The trouble with you lot is that you have such a good time at home you don't want to go back to college,' said A's mother tartly, as we hung about each other's necks at the end of a particularly busy Easter.

So an unthinking Anglicanism was woven into the eccentric normality of my youth; one of the songlines of my particular patch of southern England. But then, at some point during this process, my faith was gone. The memory crystallises into a single moment on the roof of the archdeaconry, where we'd gone to smoke without fear of being caught. We were with an ethereal creature generally acknowledged by the girls as being the most desirable male in the rock tribe. Drawing on his Marlboro, he fluently expounded the sociological explanation of religion; of course it only existed to comfort the masses. I had never before heard anything so clear, so true; my conversion was immediate.

And so by early adulthood, I'd signed up to the prevailing atheism, joining the chorus of people confidently proclaiming that they had arrived at a place beyond belief. Years of studying and teaching philosophy provided an academic language with which to dismiss any sense of reverence. The return of faith came at some point around my early thirties; I couldn't pinpoint a year. There was no Damascene conversion, no dramatic insight or revelation, just a gradually increasing feeling of certainty. It didn't have anything to do with doctrines or scripture, but would more accurately be described as a sense which was at its strongest when I looked at the beauty of the natural world. Only once I started reading widely about religion, its history, anthropology and psychology, did I discover that the features of this second, organic phase of belief had been experienced by people across faiths and ages.

The other source of inspiration came from elsewhere. As a journalist, I travelled extensively in the Middle East, particularly the Palestinian Territories and Lebanon. I was drawn, not by the heady politics of this war-torn region, but the daily reality of those eastern places with their sun and dust, and the unashamed emotionalism of their dark-eyed peoples. As my knowledge of the Arab world deepened, I was struck by its easy acceptance of the spiritual as a part of life. It was a perspective which made the heated debates in the too-cool-for-God-West hard to comprehend, much like listening to an alien species mocking the human belief in love. Despite the endless cycles of war and poverty, faith seemed to be in the grain of the place, its rocks and deserts shimmering with a beauty that made it self-evident why it was here, in *this* part of the world, that the three monotheistic religions had come into being.

Talking to a spectrum of Muslims and Christians brought me up against the reality of competing religions, but it was the Druze who had the winning story. The sect worshipped in secret, directed by a religious elite who did not share their teachings with the uninitiated. This secrecy did not stop other Lebanese holding firm views about the mysterious religion in their midst: some said the Druze were really Muslims, while others claimed they had their own, distinctive faith which they kept hidden for fear of persecution. After weeks of listening to competing theories, a single theme emerged, one which told of an ancient spirituality, transmitted by the wise and potentially open to all. That this was the 'secret' of the Druze was later confirmed in an interview with their spiritual leader, Sheikh Bahjat Ghaith. Like most religious Druze, he was a master of elliptical answers, batting away my attempts at extracting definitive statements. A single word recurred throughout his explanations. 'Our real religion is the Unitarian faith,' he told me gnomically. 'It is everywhere. You can be a Unitarian whether you are Christian, Muslim or a Druze—any religion'.[1] It seemed that the people of wisdom were everywhere, to be found in all times and all places, members of an ancient faith that transcended religious boundaries.

What a bewitching idea. Of course in practice, the story of the Druze was mixed up with all kinds of sectarian tensions such as resentments about economic inequalities and political representation, along with the usual prejudices about the Other. But it nonetheless suggested something that chimed with my day-to-day experience of the place. For behind the headlines about the war-torn Middle East, peace was always breaking out between Lebanon's various sects, testimony to a mutual tolerance which could extend to an appreciation of other ways of being.

Back home, Britain seemed to be fighting its own, underground war of religion in which you were pushed into either the believers' or the atheists' camp. The twenty-first-century adult I'd become was sorely in need of a middle ground, something that gave form to the spiritual without the cant and dogma of organised religion. Doubtless she had her origins in the squatting child building her altars of slate and moss, but I suspected that this was a need I shared with many fellow Britons. Surveys confirmed that traditional forms of religious belief and belonging were in sharp decline, yet only a small proportion of respondents considered themselves atheists. In the space between lay a vast, unexplored territory. A growing proportion of Britons considered themselves 'spiritual but not religious'; according to one survey, three-quarters had had some sort of spiritual experience.[2] As a country, we might be losing our religion, but we were certainly not losing our faith.

Historically, British religion had undergone several transformations in which the dominant belief system collapsed and its place was taken by a new form of faith. The worship of nature gods and ancestors gave way to early Christianity, the Celtic Christians to the Roman Catholic Church and then, in the most sudden shift of all, Henry VIII's marital problems swept away English Catholicism. Now, in the early twenty-first century, it seemed that British spirituality was undergoing another major change in which faith was evolving into something more in keeping with the times.

What was its nature? At its broadest, it could be described as more an attitude than a set of beliefs which had more to do with meaning than conviction. The ancients had called it wisdom, a spiritual sensibility that preceded doctrines and exceeded membership of a particular sect; modern people tended to characterise it in individualistic terms, as the fulfilment of the self. While it might exist within established religious groups, the exposure to other faiths brought by a global age made it universalistic; born of a secular age, it was also open to doubt and questioning. My hunch was that contemporary Britain was home to myriad forms of this pluralistic faith that were going largely unseen and undocumented.

The challenge was where to find these new expressions of the religious impulse. I quickly decided against exploring the vast territory of New Age practices that encompassed so much modern western belief while demanding little of their adherents. Legions of people were taking yoga classes and dipping in and out of the mind–body–spirit world, but most did so on an ad hoc basis, and I felt the vague, half-articulated ideas that tended to accompany them would yield little of much depth. What I wanted was the self-conscious, focused quest of spiritual seekers who were prepared to make a commitment, take some risks, stay the course. In a sense, I would be looking for a form of faith that had long been recognised by sages across different traditions, from contemplative Christians to Sufi mystics. But the mainstream religious institutions of modern Britain, with their impressive structures and well-rehearsed doctrines, were unpromising places to look. My search would take me to the byways rather than the highways of faith, to the experiments of religious life. It would seek out the stories of the people who were themselves on a quest, looking for a faith they could make their own.

The journalist in me wanted to find the faces and places of an under-reported trend; the traveller to explore some uncharted territory. Yet this wasn't a distant, foreign land: it was my own country, and the spirituality I was seeking would reflect the precise nature of its geography, history, national psyche, even its weather.

9

My journey would take me to places new and old, and involve looking anew at the formative places of my own life.

BACK TO THE FUTURE

It was clear that my project of investigating the spiritual state of Britain would involve going beyond an official story that acknowledged only religious traditionalism or growing secularism. I knew that my country's history was full of other ways of believing and belonging, and that its dissenting elements had helped to create a modern, pluralistic society. But despite the key role they had played, Britain's nonconformists were largely forgotten, their achievements masked by the dominant narrative of Big History in which a king's lust led to the creation of a church which eventually reconciled Protestantism and Catholicism to become the accommodating institution into which I was born.

Just as Britain's turbulent religious past had been smoothed over, a similar forgetting had taken place in my family history. The generations before my mother had been active members of dissenting churches who questioned the status quo. The family's entry into the religious establishment had only come about with my grandmother's marriage and was the result of pragmatism rather than sincerely held belief. The Eameses were Anglican and conventional; they disapproved of their son's choice of bride, reasoning with impeccable snobbery: 'She's a schoolteacher, she's plain and she's nonconformist.' To placate them, my grandmother brought up her only child in the Church of England and there my mother, conservative by temperament, stayed.

But glimpses of this other religious heritage appeared in the tales my grandmother told me throughout my childhood. One word recurred in answer to my questions about why the people who came before me lived the way they did. 'We were nonconformists, you see,' Nan would say airily, her mind already on the next anecdote. Her half-answer helped to explain the obstacles that often stood in my ancestors' way: a residue of the discrimination that had always afflicted nonconformists lasted into the twentieth century. At the same time, it was clear that the women of the family revelled in their distinctive identity, introducing themselves as nonconformists – my grandmother would do an imitative toss of the head – with pride.

It wasn't until my thirties that the extent of the family's nonconformity started to emerge. My mother and I hosted a family reunion for the descendants of her great-grandfather, a Victorian public library campaigner who remained a unifying figure for a large, scattered group of cousins. Relatives came from far and wide, and suddenly the garden of the Big House was filled with members of the free churches: a Quaker here, a Jew for Jesus there. The party also contained an unusually high proportion of professional do-gooders. 'Funny ... blood will out,' murmured my mother regretfully, as we surveyed my brother amid a crowd of cousins. At the age of seventeen, he'd surprised everyone by going to a Billy Graham convention in Bristol and standing up for Jesus. A couple of years later, he was re-baptised. My mother cried. Then he'd gone and become a social worker. The nonconformist streak, having skipped a generation, was back.

There was some evidence that it went back to the beginnings of the dissenting tradition. 'I come from a long line of religious idiots,' my mother said crisply, as we examined the family tree spread out on the kitchen table. The tree led, via a series of strokes in the neat hand of a cousin, through the Victorian nonconformists back to the Chartists, the movement which tried to revolutionise British society. Thereafter, a few firmly drawn black dashes indicated that the next genealogical steps had been lost in time, ending with a tantalisingly brief sketch of the last known ancestor: John Greenwood, 'Martyr, sixteenth century'.

The details came from the biography of Thomas Greenwood written by his daughter, my great-grandmother, whom I remembered, a desiccated creature in her nineties sitting silently in the corner of the room. The biography, written towards the end of a long writing career in which she'd produced novels, plays, essays and a biography of Engels, focused on her father's contribution to the public library movement. I had read it long ago, but forgotten the details as quickly as I read them.

Now, with a writing project of my own that involved Britain's religious past, I wanted to know more. I went to the bookcase in my living room. There it was, one of the several copies that lay around the family bookshelves: *Spadework: The Biography of Thomas Greenwood "the Apostle of the Library Movement"*.[3] The face of my great-great grandfather stared out of the tattered cover, bandaged with yellowing sellotape: a lightly bearded, smartly dressed Victorian gentleman, gazing earnestly into the distance. Something about the set of his eyes and the way his hair curled behind his ears reminded me of my mother. I opened the book and began again. The style was rather odd: my great-grandmother had chosen to adopt the approach of an objective biographer, but had clearly relied heavily on the first-hand knowledge of a daughter.

Greenwood's life began in the Lancashire hills where, as the youngest of five, he was allowed to stay on at school until the age of eleven instead of joining his siblings in the mills. He was a bookish boy and, even when he'd started work in the local hat factory, took advantage of the early morning tuition offered by the local Congregational minister. He made full use of the public libraries that were beginning to open in nearby towns and cities, and thought nothing of walking six miles to the nearest library to change a book in his lunch hour. After three years as a travelling salesman, he became assistant librarian of Sheffield Public Library and then Librarian of the Upperthorpe branch. But the pay was poor and, once engaged to a young Quaker missionary he'd met through the Field Naturalists' Society, he resolved to improve his prospects. He moved to London to take up a job as business manager of a magazine. Then, spotting a niche in the burgeoning new sector of trade journalism, he decided to start his own magazine; 'his mind', wrote my great-grandmother, 'turned naturally to hatting'.[4] The *Hatters'* and *Pottery Gazettes* had their offices in Fleet Street and were staffed by an editor, business manager and salesman who all, curiously, had the same signature. Other titles followed and, by the time he was in his early thirties, Greenwood could afford to buy a house in Stoke Newington for his growing family.

In the 1880s, the semi-rural suburb was a hive of nonconformist activity. It had its own 'cathedral of nonconformity', a large red-brick chapel on a hill which the local Congregationalists had built to replace its ramshackle tabernacle. Smaller churches lay in its shade, providing a rich social and cultural life that ran throughout the week. There were Bible classes, nature groups and the usual self-improvement society; Greenwood felt immediately at home. His biographer-daughter was at a loss as to where he found the time, but he joined committees, mentored young parsons and started a Young Men's Bible Class. His life was now a perfect expression of that peculiarly Victorian combination of enterprise and reforming zeal rooted in a counter-cultural religiosity.

But as time went on, Greenwood withdrew from church life and devoted all his spare time to the cause of public libraries. 'Book hunger', he wrote in what became an influential book for the library movement, 'presents a demand as clear as ... the demand for good drainage and good water'.[5] The Sunday reading group he ran was taken over by someone who kept to Christian biographies and devotional exercises instead of Carlyle's history of the French Revolution which it had discussed under Greenwood.

My great-great grandfather's disengagement from the Congregationalist church reflected a wider shift that was dividing the English nonconformists. By the late nineteenth century, the movement had split into two camps, with religious traditionalist in one and liberals in the other. The first favoured a scripture-based approach and the doctrines of original sin and damnation; the second, largely represented by Unitarians and Congregationalists, contained those with a questioning, open mindset. One of the most divisive issues concerned the role of nature in religion: the traditionalists considered Pantheism – from the Greek for *pan* = all, and *theos* = god – heretical, while the liberals tended to see in nature the presence of the divine.

It seemed that Greenwood may have made a secret contribution to this debate. The year 1898 saw the publication of a little book which was widely reviewed, despite being written by an unknown author called Stephen Claye, a name generally assumed to be a nom de plume. It was clear, argued my great-grandmother, why the writer of *The Gospel of Common Sense* would want to remain anonymous.[6] The book was an attack on nonconformity by an insider, someone who counted nonconformist ministers among his closest friends. Its real author, she claimed, was her father. She cited, by way of evidence, a folder of press cuttings of reviews found in his study, all neatly headed in his secretary's handwriting, and highlighted the similarities between the book's criticisms of religion and those in a novel he had published previously. She concluded her case by pointing out that, had Greenwood published such a contentious work under his own name, he would have horrified 'his circle', alienated his wife and damaged his standing in the public library movement.[7] Speaking out under his own name, she added with a daughter's acuity, would have run counter to his temperament: her father was a taciturn man who tended not to share his feelings readily.

It's a grey day in the British Library when I finally get my hands on *The Gospel of Common Sense*. The slim volume, barely bigger than a handbag diary, is delivered in an envelope because its cover is coming away from the spine. PRICE ONE SHILLING unfurls across its grubby front.

I turn the yellowed pages and start to read. The prose is purple Victoriana, the tone reason itself, but the author doesn't pull his punches. While he is a true believer 'with intense feelings of reverence for the Divine', he no longer considers it 'an honour to be classed a Christian', having become disillusioned even with the nonconformist church to which he belongs.[8] He considers its ministers hypocritical and narrow-minded men who promote a harsh version of Christianity while displaying an 'excessive parade of piety' that at times amounts to 'religious drunkeness'.[9] Their sermons recall the fire-and-brimstone preaching that had often sent him to bed as a child 'in abject and quaking terror'.[10] Decades on, he has come to reject the literal interpretation of the Scriptures on which they were based, along with an unquestioning faith in miracles. He has even – and here, briefly, the tone becomes hesitant – come to question the literal truth of the Resurrection. In short, he feels obliged to detach himself from a church which encourages the least intelligent members of the congregation to subscribe to the supernatural and see salvation and damnation in black-and-white terms.

I'm impressed with this critique of organised religion and the punchy condemnation of the 'religious terrorism' enacted by nineteenth-century Christian fundamentalism. But as I make my way through page after page of criticism, I start to feel that the essay is missing something: there is no sense of the wellspring of their author's frustration, no account of the basis for the 'intense feelings of reverence' he professed to hold at the beginning.

And then, in a burst of lyricism, the source of Claye's faith erupts onto the page:

> Nature may be better trusted than the clerics ... There are days in each of the seasons when all Nature seems to demand the worship of mankind. Foliage, verdure, the song of birds, water, hills and valley full of a Divinity so real that to doubt the presence of a Creator would be to doubt one's own existence. If religious services could only be held at such seasons out of doors, how straight from the heart on many occasions would be the worship.[11]

So there it was: behind the buttoned-up Victorian gent was a spiritual sensibility based on an instinctual, joyous response to the natural world. What a shame he had changed his name, I thought as I shut the volume; Greenwood was the perfect name for a closet pantheist. I couldn't know for sure if the man behind the polemic was my biological ancestor, but I was happy to claim kinship with his ideas and his determination, despite the pressures of his society, to stay true to his own experience. In my own secular time, the spiritual battlelines had shifted once more, presenting a stark choice between being a righteous believer, narrowly defined in theistic terms, or a clear-sighted atheist. Literalism had succeeded in recruiting the non-believers, and their loud, confident voices drowned out the quieter ones whispering of the other possibilities that lay in the territory in between.

My great-grandmother's biography also touched on the lives of the dissenters of the previous generation, the family of mill-hands into which Thomas Greenwood had been born. His father William was a yeoman-farmer whose land, while not bringing wealth, had assured a degree of security and independence. When he and his brother John joined the Chartist movement that was forming around the Manchester mills in the late 1830s, they unwittingly tipped the family fortunes into decline. Tensions between the Chartists and the authorities grew and finally came to a head in 1839. Three thousand protesters marched on Newport in an attempt to free some fellow Chartists detained in a hotel, and were ambushed by the soldiers who lay in wait. The leaders of the Newport Rising, including John Frost, were arrested and charged with high treason, a crime which carried a sentence of death by hanging, drawing and quartering. The Chartist newspaper *The Northern Star* launched the Frost Defence Fund to raise money to pay for legal help and, for a short period, the paper published the details of the donors.

Would there be any trace of William or John in the historical records of the movement? It wasn't hard to find a list of contributors to the Frost Defence Fund, published on a website devoted to Chartism. I scrolled down, scanning the tiny print. Since merely being a signatory carried the risk of arrest, many donors gave brief self-descriptions instead of names. Donations came from 'a few patriotic warehousemen' from Stockport, 'a lover of liberty' from Codford and 'a female Radical' from Ashton. 'A boy, twelve years of age' donated in Dundee; 'a widow's mite' found its way into the coffers in Knaresbrough. Others described themselves in terms of what giving cost them, calling themselves 'a week's tea and sugar' or, even more poignantly: 'All I have'.[12]

I scrolled further down. Towards the end of the list there he was, John Greenwood, listed under his own name as a donor from Rochdale, on 25 January 1840. Thereafter, the *Star* stopped publishing details of supporters because, the editorial announced proudly, they were now so plentiful that their names would fill the entire paper.

Later, the leading rebels' death sentences were commuted to transportation, and Frost was shipped to Australia. The Chartists at home paid for their defiance in other ways, pursued by the authorities or shunned by their communities. John went on the run disguised as a pedlar, disappearing and re-surfacing with such skill that he became known in the family as 'the badger'. William, my great-grandmother suggests, was effectively chased off his farm. With no other way of earning a living, he moved the family to another village and went to work in the local cotton factory. When he died in his forties, his death certificate described him as a 'factory hand'.

Things just got better as I delved further into my seditious ancestry, or – depending on your point of view – considerably worse. My great-grandmother had evoked a romantic vision of a Robin Hood-style past in which the Greenwoods – 'those men of the greenwood from which they took their name' – lived out the rebellion that was in their blood.[13] Documents left in the farmhouse abandoned by William referred to a long dissenting history that went back to an Elizabethan ancestor 'who had suffered martyrdom for his heresy'.[14]

John Greenwood was hung at Tyburn, London's main place of public execution, for 'devising and circulating seditious books' in 1593.[15] He was part of the emerging Separatists, the radical Puritans who sought to 'purify' the Anglican church of the corruption that had built up under Rome and who, unlike most sixteenth-century Protestants, rejected the possibility of reform from within. They called for the establishment of self-governing congregations run by 'presbyters' of elders chosen by the congregations they served, arguing that only these communities of 'true believers' would reflect the spirit of the early Christian church. They rejected the Anglican liturgy made compulsory by the Act of Uniformity of 1558. They wanted to be free to pray as their consciences dictated, expressing the direct relationship with God they believed lay at the heart of the Christian faith.

Back to the British Library. There wasn't much on the Elizabethan Separatists save a few dated pamphlets and a couple of obscure monographs.[16] This was clearly a minority area of historical research, conducted by nonconformist historians motivated more by love of their subject than a desire for academic prestige. Still, I set to work to glean what information there was. There was no record of John Greenwood's date of birth but, after graduating from Cambridge, he was ordained as a priest around 1581, holding a parish in Norfolk for several years. Then, increasingly disillusioned by the Anglican church, he resigned and became a freelance preacher in London. He joined forces with Henry Barrow, a friend ten years his senior, and the pair set about fostering a new, independent form of English Christianity, preaching to small groups and writing prolifically. Before long, Greenwood was known as the leader of the London Separatists.

It was a dangerous time to be fermenting dissent. Elizabeth I might have been uninterested, as Francis Bacon famously observed, in making 'windows into men's souls', but she required outward conformity from her subjects.[17] After the religious turmoil of the previous decades, the new queen was determined to reconcile the Catholic and Protestant elements of her kingdom into a single church. Wearied by years of Catholic plotting, she and her bishops were alarmed by the emergence of a group of extremists at the other end of the religious spectrum. In 1586, three years after a proclamation against the printing of 'seditious, schismatical and erroneous books', Greenwood was arrested while preaching in a private home and taken to the Clink in Southwark.[18] Visiting him in prison, Barrow was also detained. The pair were moved to Fleet, where they continued to write on scraps of paper. The manuscripts were then pushed back through the prison bars to waiting hands who sent them to Holland for printing and then smuggled them back into England for use, in secret, by the Separatist congregations that were springing up around the country.

Over the next six years, Greenwood and Barrow were subjected to repeated interrogations. A rare record of an examination that took place around March 1588, with the two Lord Chief Justices of England, the Archbishop of Canterbury and other bishops, gives a flavour of the ideological and temperamental differences between the two sides. The adversarial tone is set from the outset, when Greenwood refuses to swear on the Bible.

> Question: What is your name?
>
> Answer: John Grenewood.
>
> Question: Lay yowr hand upon the book. Yow must take an oath.
>
> Answer: I wil sweare by the name of God if ther by any need, but not by or upon a book ...
>
> Question: Is it lawful to sue the Lorde's Prayer publickly or privatly as a prayer, or no?
>
> Answer: It is a doctrine to direct all our by prayers by: but seing it conteyneth the doctrine of the holy Scripture, no man can use the same as a private or publick prayer, because he hath not present need to aske al the peticionns therin conteyned at one time: neither can comprehend them with feeling and faith.
>
> Question: Is it lawful or no? I wil heare no pratling.
>
> Answer: It is not lawful, for any thing I can see by the Scripture, for ther is no commaundement to say the very wordes over: and Christ and his apostles prayed in other wordes according to their present necessitie ...
>
> Question: What doe yow say to the Church of England as it is now guided by bishops; is it antichristian?
>
> Answer: By such bishops and lawes as it is now guided, it is not according to the Scriptures.
>
> Question: Thow has Scriptures often in thy mouth: is it then antichristian?
>
> Answer: Yea, I hold it contrarie to Christe's word.[19]

The page spat with rage, and the main issues of the English Reformation – the monarch's determination to retain authority over the church, the radicals' calls for self-governance and the disagreement about worship – were suddenly alive. The prisoners' use of the arguments that unfolded during these sessions as material for their illegal tracts must have inflamed the Establishment still further – small wonder that by the 1590s, with the Separatist movement growing, the bishops decided to shut up the ringleaders once and for all. Greenwood and Barrow were sent twice to their deaths at Tyburn, only to be granted last-minute reprieves by the Queen. On one occasion they were on the scaffold, the nooses placed around the necks, when the stay of execution came. On the third attempt, the bishops got their way. Greenwood, still in his early thirties, left a young son called Abel and a widow of whom nothing is known. But both men had secured their reputations as the fathers of English Separatism, and Britain's dissenting tradition had begun.

It was hard, from my twenty-first century perspective, to understand the depth of religious fervour that had made my putative ancestor willing to sacrifice everything for the sake of spiritual freedom. Four hundred years later, Britain's religious landscape had changed immeasurably: I was free to opt out of religion, convert to a different faith, or work out my own spiritual position, exploring freely and expressing what I felt, risking at most a bit of social mockery. But more than the clash with the authorities that had cost him his life, it was Greenwood's struggle for inner freedom that interested me most. His first published writing was a long correspondence with a Puritan minister who wanted to stay within the established church. In 'Reasons against Read Prayer', the young dissenter upbraided George Gifford for condoning the set prayers imposed in Anglican services: 'You would teach men in stead of powring forth their harts, to help themselves upon a book, yea, to fetch their cause of sorrowing and sighing from another man's writing, even in the time of their begging at God's hand', he argued.[20] The Lord's Prayer forced people into hypocrisy and idolatry, whereas true prayer was 'uttered with the hart, and lively voyce unto God'.[21]

I felt a shock of recognition as I took in the words. Nearly three decades before, as a budding young atheist reluctantly going to church with my family, I had arrived at a similar conclusion. No longer would I recite the formulaic prayers I had known as long as I could remember, nor join in with the congregation's awkward responses as we traipsed, step by well-rehearsed liturgical step, towards communion. The declarations seemed empty and it felt hypocritical. So, in a nod towards inner prayer, I adopted a practice of non-saying: a private, instinctual decision that I never discussed with anyone and which endured when attending the odd church service in the non-Christian faith of my adulthood.

It was strange to feel similar sentiments catapulting across the centuries in the words of this angry young Elizabethan. The history of dissent tended to focus on outer power, the disagreements about who had the authority to run churches, rulings about doctrine and liturgy and, above all, the behaviour of the general population. The historical narrative made explicit the connection with politics; God had long been caught up in the question of who had the right to rule, with a tiny elite using the widely accepted notion of the Divine Right of Kings to claim absolute power. In reclaiming spiritual authority for themselves, the dissenters were helping to bring about the shift to a more equal society that would eventually make Britain a modern democracy.

But this well-trodden interpretation left out the powerful world operating in the realm of belief. The change that took place on this inner territory wasn't so much to do with political power as with the existential freedom to seek God for oneself; the Protestant desire for a direct relationship with the divine became the individual's quest for authenticity: necessarily personal, possibly idiosyncratic. As this required the acceptance of difference, the peaceful centuries that followed Britain's political–religious wars saw a protracted wrangle between those who wanted the right to be different and those who wanted unity at all costs.

Pamphlets of the time – the only means by which seventeenth-century Britons could conduct a heated debate – gave an indication of just how painful this struggle to come to terms with difference was. I put the word 'nonconformist' into the British Library catalogue, and the screen lit up with voices urgently debating whether it was acceptable to depart from the religion approved by the state. *An Apology for the Nonconformists, shewing their reasons, both for their not conforming, and for their preaching publickly, though forbidden by law,* announced John Troughton the Younger of Bicester in 1681. *A discourse of Secret Prayer. Together with two essays on prayer* whispered Henry Grove – 'nonconformist minister' – in 1752. Primitivus, in 1840, was bolder: *The Non-Conformist: an answer to the inquiry Why are you a Dissenter? Or Twenty reasons for dissenting from the Church of England.* As late as the twentieth century, nonconformists still felt the need to recant: *The Nonconformist Conscience, considered as a social evil and a mischief-monger. By one who has had it,* wrote an unnamed author in 1903.[22]

Even once basic agreements about outer behaviour had been reached, the anxiety about what went on in other people's hearts and minds continued. The possibility of others *being* different, as distinct from merely acting differently, seemed to touch a raw nerve, one which threatened the national identity at its core.

Perhaps the anxiety about who *they* were was at bottom an anxiety about who *we* were. Could Britain really be Britain, if everyone believed just what they liked? But the genie was out of the bottle. In its fracturing of monolithic religious authority, the dissenters were taking the first step to pluralism. Their ideas created the conditions for a society in which all kinds of belief, including agnosticism and atheism, became possible. It was time for me to leave the library and, following the trail of my dissenting roots, go back out into the world. The obvious place to start my search for spiritual authenticity was among contemporary nonconformists. But which denomination to choose? The Congregationalist church to which my ancestors had belonged had merged with the Presbyterians to become the United Reformed Church, holding a theological position not so different from the liberal end of Anglicanism. A brief, unhappy stint working in their press office revealed an organisation on the retreat, the usual failings of organised religion, if anything, heightened. The gap between the established church and nonconformity was closing; there was even talk of a reunion between Anglicans and Methodists. But the Unitarians, whose denial of the trinity made them the most persecuted religious group of the seventeenth century, looked more promising. In the centuries that followed, while other dissenting groups gradually gained acceptance, they had continued to be persecuted for their radical beliefs. These days they were an open, tolerant group of believers who made no exclusive claim on the truth and drew on resources from other faith traditions, incorporating insights from science and taking inspiration from nature and the arts. It was an eclectic approach akin to that taken by many a modern Briton as she went about the tricky task of making sense of life.

The denomination was nothing if not keen on the past. Essex Church, the country's first openly Unitarian place of worship, was to host a 'pilgrimage' to the dissenters' burial ground to mark the two hundredth anniversary of the death of Theophilus Lindsey, the Anglican minister-turned-Unitarian who founded it in 1774. He shared the cemetery with some illustrious company: William Blake, John Bunyan and Daniel Defoe were all buried in the same piece of non-consecrated ground in London's Bunhill Fields.

And so it was that one Saturday afternoon I set out to join them. I cut it fine, pounding the pavements of lower Islington to arrive at the cemetery gates just in time. About thirty middle-aged citizens are blocking the pavement.

'Are you dissenting pilgrims?' I ask anyone who is listening. 'Yes,' beams a stout, grey-haired woman. 'Don't we look like them?'

They do. The group, clad entirely in greys and navies, has an air of cheerful resolution that it is going to enjoy this afternoon tour of tombs. It's a mild day at the tail end of autumn, and a pale, on–off sun lights a silvery sky. We shuffle into the graveyard. Inside, the season's delicate beauty comes into its own, the green of the lichens bright against the tombstones. Underneath the large-limbed London planes, a few small trees are putting on a last-ditch display of shameless, shocking yellow.

But we are here to admire the achievements of men. As we tour the tombs, Unitarian historian Alan Rushton provides an expert commentary, acknowledging their inhabitants' legacy. Since they were buried at a time when new denominations were emerging and labels shifting, it is difficult to know exactly who believed what; Rushton pauses at a tablet that marks the remains of hymn writer Isaac Watts, remarking with relish: 'He was accused of being a Unitarian: he was dodgy on the trinity.' We linger longer at the resting places of official Unitarians such as Richard Price, before finally stopping at the unadorned grave which houses Lindsay's bones. Essex's present-day minister Sarah Tinker steps up to the tomb to say a prayer. 'I'm used to talking to the dead,' she begins with a laugh, and thanks Lindsey for helping those who came after him to have the courage to be authentic.

I'm impressed by the Unitarians' relationship with history, their loyalty to the people who struggled to make Britain the more tolerant place it has become. Most of all, I admire their forthrightness in celebrating the unfashionable, spiritual side of the injunction to be true to oneself, and for being brave enough to maintain a position derided by the mainstream, secular culture. On the Sundays that follow, I pay visits to various Unitarian churches. But as service after service fails to resonate, I realise that as a living faith, Unitarianism isn't making the connection I had hoped for. Maybe a ritual focusing on the present will be more meaningful. So, on the Sunday closest to the eleventh of November, I set off to see how the Newington Unitarians mark Remembrance Day. This year, the day has acquired an added poignancy, with record poppy sales attributed to a rise in support for the soldiers returning from Afghanistan and Iraq. A generation that has never known war finally has a conflict of its own, with real dead people to commemorate.

Fate, or rather my own incompetence, is against me. I miss the train by seconds, my hand smacking against the closing door. I know there is another Unitarian church just a bus ride away, although I don't have the address. And so it is that, at a few minutes to eleven, I find myself careering around the concrete jungle that is Croydon, asking directions of the policemen posted at street cordons in readiness for the military parades. One officer helpfully walkie-talkies another to ask the location of the Unitarian Church, but he doesn't know either. Cantering off in a likely direction, I enter the United Reformed Church just as the two-minute silence is ending. The minister, seeing a woman in spiritual need, comes and put his hand on my arm, looking empathically into my eyes. But I am just physically lost, and in a hurry to get to a rival church.

Croydon Unitarian Church is a few hundred yards further on, a modern building crouching by the flyover. The service is well under way as I take a pew behind a sea of white heads. The interior has a utilitarian plainness and an abstract mural hangs in place of the east window; I feel momentary disappointment at the lack of the visibly numinous. But the proceedings have pace and interest: an American minister with a walrus moustache reads a poem by Mark Twain with aplomb, and introduces a silence with eloquence.

Yet as he moves to the pulpit to give the address, the Revd Art Lester seems gripped by hesitancy. It is a day on which it is easy to give offence, he begins slowly, a difficult day for ministers obliged to preach. Perhaps it has something to do with Britain in November, the loss of the last of the warmth which gives the time of year a bleakness like no other: he pauses, and mops his brow before finally getting to the point. Remembrance Day is very different in the Spanish village where he and his wife once lived, he tells us. Every year, the whole village troops up to the hilltop cemetery for a service followed by a picnic among the dead. Graves become tabletops and commemoration gives way to fiesta because, for the locals, the dead are all around. 'Here's my father,' a village woman had once said, and the minister had turned, hand outstretched, to find, instead of the bent old man he expected, a tombstone.

I am rapt. This is how I feel about the church graveyard in the village where I grew up, full of people I have known since a child. Now my father, the Austrian veteran, shared the same plot of English soil. It had been a struggle to get him there: local church politics meant there was opposition to burials in the main cemetery for fear of disturbing old, unmarked remains and my mother, having taken to her bed, was showing little interest in the funeral arrangements. It looked as if my father would be relegated to the adjoining field which had been pressed into service as an extension.

Catching my eye as we sit at the foot of my mother's bed, the vicar intervenes, saying firmly: 'I think we can do better than *that*, for Otto. He should be with the other old Maisemore boys.' I am to choose the spot and show it to him; he is having none of the churchyard politics: graves are meant to last only for the next couple of generations and give grandchildren somewhere to visit.

A couple of days later, I go to the churchyard. There's a lot of greeting to do before I can start my search for the plot: the elderly Welsh couple who played the role of village grandparents, the spinster schoolteacher we used to play scrabble with, and several kind men who died in their fifties. It is a pleasure to see the names on the gravestones; it gives me a sense that their owners are all right, somehow connected to this place and time. Then I get down to business, walking here and there, trying to discern the right place. Here, under the giant limbs of the old oak? Or further over towards the wall? Slowly at first and then suddenly, it's clear: here is the place, this open, sunny spot by a rose bush. I look up. It's exactly opposite the bell-tower where my father used to ring.

I return the following Saturday to meet the vicar with my old schoolfriend B, who has driven from west Wales to spend the day with me. ('You sound like you could do with some support,' she says on the phone. 'I think I'll come over.') We are standing on the chosen spot when, red-faced and tired-looking, the vicar stomps across the grass in his black cassock. He thinks the plot will be fine – he'll deal with the opposition – and he wants a chat about the state of the world. Lebanon. Why is there trouble there again? They obviously don't want democracy. In vain, I assure him that I know lots of Lebanese who passionately want change; the average Arab teenager is much more politically sophisticated than his British counterpart. The vicar is unconvinced. 'The Arabs don't want democracy,' he insists, shaking his head.

The funeral goes well. The church is full, the singing full-throated and hearty, and there's a good spread at the village hall afterwards. My brother tells my father's joke about the curate's wedding night. I go to bed relieved and exhausted; I haven't slept properly for several days. At last, I'm going down, drifting comfortably into sleep, when I'm jolted awake.

It's my father's voice, with its sing-song, reedy Austrian intonation, out there, in the room.

'Thank you very much,' he says.

He sounds very pleased. Mentally, I tell him he's welcome, and continue my journey down into sleep. As I go, I register something akin to a click, a sense of someone having hung up, and he's gone.

Unlike the Spaniards with their enviable connection with their dead, the Croydon minister continues, Britain's remembrance of its war dead is dominated by a feeling of them 'not being all right'. The country strikes him as being stuck in the first stages of grief – anger – and the triumphalist trappings of its annual commemoration suggest there are unresolved feelings. Their belligerence left out something that was important yet difficult to think: the fact that the conflicts had created deaths which were 'early and probably senseless'. Maybe, he suggests, it would be better to 'remember differently' rather than continue to mark the day with brass bands and bugles. He pauses. He had often met with anger when expressing this unorthodox view, and had hesitated to give this sermon today, even though he knew he was among friends. Then he leaves the lectern and goes and sits down at the back of the dais with the air of a man who has got something difficult over with.

I gauge the silence that follows for signs of tension or discomfort, but find only calm. As the next hymn fills the air, I find to my surprise that I am suppressing a strong urge to cry. I master myself in time to notice the elderly lady in front dabbing her eyes with a white cotton hanky. 'Is it the emotion?' asks her neighbour sympathetically. The white head, doubtless full of its own war memories, nods wordlessly.

As the congregation gathers itself to leave, an elderly gentleman sporting an outsized poppy gets to his feet. The sermon leaves us with an important question to take away, he declares: how do you remember the dead without celebrating the war? He had been to a number of services in various churches that week but – he inscribes the air with a rhetorical flourish – he was certain you wouldn't find anything like this anywhere else.

I should mention The War.

Or rather, the first and second world wars and how the deaths and enforced separations they brought worked subterranean influences which rippled down through the generations of my family, leaving their traces in absences and silences. It was a common enough story, shared by many British families.

What made mine different was having a parent on each side of World War Two: a mother whose childhood was shaped by Blitz-time London and evacuation to the country, and a Viennese father who had been conscripted at seventeen to fight for the Nazis and subsequently taken prisoner-of-war by the Americans. Both histories came together in an odd postwar confluence in San Francisco in 1960. She was fleeing the gloom of 1950s' Britain, with its greyness and rationing: with her best friend, she packed her trunk and sailed across the Atlantic. Other young Europeans were also escaping to the New World. At a party in San Francisco she met my father, who was building a new life in a society which, he said, had treated him better as an enemy than the one for whom he had fought.

Elements of life on the Home Front often entered my youth in fragments, like findings from an archaeological dig: vivid, yet lacking in context. There was the story of how a freshly docked sailor endowed my mother, then about eight, with the ultimate wartime rarity of an orange; references to the moving around and making-do of the time were always getting into admonitions about how you should be grateful for what you had, and look after your things. But while the facts of my father's very different war were never hidden, he rarely talked about his experiences. Sociable and ebullient in company, at home he was a man of long silences from which it was difficult to recall him. One day, in possibly my tenth year, as yet another battle played out on the TV screen, it dawned on me that being a soldier involved physical violence. 'Dad,' I asked, wide-eyed from my place on the sofa, 'Did you ever kill a man?' 'Oh no,' said my father, almost contemptuously, and relapsed back into silence.

His wartime legacy manifested itself in other ways. There was his habit of bolting his food and then absent-mindedly helping himself to more when the rest of us had barely started eating, which he put down to his time in prison camp where, if you didn't eat fast, you didn't eat much. Every time he did it, my mother would shoot him a look freighted with darkness, but it never changed. At village parties in the 1970s, the fact that some of the men had fought on the same battlefront entered the small talk. 'Oh, were you at Monte Casino, too?' a neighbour would ask cheerfully as he sipped his sherry. Decades later, when the village amateur dramatic society put on a production of 'Allo 'Allo! to mark D-day, my father, who could not act but was valued for his innate ability to play the funny foreigner, was General Von Schmelling. The play ended in satirical chaos, with a row of goose-stepping, uniformed Nazis – a part for every older man in the company – lining up on stage while the audience howled with laughter. The horrors of war had been tamed, rendered hilarious and made available in a village hall near you.

But within the family, the solution of not talking about the war prevailed. One day, a man from the Imperial War Museum in London came to record my father's experiences for the oral history archive. Afterwards, hoping to get some real sense of his past, I listened to the tape alone. I was disappointed. The recording had the same tone of faux jocularity that coloured the rare occasions he did talk about his past, the anecdotes of his life as soldier and prisoner-of-war recounted as if they were part of some great escapade. This was my father the raconteur, the persona he used to entertain visitors and villagers. As a personal response to a youth blighted by war, it didn't ring true, and I sensed that some sort of emotional burial had taken place.

It wasn't the only war burial in the family's emotional history. As long as I could remember, I had been familiar with the central story of my grandmother's life: her love for Jack Eames. She had waited patiently for him to finish a long-running dalliance with an older woman before he finally proposed. But four years after they married, Jack was dead, leaving her a widow at twenty-nine. It was the age before the welfare state, so she returned to junior school teaching, farming out her baby daughter as best she could. She taught until retirement.

She thought then of the prophecy, made years before by a fairground fortune teller, that she would spend all her life surrounded by young children. My grandmother was puzzled. She was getting married, and married women didn't work; that phase of her life was over. But the fortune teller couldn't or wouldn't explain, merely repeating: 'All your life, I see you surrounded by small children.'

I was twenty-one before I learnt the truth about my grandfather's death. In a storytelling session during the university holidays, my grandmother told me how, in her late twenties, she had needed medical treatment for gynaecological problems. But the NHS did not yet exist, doctors were costly and Jack didn't have the money to pay the bill. He was discovered having 'borrowed' from the petty cash at work and given the sack. Facing financial ruin and social shame, he sent his employers an ultimatum via a messenger boy: 'Reinstate me, or I will jump from Waterloo Bridge at two o'clock.' It's not known how the employers would have responded, but by the time the boy arrived at the office just after two, Jack had jumped. His parents refused to talk to his widow about the death, but my grandmother's sanity was saved by some good friends who invited her to stay and encouraged her to talk. She talked for a week. My grandfather's suicide was later put down to shell shock stemming from his time in the trenches of the First World War.

I can't honestly claim that some shadow-knowledge of these events played a part, but as soon as I was old enough to think about it, I was uncomfortable with Remembrance Sunday. Every November brought a drawn-out moment at the memorial cross, torn between reverential silence and embarrassed fidgeting until the Last Post cut through the damp air, signalling the resumption of normality. Later, as a young adult living in London, there were parades in the streets. In my early twenties, I once tried wearing a white poppy, but it wasn't my thing: it was too partisan, oppositionist and, anyway, I wasn't a pacifist. So I gave up any kind of observance and the biggest challenge on Remembrance Sunday became working out why the Archers were on early and then reaching for the off-switch. Not this, this faux 1950s' solemnity from Whitehall.

Now, decades later in Croydon, I leave a Remembrance Sunday service having heard something that makes emotional sense for the first time. Maybe I have finally found a name for that sense of emptiness that always beset me when standing in silent communion around a village cross. Maybe I was a Remembrance dissenter.

Outside the Unitarian Church, the parades are in full swing. I stand and watch them go by under a pale November sun. First come the brass band, weaving carefully between the cordons, then the various regiments and finally the youth corps of teenagers, their arms moving stiffly as they march.

But no other Unitarian service had the same resonance. The others I attended all shared the same gentle quality, offering people the chance to express their experiences without the constraints of formal prayer. As the credit crunch hit Britain, one woman described how her bank card had played up in the supermarket, prompting the realisation in the lengthening moments that followed that the harder times to come would bring people who genuinely couldn't afford the basics. But it hardly amounted to a spiritual revolution, and gradually I concluded that contemporary nonconformity had lost much of the muscle that comes from swimming against the tide. Modern Britain had largely become what the early dissenters had been fighting for: an open society in which people could believe as they chose.

Perhaps in our noisy, fast-moving society, the people who were really going against the grain were those pursuing a quieter spirituality. The monks and nuns of the contemplative Christian tradition had long recognised silence as a way of screening out the demands of the ego-driven world and creating a space to let God in. For millennia they had been quietly forging a way of life that set them apart from the mainstream, keeping much of their spiritual life hidden. Despite the official view that monastic life was in terminal decline, I suspected that contemplatives had something important to say about faith in twenty-first century Britain.

I didn't know many nuns. True to the strand of religious idiocy that ran through the family, there was a nun-ancestor, a great-aunt on my mother's paternal side who went into an enclosed order in Salford and eventually became Mother Superior. My mother had visited Great-Aunt Ethel as a girl, and the memory of the veiled figure behind the grill had stayed with her forever. My own impressions of monastics were rather more flesh-and-blood, but still superficial. Growing up in the Severn Vale, I'd long been aware of Prinknash Abbey, a large, purpose-built monastery that looked confidently out from its Cotswold hill and was inhabited by an order of male Benedictines. My grandmother had taken me to its gift shop to buy my confirmation present: a tiny silver Bible on a chain. At school there was Sister Ann Verena, the nun who taught us maths, physics and chemistry: red face, black habit, always laughing. She was patient with inept pupils like me, and unfailingly good-humoured in the face of the pranks that left other teachers tight-lipped. When one day in the lab A produced a toy pistol, declaring that chemistry lessons made her want to kill herself, Sister Ann Verena just laughed. In our youthful self-absorption, we took her presence as nun-in-the-community for granted, blithely unconcerned about how she lived when she wasn't in front of us.

Little is known about the first monastic communities: the first probably formed in India, while the Jewish Essenes of second-century Palestine and Syria, with their secluded, celibate communities, are sometimes cited as pioneers of monasticism.

Christian monasteries emerged in the third and fourth centuries, when ascetics such as Saint Anthony retreated from the noise and corruption of Middle Eastern cities into the Egyptian desert. The holy men attracted followers, and gradually the hermits came together as communities to support each other in the difficult business of living apart.

Monasticism came to Britain in the sixth century with the Irish monks who brought Celtic Christianity to the mainland. Handfuls of men settled in remote places, loosely knit communities who strove to live a holy life. The introduction of St Benedict's Rule to Britain by Augustine in 597 marked a turning point in the history of western monasticism. Put together by a sixth-century Italian called Benedict, the Rule laid down guidelines that still inform religious life fifteen centuries on. Two principles are central: the absolute authority of the abbot who, like the pater of the Roman family, is the head of the community, and the 'unhesitating obedience' required of the monks. The recommended sanctions for disobedience – corporal punishment and excommunication – are harsh. The Rule requires utter commitment to monastic life, obliging the novice to give up private possessions and make a vow of stability which commits him to that institution, a single place and set of people, for life.[23]

Despite its rigour, the Rule was gentler than the ad hoc regimes followed by most early religious communities. Its humanity and attention to detail took into account the psychological and practical difficulties faced by an all-male community: Benedict recommends that the porter – a key figure who welcomed visitors while keeping an eye out for runaway novices – be 'a sensible old man' whose age 'keeps him from roaming about'.[24] The Rule proved so successful that, by the late Middle Ages, it had become the most popular guide to monastic life. Meanwhile, the institutions that followed it had become part of the social fabric, acting as a spiritual beacon for their communities and providing them with services such as learning and healthcare. Monks had the time to tend the herb gardens that were central to medieval medicine, while scriptoriums provided the resources to produce books before the age of printing. Even after the English Reformation brought about the closure of all the religious houses in England and Wales, the Rule lived on, as the monastic tradition gradually re-established itself on British soil.

I was curious about the motivations of the people who signed up to this peculiarly demanding way of life: did it really make monks and nuns different from the rest of us? Those who have got close to them have various theories. In an idiosyncratic book that distils a lifetime's observation of monastic behaviour, poet and former Jesuit Peter Levi says: To the question what are monks like? I have found to my surprise that the answer is curiously simple. They have a great deal in common which cuts across differences of rule, culture, climate, language and religious belief. What marks the monks ... is a silence of the spirit, a childish innocence, an apparently meaningless goodness. They become like good children playing at being good. [25]

In *The Heresy of Monasticism*, Jesuit historian James Mohler puts it differently. Monasticism is counter-cultural, even subversive, in its pursuit of a religious ideal, 'an attempt to live a religious life in a perfect, intensified, and usually communal manner, often hoping to recapture the lost spirit of the founder which has been diffused by some foreign influence'. [26]

If I wanted to get any insight into monasticism in twenty-first-century Britain, I needed to get up close myself. I knew exactly where to go to get a first glimpse of life beyond the gift shop. Tyburn Convent, home to an enclosed order of Benedictine nuns, was in central London near Marble Arch. Its twenty inhabitants spent their lives entirely within the walls of the convent, maintaining a round-the-clock vigil of prayer on behalf of the outside world. I liked the idea of an oasis of calm amid the relentless consumerism of the West End; it seemed a nice contemporary take on the time-honoured mission of praying for a world too busy to attend to its own spiritual needs. And I was intrigued by the location of the convent on the site of Tyburn Gallows. Established a hundred years ago, it commemorated the hundred-and-five Catholic martyrs hanged on that spot during the Reformation, marking a period in Britain's recusant past when the dissenters were Catholics. Once a month, the nuns held a 'monastic afternoon', opening the crypt to the public, and giving a talk about life on the inside.

So one Sunday, I go to the west end of Oxford Street, ignoring my usual haunt of the Marks & Spencer flagship store, and walk on to Bayswater Road. It would be easy to miss the convent, an unremarkable building in a row of red and white town houses; I must have passed it hundreds of times. But the nuns on the door reassure me this is the right place, smiling a hesitant welcome as I step over the threshold and take the steps down into the crypt. The main room is a cross between a church and museum: rows of pews face a small altar, and displays and cabinets line the walls. People are dribbling in in twos and threes and there's a gentle buzz of anticipation. I wander around looking at the exhibits, lingering over one glass cabinet. Its centrepiece is a large piece of blood-soaked linen, surrounded with carefully placed pieces of hair and bone. I can't tell much about the life or death of the person to whom they belonged, as the explanations are in Latin.

The chatter dies away as a nun glides in front of the altar and takes the microphone from the stand. Mother has a wide, smooth face and a short, fleshy figure which, draped in the simple lines of her habit, has a pleasing, doll-like rotundity. Her voice is melodious and soothing. It is just as well, because the details of the stories behind the exhibits are gory. Margaret Clitheroe, a leading Catholic martyr from York, was put to death on the Good Friday of 1586 by plank, a process which involved stripping and covering her with a door, and then slowly loading it with stones until she was crushed to death. Her preserved hand, adds Mother, is in York. The fates of Tyburn's other Catholic victims are recounted in equally impressive detail. The Carthusian prior John Houghton, who became the Reformation's first martyr in 1535 for refusing to acknowledge Henry VIII as supreme head of the Church of England, was hanged and taken down alive for quartering. Once Catholic martyrdom was established, the demand for body parts among the faithful grew. In 1681, Oliver Plunkett – the last Catholic martyr to die in England – was buried in the nearby church of St Giles before being dug up and moved to Germany. Thereafter, his head went on tour in Rome and Ireland, while his other remains were split between Downside Abbey in Somerset and various sites in Germany, Ireland, the United States and Australia.

As Mother talks on, I lose track of the details of the fate of these various body parts. Staring at the altar behind her, I realise what has struck me as odd about it since I walked in: the strange three-sided wooden cross is a miniature replica of the notoriously ergonomic Tyburn tree, which was capable of hanging several miscreants at once. When my thoughts drift back to the subject of the talk, they're clouded by bemusement at this preoccupation with the physical. Why, in a tradition so insistent on the immortality of the soul, is so much attention given to the body, with this sanctification of heads, hands and bones loyally conserved by the faithful? Can it be healthy?

As the question and answer session gets underway, I have a growing desire to ask Mother about the other martyrs hanged at Tyburn. I want to somehow acknowledge the likes of Greenwood and Barrow, not out of loyalty to some Protestant cause, but to honour the spiritual integrity that led to the deaths of all who died here. My journalistic instincts tell me to ask, now: I may never get another chance. But I am loathe to put the nuns' ability to empathise with victims on the other side of the sectarian divide to so public a test. While I debate the matter, the enquiries from the pews become more probing. What does being enclosed mean: do the nuns really never go out? Someone else wants to know how they get their news of the outside world. Fielding the more challenging queries, Mother becomes visibly more animated, her smile gaining in assurance.

The nuns don't go out, she tells us, except for hospital appointments or the occasional business meeting. While they are permitted to go to a dying relative, they often choose not to, having decided that prayers may have more effect than physical presence. Information about the outside world – vital in determining what to pray about – comes from the Catholic press. What about the money? asks someone, anxiously. 'Divine Providence!' responds Mother jubilantly. Sensing a mystified silence, she elaborates: friends of the convent bring them what they need, often buying supplies – she gestures outside – from nearby Marks & Spencer.

She's a big nun, I decide, and can surely cope with the ecumenical question.

'I know from history that there were other people – Protestants – who died for their religious convictions at Tyburn. I wonder how would you think about them?'

Mother looks uncomfortable. 'I'm not aware of any others ... '

'There were some towards the end of the reign of Elizabeth I,' I persist. 'And, in a way, they were dying for similar reasons to the Catholics – for keeping their faith in the face of persecution from the authorities.'

Now decidedly ill at ease, Mother responds with a series of unconnected points. She had heard that under Mary's reign there was a mass grave of those who died at Tyburn which made it impossible to tell whose bones were whose. Some were martyrs who died a traitor's death, while others died a heretic's death. 'Is that all right?' Her voice trails off uncertainly. And now, she announces, it's time for tea.

In the next room, a pair of Irish Catholics, a mother and son out for the afternoon, greet me with hearty friendliness. 'Well, that was an interesting question!' exclaims the mother ebulliently. 'You didn't get your answer, did you?'

Stirring my tea, I catch a fragment of conversation between a postulant and visitor. The face of the new recruit, despite having been there only two weeks, already has the scrubbed-clean glow of a long-serving nun. She is explaining the various whereabouts of a martyr's earthly remains. 'I think his head is here,' she says eagerly.

That's it. I'm off.

But it would be a shame to leave without stepping into the little chapel next door, where the community keeps a twenty-four-hour prayer vigil. The tiny nave is almost full of people waiting for Vespers. Behind the grill that separates them from the altar, a lone nun kneels in prayer. Draped in a cream cowl and black veil and entirely motionless, the human form has a stark, poignant beauty. Yet the atmosphere in the shrine is curiously static; I feel stifled, as if moving would be a transgressive act. It's an uncomfortable feeling that I recognise from visits to the more impressive Catholic cathedrals of Europe: a sense of being dwarfed, almost belittled, by the vaulting spaces above. And it has nothing to do with the feeling of being uplifted.

After a few more minutes I make my exit, hugely relieved to be back in the melee of Oxford Street. Recession or not, I will redeem the rest of my Sunday afternoon by shopping. I head purposefully towards Marks & Spencer.

I had, meanwhile, heard of a new monastery, a start-up community of Benedictine nuns in an Oxfordshire village. Founding a new monastery was a bold step to take, given that existing religious houses were struggling to survive, their numbers dwindling as they failed to attract new recruits. Unusually, Holy Trinity had been established without the backing of a major institution: there was no funding, no guidance, no ready-made ecclesiastical network to help it get off the ground. This was the urge to withdraw from the world tested to the limit. It would be in such a community, if anywhere, that I might discover what motivated people to choose the monastic way of life in contemporary Britain.

There was, if I'm to be entirely honest, another reason for my interest in Holy Trinity. The origins of the new monastery lay in the ultimate no-no for a religious community: relationship breakdown. Its three founders came from Stanbrook Abbey, a contemplative Benedictine order who had inhabited a beautiful Gothic abbey in Worcestershire since 1871. For reasons that were not clear, the three nuns had left under a cloud in early 2004. Several years later, a row erupted on the website of the *New Statesman* magazine after Holy Trinity's prioress Dame Catherine contributed a series of blogs to the Faith Column. She wrote eloquently of the call that had led her to reject the banking career that had followed her PhD at Cambridge, of the joys and hardships of her vocation and how, over time, the Benedictine combination of prayer, study and manual labour worked on her and her fellow nuns, bringing them more spiritual fulfilment than they had ever imagined possible.

A single, brief paragraph alluded to the event that had posed the ultimate challenge to her faith: exile from Stanbrook. 'My world fell apart', she wrote. 'The next few years were lonely and difficult, made all the more so because I was forced into a position where I could not openly tell all I knew and had to endure a number of false accusations. This shook my faith in the Church and her institutions, but a single sentence of the Rule, to which I had clung during a bad patch as a novice, came to act as a lifeline. "Never despair of God's mercy"'.[27]

The comments readers had posted in response testified to some unedifying ecclesiastical politics. Some came out in support of Dame Catherine, claiming a privileged insight into the events leading up to the nuns' expulsion. 'The treatment of Dame Catherine and others by the Superiors of Stanbrook Abbey and the wider Benedictine establishment was unspeakable to its very foundation, Un-Christian', wrote one commentator, concluding biblically: 'Did anyone hear a cock crow?' Another ally firmly refuted the suggestion that Dame Catherine was a 'bad nun': 'Dame

Catherine is a devout, good and holy Benedictine nun,' wrote another. 'I, too, heard the cock crow.'

One voice stood out, sharp in its condemnation of Dame Catherine. 'She has managed through inference to suggest that her former community have not acted as they should and I cannot believe for one minute that this could be so,' wrote someone under the pseudonym of Alba. It was impossible to tell whether 'Alba' had any first-hand knowledge of the situation, but in her angry tones I could hear the voice of an archetypal character: the defender of the status quo, someone temperamentally opposed to speaking out, regardless of the issue, driven by a fear of nonconformity so deep that it turns into rage at the dissenter.

Lunch with a wise elder unexpectedly revealed more. My friend, it turned out, had connections with Stanbrook that went back decades. Many people had been concerned about the situation there, she confided; the abbey had traditionally been a liberal institution, fostering a spirit of inquiry amongst its famously learned nuns. But in recent years a new, narrow orthodoxy had sought to stifle imagination and independence of thought. The struggle for Stanbrook's soul had come to centre on the decision to sell the Worcestershire abbey and move to a new, smaller building in another part of the country.

Afterwards, she emailed me with more details. 'A friend of mine went there as a postulant and was simply crushed and driven away. Another member of the community, who was there for years, was prevented from introducing creative activities that could have made the life there more lively and interesting, especially for younger people. And now, because the community failed to draw new people in, the remaining nuns are moving away from a place that has been tended for generations and loved by a host of visitors, as well as the nuns themselves, some of whom are really sad about the move.'

It was a familiar enough story: a clash of visions and temperaments found in offices and organisations up and down the land. But in monastic circles, this kind of division was all but unheard of. If most accounts were to be believed, tensions in religious communities were minor and personal, safely contained by a leadership as benign as it was capable, and who dealt with problems in the manner of a good parent overseeing squabbling siblings. 'He must vary with circumstances, threatening and coaxing by turns, stern as a taskmaster, devoted and tender as only a father can be', stated the Rule.[28] Hearing of the disunity at Stanbrook was disconcerting, but the story crystallised some questions that had been hovering in my mind for some time. Were nuns and monks nicer than the average person? Could the special way of life they carved out for themselves escape the realities of the venal world? It was the question that lay at the heart of all utopian communities, religious and secular: is it possible to *be* better by living better?

The nuns looked fun, smiling toothily at the camera as they cuddled up for the photo. Energy and good humour emanated from the Holy Trinity Monastery website, which had risen to the challenges of the digital age with a prayer podcast, an ebook and a blog about the realities of the life of contemplation. The latest post reported the conflicting demands of catering for a rush of visitors, running a business and carrying out a multitude of chores in house and garden, all while preserving a prayerful stillness at the core. 'I hope there's humour in heaven. If not, some of us are destined to linger a long time outside the door', concluded the blogger wryly. A Frequently Asked Questions section gave patient, slightly tongue-in-cheek answers to idiot questions from the general public, such as 'Do you wash in cold water?' 'Do you have holidays?' I hoped that, when I met the nuns, my questions wouldn't be as daft, but I couldn't count on it.

I wrote Dame Catherine a letter, asking if I could visit, making it clear I wanted to interview her. The reply came, almost immediately, by email. Of course I could come. I would be the first to use the monastery's new guest room, as previous visitors had stayed in nearby B&Bs, joining the nuns for worship and meals. I should let them know if I had any allergies – they had a dog – and she could meet me from the station. She sounded brisk, businesslike, and dauntingly on-the-ball.

As the time for my visit approached, I developed some mixed feelings. Spending the weekend with some strange women in a chilly building wasn't the most inviting of prospects, but what I most feared was a kind of psychological austerity. Surely a degree of coldness must inevitably stem from the nuns' disciplined life apart? Detachment, rather than engagement, must be their way. But at least it would be restful; I expected to be left largely to my own devices, with the rhythm of the day, organised around the seven daily offices, rolling on impersonally around me. And there would be – unparalleled of luxuries in my metropolitan existence – Quiet.

Silence has long been prized by spiritual traditions, but living in urban Britain I had come to appreciate its more modest variant, a kind of elastic peaceableness capable of accommodating the myriad sounds of life going on around. Quiet can easily accommodate a laugh, the bang of a door, or the burst of an engine, regathering itself like a pool after a stone has broken its surface. Over the years, I had come to experience it as an almost sensual pleasure, synaesthetically experienced: a creamy sound to be lapped up, or a quilt that descends and envelopes you with comfort. But my recently acquired London flat, a badly done Victorian conversion, was turning out to be an acoustic nightmare. At any point a thought could be aborted or a mood fractured by the thuds and crashes of the endlessly circulating family above. The phrase 'break the silence' took on a new resonance as the continual disturbances ate into my well-being. The constant noise had gradually rendered my craving for quiet visceral, a physical need akin to the longing new parents have for sleep.

The noisy family moved out, but the bachelor that replaced them brought a new set of problems. One particularly dramatic intervention came one evening, ironically while I was reading the chapter on 'recollection and quiet' in Evelyn Underhill's classic on mysticism.[29] Mr Upstairs was having sex on his living room floor; vocal and vigorous, it was a performance designed to impress.

At least in the monastery, there would be no clumping or bumping overhead, and I could leave my US-imported ear plugs at home. And unlike my flat, which only ran to a shower, Holy Trinity's rambling Victorian premises were sure to satisfy my very unascetic desire for a long soak in the tub. A weekend break in a nunnery? Why not?

The Friday afternoon train to Didcot is hot and overcrowded. It's one of the first warm days of the year and sun-reddened shoulders and exposed knees fill the carriage. Some of my fellow passengers are in a holiday mood, chatting animatedly about their plans for the weekend, while others are conked out, heads thrown back against the seats, mouths dropped open. Outside, the passing countryside has a new-found lushness; fields, trees, hedges unfurl with the lime-green vigour of high spring. Every now and then, the landscape disappears behind the red bricks of rural suburbia. As we chug towards the cooling towers of Didcot power station, the gabled roof of a Tesco superstore slides into view amid a worshipful community of Barrett homes.

Having declined Dame Catherine's offer of a lift from the station, I make my way down into the Vale of the White Horse by bus, to the village of East Hendred. The nuns are continuing the village tradition of recusancy: the manor house has been inhabited by the same family of staunch Catholics for the past six hundred years, and its chapel is said to be one of three in England never to have been 'contaminated' by Protestant worship. In a neat sectarian reversal, the Benedictines are renting a former presbytery, a building governed by a trust on terms that prevent it from being put to more commercial use.

The village seems almost deserted when I get off the bus. But it is, I soon discover, large and decidedly prosperous. Half-timbered houses and smartly converted barns line the leafy lanes and roads snake off in various directions. After wandering a while, I get directions from a woman tending her garden and make my way to the upper end of the village, where the houses give way to sloping fields. The presbytery is a large Victorian house hidden from the road by a high hedge. I slip into the grounds and up the drive; the narrow mullioned windows show no signs of life. But the sign by the door clearly says 'Monastery'. Hesitantly, I ring the bell.

Almost immediately, the door is flung open by a nun with a big smile, her hand extended in greeting. Dame Catherine is a blur of energy and friendliness, but I'm conscious that her habit deprives me of the usual social clues given by hair and clothes. All I have to go on is a pair of large blue eyes, and a fresh, slightly freckled complexion. She ushers me in, making solicitous, hostessy enquiries, and steers me along the corridor to the newly refurbished guest room.

'If any of the flat pack furniture falls down, you'll know why,' she remarks cheerfully. We stand in the doorway, surveying the pale green walls and chunky pine furniture. I'm the first visitor to use the room, and it has been a rush to get everything ready in time. When she leaves me to settle, I pick up the 'Information for Guests' leaflet lying on the desk. It details the divine offices that punctuate the day from Vigils at six to night prayer at quarter past eight. After that, everyone must observe The Great Silence that lasts from after Compline until the end of Lauds. A helpful caveat follows: 'If you hear nuns talking after this time, it is probably because of the boiler.'

In the living room along the corridor, Dame Catherine is waiting with a tray of afternoon tea. It's an elegant, generously proportioned room, furnished with a motley assortment of armchairs and sofas, and a rainbow of carpets and rugs. Dame Catherine introduces me to Duncan, the hairy white French basset who has been sniffing me politely and, sitting forward, gives me her full attention. I don't want, having just arrived, to sit and fire questions at her. So instead, we talk about my attempts at learning Arabic, her father's time in the Levant, and the web design business that keeps the monastic household afloat. Her skills are all self-taught, but she talks about internet security breaches and Google rankings with a fluency I can't hope to emulate. She sees IT work as the modern equivalent of the copying monks used to do in the scriptorium to earn a living. 'I don't know why, but I seem to do a lot of psychotherapists,' she says ruminatively, adding as an afterthought 'Tonight, I won't be praying: I have to finish a site for a dog club.'

She's a natural communicator, and the conversation moves easily. But something about her demeanour puzzles me, and it takes me a while to work out what it is: an unusual combination of wit and speed of thought with an attitude of humility. Propelled by her openness and my curiosity, we soon abandon small talk in favour of the concerns that fill the nuns' days. The internet has extended their traditional pastoral role, bringing requests for prayers from all over the world, and they deal with a lot of recession-induced woes of debt and repossession. A few communications are hostile. An academic in the US had emailed the nuns some statistics which claimed that eighty-five per cent of people don't believe anything at all: 'You only believe if you're stupid or uneducated,' he'd informed them. 'Well, I'm one of the fifteen per cent,' Dame Catherine had replied crisply. 'I can't claim to be uneducated, so I must be stupid.'

'What did he say?' I ask, almost in stitches at the rudeness and sheer futility of emailing some strangers halfway across the world to tell them they are wrong.

'I haven't had a reply yet,' she responds with an amused glint.

There is a pause. 'The ones I can't handle are the Satanists,' she volunteers suddenly.

I nearly fall out of my velveteen armchair. Is this Christianity's old fear of the Other surfacing, its projection of evil onto the indigenous faiths it sought to replace?

'You mean Druids, Pagans?'

'No,' says Dame Catherine, firmly. 'I mean Satanists.'

'You mean Wiccans, and those who revere nature, seeing in it a life force which could be called divine ...' I ramble on, struggling to articulate the difference between a benign, nature-based spirituality, and a cult which actively embraces ill-will.

'Some of them may call themselves Wiccans or pagans, but they are Satanists.' She turns towards the window and rubs her face, suddenly looking tired. 'I didn't mean to talk about this. I find this very difficult.'

'But they're a tiny cult, silly or mad,' I protest, following her gaze through the mullioned windows to the garden in the spring sunshine. 'And there can't be any near here.'

'They're Not Mad.' She's emphatic, half laughing in exasperation at my inability to comprehend. 'And I know they're here. There are a lot of them. Someone told me, "The local coven know you're here. They're praying for you to be gone."'

We try to thrash out the difference between wickedness and ordinary human failings, positing reasons for genocide and characters like Josef Fritzl. Both of us tend towards the view of evil as a lack of goodness that has dominated western thinking since Augustine. And yet there are examples of wickedness so extreme, instances of malevolence so there-for-the-hell-of-it that they escape this comforting explanation. Perhaps true evil centres on intention, and that is why the stereotypical image of the witch sticking pins into a doll is so disturbing. It is strange how the notion of radical evil has suddenly catapulted its way into tea at the presbytery on a sunny afternoon. 'I find talking about this very difficult,' repeats Dame Catherine. 'At the moment I'm in correspondence with a victim of ritual abuse in the States. I can only do it because it's by email.'

The model hostess has disappeared behind the face of a tired woman and, briefly, I get a sense of how draining this aspect of her work must be. Then she looks at her watch, briskly in control once more. It is nearly six, time for Vespers, and her mind is returning to the practicalities of my visit. After the office comes supper, silence and sleep, for me at least. 'The bathroom is above the guest room – it's the only place we could find for it. So if you hear us overhead, you'll forgive us.' She smiles disarmingly, her head tilted to one side.

I nod. Of course. But inwardly, I am laughing. Someone up there certainly has a sense of humour, and likes practical jokes – the nuns will be getting up at five am, maybe earlier ... And I have noticed that, even in the house, under their habits they wear big, black boots.

Next door, in a Victorian parlour-turned-oratory and library, the other two nuns are preparing for the office. An elderly nun is sitting quietly on one of the chairs set in front of the altar, while a younger woman readies the music at a Yamaha keyboard. Duncan follows us, walking straight to the rug in front of the altar where he rolls around, scratches himself vigorously and releases a series of harrumphing groans.

As the office gets underway, he falls into a state of open-eyed canine bliss, hairy belly rising and falling as the nuns' quavery voices rise into a delicate web of sound. The service is difficult for a layperson to follow, requiring rapid switches between Latin plainchant, scriptural reading and antiphonal psalms. Beside me, Dame Catherine indicates gently where we are in the various psalters and readers, but too slow and caught up with each activity to move on to the next in time. In truth, I'm rather overwhelmed: it's obvious that I'm part of something special, but I feel outside it, a novice anthropologist who has yet to find the key to the mysteries of another culture.

The office over, she turns to me and explains that each service takes place only once a year and is followed by members of the

Benedictine community the world over, uniting them with each other and their past. 'We're singing what was sung in the synagogue in the first century, at the beginning of all of this.' Her face is aglow. 'We're keeping that connection going.'

'She's a bath lady!' announces Dame Catherine to the other two nuns in the dining room. Her informal introduction draws peals of laughter, and I immediately feel accepted. At seventy-eight, Dame Theresa has a penetrating gaze and crisp, Queen's English diction; Dame Lucy, decades younger, has limpid brown eyes and lilting Scotch cadences. The nuns have swopped their one 'talking meal' of the day – usually lunch – to accommodate their guest. Over a supper of baked potatoes, boiled eggs and salad, the conversation ranges over current affairs. The nuns are intrigued by the fleet of buses that has been touring the country, bearing the slogan 'There's probably no God. Now stop worrying and enjoy your life' as part of a campaign headed by Richard Dawkins. Dame Catherine thinks the atheist buses have done a lot of good by starting a debate about things people are reluctant to discuss. I suggest there are plenty of non-believers trying to be good without God, and that it doesn't matter whether behaviour is explicitly motivated by faith. Dame Lucy takes the orthodox Christian position, arguing that good works are necessarily about 'bandaging the wounds' for Christ. Dame Catherine takes up the counter-argument with me. What about secular aid workers, trying to relieve suffering in the most extreme conditions? Might not a desire to do good without the fear of hell and hope of heaven be purer? 'So,' she says, energetically concluding our case: 'If I do a good deed, I might have a double motive, because I want to get to heaven.'

Dame Lucy's brown eyes are wondering as she sees the point. 'So there are some hidden Christians – hidden even from themselves,' she muses, nodding thoughtfully. 'I think they'll be in heaven.'

'While some nuns will be howling in their habits outside!' rejoins Dame Catherine with a short laugh.

Rain threatens the next day, but Duncan must be taken for his morning constitutional. So after Lauds, breakfast and the harvesting of rhubarb, Dame Lucy lends me a waterproof jacket and we set off in the car: me, two nuns and a dog.

The walk takes us along an avenue lined with parasol pines in the lee of the Ridgeway. The nuns hitch their habits up for walking, but progress is slow, as we make frequent stops for Duncan to raise his hind leg or snuffle in the hedgerow. The only other people about are an affluent breed; a smart-jacketed equestrian trots past on her shiny-coated steed, instructing us peremptorily to 'Talk to the dog,' as she approaches. Wry laughter passes between us.

I'm struggling to understand the nature of the nuns' enclosed existence. They cannot go out unnecessarily, and yet they seem so active and attuned to the world. I think I hear the faintest of suppressed sighs as I express my bemusement to Dame Catherine. As *moniales*, she explains patiently, they have taken solemn vows which form the basis of their lives: a constraint on freedom of action designed to create greater spiritual freedom. Paradoxically, the restrictions on social interaction allow them to be more truly engaged with the world than they would otherwise be.

But there is, she acknowledges, a danger of members of enclosed orders becoming inward-looking. 'Then people become obsessed – with the food in the refectory, or sister X or Y who's not my cup of tea. But our kind of order recognises liberty of spirit. You see how the three of us are very different. We even wear our veils differently' – she taps the side of her head – 'It's not about turning out a standard product, identikit nuns. The interpretation of the Rule allows for the recognition of individuality, and then we see if we can work as a team.' Despite the compromises of communal life, contemplation remains at its core. 'A lot of our life is hidden, even from you. For example, you didn't see us this morning, at our prayer and reading.'

We turn back, pausing to admire a red kite wheeling on an air current high above the neighbouring field. Dame Lucy wants to know how I get around London, and I tell her about life as a commuter, of the wasted hours freezing on platforms or boiling in tunnels waiting for trains to move. Her eyes widen with concern as she listens. 'I wonder how people find God,' she says, trying to stand firm as the lead nearly pulls her over. 'There's so much stress, worry, filling their minds, that by the end of the day, there's room for nothing else.'

Dame Catherine describes the five hours she spent on her mobile at premium rate to an Indian call centre, when the monastery's landline went down. Finally, the customer service adviser, unable to deal with the problem, told her to go into the junction box and attempt some electrical repairs herself. 'I'm afraid I lost my cool,' she confesses wryly. 'I can't remember my exact words – there was no shouting – but it was something to the effect of after five hours, it was a pretty poor show, and that at least they could do the decent thing and try to sort it out. And then I berated myself.'

The fault had turned out to be the phone company's, but she hadn't tried to get the cost of the lengthy call refunded. 'It's difficult to complain if you are in a monastery. People don't think that you should express any anger.'

'There is such a thing as righteous anger,' I say.

'Yes, there is,' she agrees. 'But people often don't recognise that.'

I am comfortable with the nuns. Their habits become invisible to me, in the way that the veils of Palestinian friends in the West Bank soon disappeared from view, leaving only the person. At the same time, I notice how the nuns' religious dress changes the way they used their bodies, allowing them to sit with their legs comfortably apart, the voluminous folds of the fabric a shield against unladylike posture. It is easy, too, to fall into the custom of addressing them with the same formality they use to each other – either Dame, the traditional title for a Benedictine nun, equivalent to the male 'Dom', or the more commonplace Sister – and soon I can't think of them with just their first names. Their monastic identity is part of them, not a set of restraints imposed on a separate person that lay below. And I am finding in their company more freedom to raise challenging questions about spiritual matters than the world I usually inhabit, with its dogmatic, disapproving atheism.

Yet my close-up view of the nuns reveals some of the tensions in their way of life. For all its wisdom about maintaining a balance of prayer and labour, following the Benedictine Rule in modern times is a pretty tall order, the visitors more frequent, the demands of pastoral care more complex. The Rule had, after all, been designed for a much larger community with considerable support from servants and lay folk. At Holy Trinity, all the burdens of institutional life fall on three individuals, sometimes two, if you take into account the failing strength of the eldest nun. The number and variety of tasks to be carried out each day, from the mandatory half hour of *lectio divina* to picking fruit and veg, is mind-boggling. As prioress, Dame Catherine seems to be constantly making lightning decisions to re-assess priorities, cancelling an office or putting aside her paid work to welcome an unexpected caller. The light from her bedroom late at night suggests she is sacrificing an already short night's sleep to the website for the dog club.

Then there is the challenge of outsiders' expectations. The presbytery's ancient boiler struggles to produce much hot water: my longed-for bath had quickly run tepid. Even washing up involves boiling several kettles, yet it is always done as soon as a meal is finished, and everything dried and put away. 'Somebody might call, and people expect nuns to be tidy,' Dame Lucy says as I help her to wash up after lunch. The perception of nuns as exemplary housekeepers extends to the media: they had recently taken part in a BBC television programme about the cooking of soft fruit. Wisely, they had turned down an invitation to do a cook-along with Gordon Ramsey. 'This is where we've got to be careful,' she explains. 'People like to make sport of nuns.'

We pause, tea towels in hand, to watch a little group of people at a tombstone in the graveyard of the Catholic church next door; they seem to be almost talking to it. There have been several untimely deaths in the village, Dame Lucy explains; the parents and girlfriend of the young man buried in that one are always coming and leaving flowers. She doesn't know whether they are regular churchgoers or if they just come to visit the grave.

The scene reminds me of my father and his paradoxical attitude to faith, I tell her. My younger atheist self had been gratified when he'd once confided that he didn't 'really believe in anything'. Yet after moving away from the village of the Big House, he had insisted on going back for a church service every second or third Sunday. My mother thought he was anxious to ensure a proper burial in the churchyard: once a Catholic, always a Catholic. 'You don't really know what people believe,' I conclude.

'Oh yes, when it comes to it, they often really believe deep down,' agrees Dame Lucy, stooping to put a bowl into a lower cupboard.

It is time for my interviews, a chance to talk to the nuns about their interior life. I sense an undercurrent of alarm at the prospect from Dames Theresa and Lucy, but Dame Catherine's tone, in arranging the interviews, is firm. As prioress, her word goes; it is all part of Obedience. I am set up in the sitting room, where the nuns are to join me, one at a time.

Dame Theresa comes first. At breakfast, as we'd exchanged polite enquiries about how the other had slept, it emerged that she had passed a sleepless night. 'Is there a particular reason?' I had asked with concern.

She had nodded sadly, as if to acknowledge an all-too-familiar cause of insomnia. 'Oh, you know how it is, when something goes round and round in your mind.' Then she adds briskly: 'It's not a tragedy.'

But she shows no signs of fatigue as she describes how, just after the second world war, at the age of nineteen, she left her home in Trinidad and entered Stanbrook Abbey. The call to enter a holy order, heard since her early teens, was clear, and the following decades brought no crisis of faith, no regrets about the other life she might have had.

'The more you live the life, the more it becomes part of you,' she explains. 'You change in the sense that you become more deeply what you are. The core of the thing remains so stable. The core of the thing is prayer.'

'What kind of prayer?'

'You have two kinds of prayer – prayer in the community, and solitary prayer,' she replies. 'The one supports the other. If you only had communal prayer, it wouldn't be so powerful. It has also to be supported by private prayer.'

'Does it ever fail you?'

'That's part of prayer. You've got to go through those phases when it's most unrewarding. There's an absence, rather than a presence of God. You have to continue praying through it.'

'Were you never tempted to give up?'

'I think there was one point when I was tempted to give up,' she replies carefully. 'That had nothing to do with prayer: it was the situation, new developments and so on. Then I was given a job outside the community, and that gave me the opportunity to carry on. By the end of that experience, I was ready to take it up again.'

'Couldn't you do the same thing in the world?'

'You have posed a very difficult question, and I don't know how to answer it.' She pauses. 'It's easier in religious communities because you all think the same. You have made the same profession, and you follow the same Rule. If you're on your own, it's easy to get side-tracked. Yet it's no good living in community without prayer.'

'Have you seen people lose contact with that prayerfulness, over the course of your career?'

'No, but I've read a lot of history.' She reflects for a moment, and then says decisively: 'Yes, I have seen it. I've seen people become shells of what they should be.'

We have stepped onto the territory of Obedience, the realities of submitting oneself to authority, and the difficult issue of the nuns' break with Stanbrook lurks unspoken in the background. Yet Dame Theresa gives no sign that her faith in monasticism has been shaken, talking with enthusiasm about the checks and balances in the Rule that prevent the abuse of power, and the spiritual fruits of yielding to an unpalatable instruction.

'St Benedict says: "Trust in the Lord and God, and something will come out of it in a way that you hadn't dreamt".' Her eyes sparkle.

'It's not always a good policy in the outside world. If I did that, I wouldn't survive,' I remark.

'Yes. Mmm ...' She is thinking hard how best to explain this to an incorrigibly secular mind. 'I think you have to change the modality. *Imitatio Christi.* Christ did not want to be crucified, but good came out of it. How many of us can do anything about the credit crunch, what the bankers did? You find yourself in a situation of helplessness. God will always bring good out of evil. A religious person will be more aware of that.'

'So it's a basic attitude which remains, even during the hardest of times?'

'That's right'.

I thank her, not wanting to push an obedient nun into talking about dissent, and she exits the room with the bright air of someone released from a dental appointment rather earlier than expected.

Dame Lucy sits with me next, her head wrapped in the bright blue veil she wears for gardening. It turns out she is in her late fifties, older than I thought, her skin so fresh that I had taken her for a dozen years younger. It is something I've noticed in other religious women I've interviewed, from ultra-orthodox Jewesses to a Druze sheira. We wonder together whether good skin is a reflection of spiritual well-being, or simply the product of abstemious living. She is easy to talk to, with a fluid mind that is alive to different possibilities. Her capacity for reflection makes listening to her entrancing, the conversational equivalent of watching a clear brook bubble its way over a many-hued bed of pebbles. Her hands clasped against her knees, her gaze fixed on the middle distance, she tells me how her upbringing in the Scottish Episcopal church had been followed by a lapse of faith. Her life became chaotic as attempts to find a sense of purpose repeatedly ran aground, even during a year spent in a Catholic lay community. Finally, at the age of thirty, while working as a science teacher in a London school, the mists started to clear.

'I can't explain it; it wasn't a thought process. It was a sense that God does exist, and there was a tremendous amount of calm then, and great joy. It was so powerful, and so certain.' Within months, she had entered Stanbrook.

'Did you find what you were looking for?'

'Yes,' she replies without hesitation. 'Over those twenty years I can see, looking back, how much things changed for me. I can see some people would find organised religion very confining, and could find their own God, but I feel I needed all the structure, all those helps, and I think I still do. And the evidence is that it has worked, for me.'

'Why is having quiet so necessary to you?'

'Because I'm so noisy, probably!' She laughs, and then adds gravely: 'Those little moments, they tend to come when you're quiet, and not focused on anything. My mind is very active, talking about things, so I need to slow down. Often it's in this sort of meditating you can get an insight that helps you. It's difficult to describe, because it's different for different people. I'm sure God speaks to people differently ... I'm talking as if he's a person, but it's the only way to understand it.'

I am puzzled. I'd expected a more conventional understanding of a personal God, centring on a relationship with Christ.

'I don't think about God like that,' Dame Lucy explains. 'There's almost a resistance in me to thinking of Jesus as a person. It's quite a dark—' she breaks off, and shrugs. 'I don't know how to describe it. It's almost as if there's no contact. It's so fragile.' She pauses. 'I remember Mother Teresa saying she had no experience of God, and people were saying "how can someone so holy say things like that?" But it's encouraging that some of the great saints have nothing tangible. So a lot of it is faith – you keep going on.'

'Has that experience of the absence of God ever caused you to doubt?'

'Only in terms of surface thoughts. I ask myself, "Do you want to give it up?" The answer, deep down, is always no. It's like a rock, deep down, so solid. Even if this community broke up – we're quite fragile – I think I would continue being a nun, even in a secular state. I think for me there's a search going on, and I have to hold on right to the end.'

A quiet settles on the room. I watch the dust motes float slowly down through the sunbeams slanting through the windows, and try to absorb Dame Lucy's words. I don't know how to respond. She is the first person to clearly articulate my own experience of a kind of certainty amid the darkness, devoid of any image or doctrine. Eventually I say, 'I didn't think I would find a Benedictine who would talk about faith like that.'

Sister Lucy nods sadly, as if taking the point as a comment on her inadequacy. 'I think if I was stronger, I could do it on my own.' She speaks without a trace of defensiveness. 'I wouldn't need all the props. It's a very difficult, windy road.'

In the *Dark Night of the Soul*, the sixteenth-century mystic St John of the Cross makes what has come to be regarded as the classic statement of how, at the heart of faith, lies doubt.

In a little over a hundred pages, the Spanish monk documents the process by which the soul draws closer to God, explaining phenomena that first appear as a loss of faith or meaningless misery as an intrinsic part of the spiritual journey. True union with the divine, he writes, involves entering territory so far removed from ordinary experience that a period of purgation is needed to free the self of its limiting habits: 'It is most fitting and necessary, if the soul is to pass to these great things, that this dark night of contemplation should first of all annihilate and undo it in its meanness, bringing it into darkness, aridity, affliction and emptiness'.[30]

His account of the *via negativa* echoes descriptions of spiritual experiences by sages from all times and traditions. According to thinkers such as Meister Eckhart and Paul Tillich, God – or the divine, groundless ground, Source, whatever you want to call it – is not an object among other objects, a thing that exists in the world in the manner of other good things like a beautiful view or the curve of a loved one's face, but an aspect of experience that defies human powers of comprehension. While the cataphatic tradition attempts to define the divine positively, freighting it with descriptors like omniscient and omnipotent, exponents of the *via negativa* content themselves with evoking it in negative terms. In talking of God as not-this and not-that, they acknowledge the existence of this other reality while signalling the limits of language to represent it.

For intimates of the dark night, St John's focus on the psychological aspects of the *via negativa* is reassuring. Put aside the intensity of the religious language, and the description has a peculiarly modern feel. He separates the pain of the troubled soul from its underlying significance in the manner of a modern psychoanalyst helping a patient to find healing by returning to the origin of suffering. Despair is a theological necessity; a sign that *kenosis*, in which the soul detaches itself from the demands of ego and world, is happening. Those prepared to endure the anguish of the dark night will end up closer to God, ultimately attaining the 'happy night of contemplation'.[31]

Nirvana! You would think that, having attained this state of bliss, the spiritual adepts' problems would be over. Instead, they find themselves with a new difficulty: their new-found enlightenment doesn't translate into the language of the world and they must resign themselves to being lonely and misunderstood. St John cites the Old Testament's acknowledgement of the communication problem that accompanies mystical knowledge:

'For the incapacity of man to speak of it and describe it in words was shown by Jeremias, when, after God had spoken with him, he knew not what to say, save "Ah, ah, ah!"'[32] The knowledge revealed in the dark night is a 'secret wisdom' which is 'so secret that the soul still cannot speak of it and give it a name' which can only be attained by 'a secret ladder'.[33] So, explains St John, the journeying soul takes on a disguise which advertises its commitment to the Christian virtues of faith, hope and charity: garments of white, green and purple to protect the soul respectively from the devil, the world and the flesh. Meanwhile the real spiritual work goes on undisturbed underneath.[34]

The Christian virtues just protectors and deflectors? For the institutionally minded, the idea that the outer trappings of Christianity are inferior to the inner process of spiritual development is a troubling one. For if, at bottom, the encounter with the divine can never be translated into doctrine and ritual which can be controlled from the top, the message of mysticism is a subversive one. No wonder, then, that church authorities through the ages have been suspicious of the most successful mystics, often accusing them of heresy. St John was imprisoned in a tiny cell by his own Carmelite order and brought out periodically for public whippings. (Eventually he escaped by climbing out of a tiny window in the adjoining cell and scaling down the building.) Despite his membership of the Dominican order, the fourteenth-century church authorities disapproved of the preachings of German mystic Meister Eckhart which, being in the vernacular, could be understood by ordinary folk. After his death in 1327, the authorities cautioned his disciples for preaching 'subtle things which not only do not advance morals, but easily lead the people into error'.[35] Even now, a strain of anxiety about Eckhart seems to live on in the Catholic establishment: 'It must be admitted that some of the sentences in his sermons and treatises were Beghardic, quietistic, or pantheistic', notes the online encyclopaedia New Advent regretfully.[36]

I like the fact that Britain's best-known advocate of the *via negativa* relies heavily on the most English of meteorological metaphors: cloud. The author of *The Cloud of Unknowing* is unknown, but quite a lot has survived about the writing of the book. It's thought to be the first work of spiritual guidance in the vernacular, written around 1370, probably in the Midlands, by a priest or monk. It is addressed to a young man who has recently entered a religious order and is taking his first, tentative steps up the spiritual ladder. One can imagine from the author's tone – avuncular, firm-but-kind – how great an obstacle the puzzled literalism of his intended reader might present to understanding his central, elusive idea:

> Do not think, because I speak of darkness or a cloud, that I am talking about any cloud formed from the vapours that fly about in the air, or any darkness such as that in your house at night, when your candle has gone out. Your can picture such darkness or clouds with your imagination, calling them to mind on the brightest summer day, or picture a clear shining light on the darkest day of winter. Leave such imaginings aside; they are not what I am talking about. When I say "darkness", I mean an absence of knowing, with everything you do not know, or have forgotten, dark to you, unseen by the eye of your spirit.

This is why I call it not a cloud of the air, but a cloud of unknowing, between you and your God.[37]

He advises, in the manner of modern self-help books, the use of a short word as a mantra for spiritual practice: 'If you reach this cloud, stay in it and work in it.'[38]

It struck me that early exponents of the *via negativa* left a legacy that was peculiarly relevant to the modern situation. It offered a useful corrective to the strand of western Christianity which, with its confident emphasis on light and progress, lays the ground for spiritual colonialism. For Christian soldiers to stride out over the world, convinced of their superiority over other ways of being and believing, is only possible if founded on absolute certainty. In highlighting the role of doubt, the *via negativa* points to another kind of faith, one between religious fundamentalism and fundamentalist atheism. Yet there are few well-known modern examples of doubtful faith. When the private writings of Mother Teresa were published in 2007, ten years after her death, they created a furore. The letters in *Come Be My Light* – which the author had repeatedly begged her spiritual advisers to destroy – make for extraordinary reading, with their revelation that deep down, beneath all the altruistic deeds and personal sacrifice, the world's best-known nun *lacked faith*.

Unsurprisingly, the Catholic establishment was quick to pre-empt any idea that Mother Teresa was really a non-believer. Edited by Father Brian Kolodiejchuk, the main advocate for the nun's canonisation, *Come Be My Light* accompanies the writings with a commentary which explains their author's doubts as an extreme identification with Christ in the form of the suffering poor. She completely identified with 'her people', he explained; just as they felt unloved by society so she felt unloved by God.[39]

Mother Teresa's staccato, broken prose makes for painful reading. Outstripping St John's descriptions of spiritual anhedonia, her journey never seems to end in that state of peace he describes as the 'happy night'. In one particularly painful extract she writes of being alone in anguish, in a place where there is nothing but 'emptiness & darkness', and concludes that she has 'no faith'. But the words belie the act: the vivid description of her lack of faith was written as a prayer and sent to her spiritual director Father Picachy in obedience to God. It ends with a rhapsodic profession of faith, telling God that she will always 'smile' at his 'Hidden Face'.[40]

On Saturday afternoon, I sit down with Dame Catherine for our formal interview. I had been wondering how to broach the difficult topic of the rupture from Stanbrook; like Dame Teresa, Dame Lucy had preferred to not to discuss the issue, telling me gently that it was 'not relevant'. But Dame Catherine seems to be expecting the question, and we slide effortlessly into the subject. She didn't believe it would be right to go into details while some of the key protagonists were alive, she tells me, and had not intended to start the debate in the *New Statesman*. But once she and her fellow nuns had become subject to accusations, she felt obliged to respond.

The disagreement between the nuns and their superiors at Stanbrook had turned on the plans to leave the Worcestershire abbey and move to purpose-built premises in the north. The decision to downsize was a sign of the times, of the need to find smaller buildings for ever-dwindling communities. But as Stanbrook's cellarer or bursar, Dame Catherine was privy to certain information. The former banker took a long, cool look at the plans and concluded that the numbers simply didn't add up.

'I was concerned about the way that it was being presented to the community, and its implications for the way in which the community would live its monastic life.' She chooses her words carefully. 'I was concerned about the agenda behind the proposal. And I tried and failed to get discussion about this into the open. As a result, the superiors recommended us to take leave of absence as – I'm quoting directly – they "did not wish to be put in the position of having to make us leave".'

The situation had made her question the keystone of her existence as a Benedictine nun. 'What is the limit of Obedience?' Her tone suggests the issue is still painful. 'When I'd done everything I could, and spoken to everybody, I felt I'd reached it.'

Ejected from their order, the nuns found a temporary home at Douai Abbey in Berkshire, and Dame Catherine went to Rome to seek papal permission to start a new religious community. To her surprise, the Vatican official who received her was sympathetic. He already knew about her case, and had a whole file of letters from people concerned about the three nuns. Permission to found Holy Trinity was granted in record time: six months instead of the usual two to three years. By the end of 2004, the nuns were starting a new chapter in their religious life.

They were still Benedictines, formed by the tough beauty of Stanbrook before it had all gone wrong. But the practicalities of starting a new monastery were daunting, especially on the limited funds the three women scraped together. The savings Dame Catherine had invested on entering Stanbrook had been returned, but interest-free after nearly twenty years, they did not go far, while the other two nuns had very modest resources. As Holy Trinity struggled to get established, it ran up against another problem: blacklisting. It never appeared in official lists of communities in Britain such as *The Benedictine Yearbook* and *Association of British Contemplatives Directory*.

'That creates a knock-on problem. When people are attracted to the community, and begin to do their research, they wonder what's wrong with us,' Dame Catherine says matter-of-factly. 'Of course, there's nothing wrong with us: canonically, we're watertight, but it creates doubt. And now we are quite wary of some ecclesiastical institutions. One of the reasons why we didn't join another community was because it was such a huge shock to all of us. We would worry that it might happen again. One of the things that we learnt from our own experience is how much power people have in the church set-up, and I would question whether that's a very good idea.'

It seems a daft, almost rude, question to put to a nun, but I have to ask it. How had these intelligent, resourceful women come to give away their power to such an extent that those prepared to take advantage could do so with impunity? 'Weren't you – in a sense – naive?' I ask hesitantly. 'Trapped by your desire to be good?'

'No one's ever called me naive before.' Dame Catherine rests her face on her hand as she considers the matter. 'The real problem here is untrammelled power. I think religious power is even more dangerous than secular power, untrammelled. With religious power, superiors have absolute power over people. With the exception of a few dictators, no one else in western democracies has that kind of power.'

'Do you still believe in Obedience?'

'Yes.' Her tone is definite. 'I still believe in everything I believed in before. What has changed is that I have fundamentally accepted that there are people who will not act in the best interests of the communities they are elected to serve. But the story doesn't end there.' She suddenly sounds upbeat. 'The story surely is that, having licked our wounds, life begins again. I hope that we will be a more compassionate community as a result of our experiences. As prioress, I take more trouble in getting agreement on things than I would have done, even when it takes a very long time.'

'So you're experimenting?'

'Oh, yes, and we're making mistakes.'

They had revised their open door policy as that required by the Rule had got too much, and the invitation to stay was now limited to three nights. Midday mass had been adapted so that fewer psalms interrupted the working day, and the nuns donned a more practical outfit of jeans and smock to do the gardening. Such reforms were essential to the survival of the community, which badly needed new recruits. 'It's difficult, if you're trying to push the boundaries a little bit, and be a monastery for our time,' she concludes. 'Our community is not going to be made up of women who've come from the past. If we accept new members, they will be from this generation. Otherwise it simply becomes a romantic fantasy of the past.'

The doorbell has rung while we are talking, and a flushed-looking Dame Lucy appears at the sitting room door. The Abbot of Farnborough and one of his novices, en route to their monastery in Hampshire after visiting Prinknash, have dropped by for tea. The abbot is fortyish, his junior possibly half his age, and both look stereotypically monkish: rotund and ruddy-cheeked. An air of heartiness prevails as greetings are exchanged. 'You don't want me to kiss your ring, do you?' Dame Catherine asks the abbot.

'Oh, no, no, no,' he responds jovially. 'You couldn't bend low enough.'

She and I decamp to my bedroom to finish our conversation while Dame Lucy holds the fort in the living room. I sit on the bed as Dame Catherine takes the rocking chair in the corner and resumes her account of the nuns' last few months at Stanbrook. The three grew increasingly isolated, unable to consult with outsiders as they could not write letters or make phone calls without the knowledge of their superiors. Because the Rule forbade talk deemed non-collegiate, they did not even discuss things among themselves until they were given permission by the Abbess. 'That's the means of control,' she concludes.

'I'm surprised you were willing to talk about this,' I tell her. Dame Catherine leans forward, the gaze from her blue eyes very clear and direct.

'So much that is not true has emanated from Stanbrook that I feel it's time for the little person to stand up and tell the truth. I have the right to defend this community. We've worked very hard and made a lot of sacrifices – and so have our friends and supporters – to get this going.'

I step out into the sunny afternoon to clear my head. The farm track that bisects the rising land behind the presbytery looks tempting, and I make for the crest of the hill. The fields on either side are crammed with ewes and lambs, jostling each other in their eagerness to suckle. But up in the woods an uncannier atmosphere prevails. Some makeshift trestle tables have been formed out of planks and disused oil cans, and I hastily dismiss the thought of covens gathering around them. I take the path through the conifers, but am uncomfortable with the oppressive energy of such a dense woodland. On a track between the trees, I see a lone, wild-faced dog and then, deciding I'm more comfortable on open land, head back to the rolling fields.

The guests are still there when I get back to the monastery and I am invited to join the company in the sitting room. The three nuns are sitting neatly on the sofas, upright and attentive, like Jane Austen heroines receiving callers in the parlour. The abbot is reporting the latest news from Prinknash, where the shrinking community of a dozen monks is adjusting to their new quarters after selling the sleek, modern building I recall from my youth. He sounds cheery as he describes the beauty of their new home and its suitability for the community. Yet he can't avoid the reason behind the move. 'They need to recruit, as do we all,' he concludes. The nuns nod sadly in agreement.

Once the visitors have gone, I say my goodbyes and Dame Catherine, waving aside my protests about having a return bus ticket, drives me to Didcot station. On the train, I slip into the only available table seat, which is littered with food wrappings as if some giant consumer-beast had been routed in the middle of a feed. I soon discover the other reason the table is free: the young women opposite are simultaneously drinking from several bottles of alcohol, while the teenage boys behind are shouting over the loud dance music they're playing on a ghetto blaster. But the nuns seem to have leant me some of their monastic calm: instead of succumbing to my usual railway misanthropy, it all washes over me.

The following week, the monastic world disappeared behind the bustle of the news desk, leaving little time for reflection. Yet it occurred to me that, objectively, the nuns were considerably busier than I was, their lives governed by the demands of hospitality and household, web design, prayer, study and pastoral care, a juggling act achieved through the simple expedient of having less sleep and relaxation than lay folk. Despite their relentless timetable, they had shown me a level of openness I hadn't expected: in matters concerning the spirit, I felt more myself with them than people I had known for years.

But I knew I couldn't be a friend of theirs in any ordinary sense: particular friendships violated the principle of equality laid down by the Rule. I had sensed the embargo come into play on parting: with her warm spontaneity, Dame Lucy had sprung forward to kiss me, while Dame Catherine – the prioress who must lead by example – held back in reserve.

The other element separating me from the nuns was perhaps more significant. Behind the Benedictine routine they shared so readily with their guests lay a hidden life, a relationship with God that blossomed in the solitary prayer of their early mornings, and numerous other, unofficial moments. It required both life-changing commitment and daily, disciplined cultivation. Yet their interior life didn't stop the women from engaging with the world. The nuns had done it: they managed to remain both open, and apart. It was some trick to pull off. And I felt I had some quite clear answers to my question about monastic living.

Could nuns be nicer than the run of humanity?

Yes.

Could they escape the power-mongers, the politics of the world?

No. Categorically, no.

It was ironic. After my exploration of contemporary nonconformism, I had found the true spirit of dissent among those pursuing the life of Obedience. The nuns had become reluctant dissenters, obliged by the dark side of monasticism to take a position very different from the one they wanted.

There is little attempt, in the literature about monasticism, to address this dark side, to engage with the dilemma of what to do when Goodness runs up against Power. This is perhaps not surprising in a body of work written mostly by insiders and admirers. But read closely, and there are a few telling admissions. 'Do you think nothing so wicked would happen among nuns? You are mistaken, but I blush to print the stories', remarks Levi with cheerful acerbity.[41] The sixteenth-century Spanish Carmelite St Teresa of Avila describes with grim hilarity how her male spiritual directors would often treat her 'curtly' because they thought she fancied them: 'I used to laugh to myself when I saw what a mistake they had made. I did not always tell them outright how little I was attached to anybody, though I knew it myself'.[42]

Modern monastic misery has perhaps been best documented by Karen Armstrong, the religious historian who became a Catholic nun at the age of seventeen. In the book she subsequently wrote about her experiences in the 1960s, Armstrong describes the coldness and cruelties of her strict Ignatian order, and the practices intended to break down the self and let God in. She was forced to eat double helpings of food that made her ill and perform demoralising tasks like scrubbing already-clean steps with a nylon nail brush or working a needleless sewing machine. Seven years and a breakdown later, Armstrong left, embarking on a period of atheism before eventually finding peace in a solitary life writing about religion.[43]

Although they contained nothing of such abuses, Mother Teresa's diaries had left me with a vague sense of unease that I couldn't quite put my finger on. Later, exploring the literature critical of her work, it started to take on a shape and a name. Testimony from both investigative journalists and insiders told of the horrors wrapped up with the good deeds: the neglect in the orphanages, the unnecessarily harsh conditions endured by the nuns, patients and volunteers who carried out the charitable work. It was the details that spoke: working in impoverished Haiti, the nuns had to re-use blunt syringes because they were not allowed to buy more; on another occasion they were obliged to throw away good tomatoes because to store them would demonstrate a lack of trust in Divine Providence. Meanwhile, millions of dollars lay in the charity's bank accounts, donated by people in the hope that their money would alleviate suffering.[44] The disconnect reflected a theology in which suffering was to be sought out rather than assuaged because it brought you closer to the agony of Christ. Mother Teresa's evocation of her own pain had made uncomfortable reading, but reading the pain she imposed on her followers was positively disturbing: goodness had become tyrannical.

It's hard to see the needs of others if you don't recognise your own. Other tales revealed how this obsessive preoccupation with goodness had created a shell of denial that was impossible to break through. When undercover reporter Donal MacIntyre revealed inhumane treatment of disabled children in a care home run by Mother Teresa's Missionaries of Charity, the nuns responded by ... blessing him.[45]

Now, thinking about the nuns of Holy Trinity, I had more questions, ones to which I didn't have the answer. Was there something – a counterpart to the banality of evil famously observed by Hannah Arendt in Adolf Eichmann – that could be called the naivety of goodness? I had seen plenty of examples: friends whose constitutional sweetness meant they failed to see when others were taking advantage; people who clung onto a rosy version of the world regardless of the evidence before them. Was there something inherent in the Christian tradition, with its message of humility and forgiveness, that gave theological form to this psychological tendency? And did that make it all too easy for the power-hungry to exploit those who took its message of acceptance seriously?

Reader, I didn't have the courage to go undercover and investigate the other issue my visit to the nuns had raised: the threat from witchcraft. To be honest, I feared for my mental health or, to put it in more old-fashioned terms, my soul. My discussion with Dame Catherine about the nature of evil had taken me back to another conversation in the dimly lit side aisle of my parish church over thirty years before. My friend S often woke at night to see the ghostly form of a man standing over her bed; he seemed unfriendly, and she wanted me to go with her to talk to the vicar. To support her, I agreed, but I was sceptical about the ghost – S was always seeing this or that, and I was confident that the vicar, who was young and trendyish, would soon dismiss her fears about this manifestation of evil. But when she told him of her nocturnal encounters, his eyes widened with alarm. 'Don't think about such things. Don't talk about them,' he instructed hastily. My friend was left with her fear, and now I was worried, too. If a grown-up and a clergyman reacted like that, maybe supernatural evil really did exist.

With the hindsight of adulthood, the incident seemed to illustrate the Church's inability to deal with the dark and the different. I really didn't know what to make of Dame Catherine's claims that local Satanists were plotting the nuns' demise: was it a symptom of Christianity's old antipathy to nature religions, or did the problem lie with people like me, refusing out of scepticism or misplaced liberalism, to recognise malevolence? Whatever the case, when soon afterwards I met someone from south

Oxfordshire, I asked him, as casually as the subject permitted, whether he'd heard of local Satanic practices. 'Oh yes, in Drayton, East Hendred, that sort of area,' my new acquaintance replied easily. There was a lot of talk about such things locally, he added, part of a long history of local witchcraft.

I did some research. *The Oxford Times* reported raids on two village churches in the area. The motive was hard to fathom: nothing had been stolen, but the tabernacles containing the consecrated bread had been prised open, and the police believed the vandals were making some sort of religious statement.[46] I rang the Revd Anthony Hogg, the vicar of St James the Great and St Nicholas, and had the second conversation of my life with a vicar about the supernatural. 'It's known there are rites in this area,' he said cheerily. 'I would say it's benign. It's just people who have a connection with nature. I never heard anything to alarm me.'

The following month, I switched on the radio early one Sunday to hear a BBC report on the Stanbrook community's move to north Yorkshire. The tone was congratulatory, stressing the virtues of the new four-and-a-half million pound eco-convent, with its solar panels and rainwater harvesting technology. The nuns interviewed described the rigours of moving for the first time in a hundred and fifty years cheerfully, and spoke of the joys of their more remote location overlooking pastures filled with sheep.[47]

But the sale of the old abbey had fallen through and the lack of funds meant there would, after all, be no library. Most of the community's prized collection of thirty-three thousand books remained unpacked and unavailable to the scholarly nuns. It seemed as if some of the doubts Dame Catherine had expressed about the move were already being borne out.

For the three exiles at Holy Trinity, the news of the move would inevitably herald another phase of grief. I thought in particular of Dame Theresa during the long, sleepless nights, turning over and over in her mind how her Benedictine vow of stability had got broken in the final stage of her life.

The following month, I took a week off work and headed north. Next, I wanted to explore a different side of the Christian tradition, one intimately connected to a place and time before the British Church had thrown in its lot with Rome. Celtic Christianity had emerged on mainland Britain in the sixth century, thriving in Northumberland, where a small band of scholarly monks developed an indigenous form of the new religion. I had never been to Northumberland, and my mental image of the place was of an empty landscape blighted by chill winds from the North Sea. But I had discovered it was the site of a monastic experiment in the Protestant tradition, and now I was eager to go.

The Northumbria Community, according to its literature, had the basic features of a monastic order: its members followed a Rule, and the day was organised around a series of offices, with periods set aside for study and reflection. But in other respects, the approach was resolutely unorthodox. The community welcomed doubters and questioners, those on the edges of the Christian faith, actively encouraging obedience to the 'heretical imperative' which demanded listening to other viewpoints and challenging assumptions. 'We don't want to box God into denominations or narrow statements of faith,' declared the introductory booklet. 'We've seen the damage these can do'.[48]

The community drew inspiration from Dietrich Bonhoeffer, the Lutheran theologian who was hanged by the Nazis at the age of thirty-nine for his work in the Resistance. During the course of his short life, Bonhoeffer sowed the seeds of the 'new monasticism', a movement seeking to bring a monastic ethos to ordinary people in their everyday lives. It was an attempt to incorporate the contemplative tradition into Protestantism, encouraging a personal quest for God which, like the eremetic and cenobitic paths open to the first monastics, could be pursued alone or in the company of others. There was no requirement to up sticks, go celibate or move to a holy house. The community was dispersed, the majority of its companions living at home and finding their own ways of building the Rule into their lives.

Nonetheless, the Northumbria Community had a mother house. Nether Springs took its name from a passage in Joshua 15:19, in which 'nether' denotes 'lower' or 'hidden'. It was home to a small number of members, a centre for retreats and, in keeping with the monastic tradition of hospitality, a refuge for anyone who wanted to stay. For its location, the community leaders had chosen a remote part of north Northumberland. They hoped it would act as a geographical reflection of the distinctive spirituality they were evolving, and a counterpoint to the spiritual glamour of Lindisfarne, with its public, missionising brand of Christianity. 'Holy Island was so clearly the place of the Upper Springs', explained the Northumbria Community's website. 'But somewhere further inland would be a place where people could seek the nether, hidden, deeper springs of spirituality rooted in the history and heritage of Northumbria'. The 'quiet and contemplative prayer' of the Nether Springs would complement the 'active and contagious' faith of the Upper Springs' because both 'the ebb and the flow of the tide of life' were necessary.[49]

Both approaches were rooted in the Celtic monasticism of the seventh century, when the Irish monks who had established

Christianity in Scotland began to take their religion elsewhere. The wild beauty of Northumbria must have been a tempting prospect for these early missionaries, offering a bleak landscape to feed the ascetic consciousness and plenty of heathens in need of conversion. The people of the region had abandoned Christianity after the departure of the Romans, and taken to worshipping the powerful cohort of pagan gods brought by the invading Anglo-Saxons. But King Oswald of Northumbria was a devout Christian and, in 635, he invited Aidan, the founder of Iona, to come and restore the faith. Aidan erected a clutch of wooden buildings on Lindisfarne, sending his monks out into the surrounding lanes to convert the locals, establishing the beginnings of the monastery made famous by St Cuthbert.

As the Christians of the Middle East drew inspiration from the desert, so the Celtic Christians were shaped by their surroundings. God was ubiquitous and ever-present, discernible in bird, tree and rock, and in continual, easy relationship with humans. Access to the divine didn't depend on institutions: you could just go to a favourite haunt, sit down on a stone and wait for a sense of its presence. St Columbanus, the Irish monk who established monasteries across Europe, gave his followers a simple piece of advice: 'Understand, if you want to know the Creator, created things'.[50] The late poet–philosopher John O'Donohue writes eloquently of the intertwining of the sacred and the mundane in the Irish tradition:

> The world of Celtic spirituality never had such walls. It was not a world of clear boundaries; people and things were never placed in bleak isolation from each other. Everything

was connected and there was a sense of the fluent flow of presences in and out of each other. The physical world was experienced as the shoreline of an invisible world which flowed underneath it and whose music reverberated upwards. In a certain sense, they understood a parallel fluency in the inner world of the mind. The inner world was no prison. It was a moving theatre of thoughts, visions and feelings ... the interim region between one person and another, between the person and nature, was not empty.[51]

For the early Celtic Christians, the divine world was tantalisingly attainable. The 'Land of Promise', 'Land of Summer', 'Plain of Happiness', or 'Land under the Wave', as it was variously known, was an earthly paradise that could be reached by finding the right point of entry, typically by sailing across the sea in a westerly direction. (And who has not felt the lure of the setting sun?) If you couldn't travel, you could access it by tuning in at the right time: at Halloween, the pagan festival of Samhain that marked the start of the dark half of the year, it was believed the boundary between the two worlds became so thin that souls could move freely between them.

Perhaps it was this sense of another reality lying beyond, oh *just* beyond, the here-and-now that drove the early Celtic Christians to set off on their perilous journeys overseas. Their exact motives are hard to fathom. 'We stole away because we wanted for the love of God to be on pilgrimage, we cared not where', was how the three Irishmen who had drifted across the sea in an oarless boat explained their presence in Cornwall to a puzzled King Alfred.[52] As *peregrini* – wanderers – they were engaging in a particular kind of ascetic practice that involved renouncing the comfort and safety of home to wander in a strange land. Travel was difficult and dangerous; the wanderer knew he might never see the people and places he loved again. The Celtic church acknowledged the risk of such journeying by labelling it a 'white martyrdom' – bloodless sacrifice – and St Columbanus devised the classic Christian formulation of *peregrinatio pro Christo*: to travel for Christ.

The monks who came to Northumbria were steadier types than the most rootless *peregrini*, tamed by the need to settle down and integrate into the local community. As the Celtic tradition gradually became assimilated into the Roman church, the custom of wandering died out. The episcopal authorities saw such madcap spiritual adventures as a form of escapism, a sign of restlessness very likely prompted by the devil. Like Bede, they declared that stability was the thing: a truly religious life involved a disciplined relationship with one place, one community.

As a something of a twenty-first-century wanderer myself, I couldn't help but feel a sneaking sympathy for the early Christian travellers. Perhaps the significance of a distant place went some way to explain Celtic Christians' intense need to forge a spiritual connection with their surroundings. After all, the faith which lay at the centre of their existence had begun in a faraway land inaccessible to almost everyone. Its central text was always boasting about the holiness of this other place, describing its deserts, rocks and bushes as if they were the only sacred sites in town. But why should the Middle East have all the holy places? Couldn't our fields and rocks be special, too? Maybe the head honcho himself came here, and sanctified the land with his physical presence. And did those feet in ancient time ... ?

I booked myself onto a retreat at the Northumbria Community, a few days devoted to exploring the version of monasticism pioneered by Bonhoeffer. But first I planned to pay a visit to Lindisfarne. Like Iona, the island had become known as a 'thin place', a site where the boundary between heaven and earth was permeable, and I was curious to see how far it merited this otherworldly reputation. Joined to the mainland by a narrow strip of land, it was only accessible when the tide was out; as I had no car and the island no public transport, the practicalities of getting on and off it were tricky. But as I pored over tide timetables, trying to marry the movements of the sea with accommodation and trains, I reminded myself that it was precisely its unusual geographical situation that had made Lindisfarne's spiritual fortunes. You could hardly hope, in the daily pattern of withdrawal and connection enacted by the tides, for a more exemplary solution to the age-old conflict between contemplation and action. Maybe there was a lesson to be drawn from nature that you didn't have to choose one or the other. Maybe it was all a question of balance.

Judging by his CV, achieving this balance had exercised St Cuthbert of Lindisfarne throughout his life. Growing up in Melrose in present-day Scotland, he was minding a flock of sheep and his own business when the soul of Aidan flew by. The vision of angels carrying to heaven the Irish monk who had founded a monastery at Lindisfarne convinced the young Cuthbert that he must become a monk. But first he went out into the world and spent several years as a soldier. When he finally entered a religious order, his worldly skills got him headhunted to lead Lindisfarne through the transition that followed the decision of the Synod of Whitby in 664 that the British Church should adopt Roman rather than Celtic ways. A decade later, craving solitude, Cuthbert withdrew to a nearby islet. People kept rowing out to consult him, so he moved further out to sea to Farne Island, where he is thought to have instituted the first bird protection laws. The ecclesiastical world summoned him back once more to become the Bishop of Lindisfarne until finally, nearing death, he was allowed to retreat to the peace of his hermitage.

The saint would have had an even tougher time finding a bit of peace and quiet on modern-day Lindisfarne. Increasing numbers of tourists were seeking out the island, says the driver of the taxi I take across the causeway. 'There are more each summer. I'm surprised it doesn't sink,' he says dourly as we speed across the sands, still gleaming from the receding waters. Too often, casual day-trippers refuse to heed warnings about the movements of the sea, returning to find their cars floating in an expanse of water. On the island, it is obvious that the locals make every effort to convey the dangers to their guests. Notice boards are covered with press cuttings recounting tales of drivers who failed to respect the tides, accompanied by photos of half-submerged vehicles. I can't help but notice that the stories ooze an almost gleeful schadenfreude: in the face of such idiocy, the car was brand new/had cost thirty grand/the insurance company refused to pay up. But it is clear that tourist revenues have brought prosperity to the village – the island is very different from the wild outpost that had attracted the early Christian settlers. The low stone houses are beautifully maintained, the eateries and B&Bs brimming with customers, and a constant stream of people tread the coastal path leading to the perched castle that had become the iconic image of the island. Blue nuns scurry around the little streets with a recreational bustle: they are on holiday, says my landlady, and even take a break from praying.

Then, to cap it all, I spot the novelist Lionel Shriver at the bar of the Ship, asking for Tabasco.

The next morning, I set out for the far side of the island towards a promisingly uncluttered skyline. Despite warnings of rain, the day had dawned fair and now the sun blazes across the land, irradiating every nook and blade with a sharp, clean light. The creatures populating my path seem unusually confident; the sheep trot along the same raised tracks as the humans, and the flight paths of the birds are just a yard or two above the earth. I stand and watch a plump-breasted thrush tugging a fat worm out of the mud, cocking a bright eye towards me, unfazed by my proximity. Soon the path gives way to dunes covered in springy sea grass and the few other walkers become tiny matchstick figures. With the wind coursing through the stubby vegetation, it is easy to see how the founders of the early Celtic church felt they were continuing the tradition of the desert fathers: the vastness of the place opens up space in the mind, too. The emptiness throws into relief the few things that are there and brings them into microscopic focus. I pause to examine some wild violets nestling against the hummocks, and then, curling up in a hollow to take a break from the wind, listen as the song of the skylark overhead becomes first stereo, then multiphonic, the sound pouring out of several throats directly above.

Ten minutes' more walking, and I arrive at land's end. And there, the bright clouds echoing the shining water, Lindisfarne's famed liminality comes into being. It is hard to tell, looking out across the mudflats, where one element ends and another begins. The silver-grey line that joins sand and sea flashes with now-you-see-it-now-you-don't brilliance. I sit on the shingle, listening to the strange, half-human calls coming from a colony of seals a little way out to sea. Then I notice an odd little construction a few yards away. Someone has built a tiny house out of piled rocks, with a doorway of driftwood held together by rope. The little igloo looks simultaneously robust yet perilous. I peer in: inside is a child's playroom, fully furnished and peopled with play folk. Pooh Bear sits at a little stone table, his mouth yawning hungrily over a lunch box, and a grubby Teletubby reclines in a little rope hammock. Plastic spades hang from the ceiling and tiny toys decorate the walls.

The next day at low tide, I pick my way, stone by stone, over the wet sands to Cuthbert's Island, and clamber onto the rocky ground. A wooden cross marks the spot where the abbot had chosen his first retreat from monastic life, and a plaque has been tacked to the side of the biggest rock. It bears some triumphal lines:

> Mightier than the thunders of many waters
> Mightier than the waves of the sea
> The Lord on High is Mighty!
> Psalm 93:4

I take a seat on a mound upholstered with sea grass. The previous night had been completely still – the stillest he had ever known on the island, one local told me – and the morning air is motionless; only a low sea breeze carries the honeyed scent of sea-thrift into my nostrils.

Ahead, artfully spun clouds hang as if suspended for an installation, and a flock of plovers are flying in formation over the sands, surfing back and forth on the air currents. When they fly at one angle and expose their upper, dark side, they disappear from view, blending with the slate of the sea. Then, as one, they turn, their white undersides hitting the sun and reappearing in a sudden, brilliant flash.

'Nether Springs' is at Hetton Hall, a large, rambling building set on a rise of land a few miles from the town of Wooler. It is a strange house, a hotchpotch of pinky brown granite, probably first built in the fifteenth century as one of the fortified homes along the Scottish border. The following centuries brought various alterations and extensions, and a disproportionately small Victorian porch now serves as the main entrance. As a result of all these changes, the house has acquired a somewhat long-suffering air, and I can't imagine any marauding Scot quailing at the sight of the original tower, which bulges out of a wall and is reportedly made of rubble.

But its situation, overlooking the undulating expanses of the Cheviot Hills, is majestic. I am discovering that Nature does things differently here, up in the chilly northern borders. It is mid-May, but the deciduous trees are barely coming into leaf, their filigree limbs starkly black against the sky, while the greening hedgerows are less prissily floral than their southern counterparts. Even the lambs are younger and smaller, standing shakily near their mothers, as unsure of the world as children whose August birthdays had sent them early to school. The landscape is on a vaster scale, with highlands of bare rock and fir-covered slopes sweeping down into basins where rivers tumble under stone bridges. The colours are simpler and bolder, the greens of the fields varied only by bright yellow patches of rape and gorse.

Hetton Hall's interior is at least as assorted as its outside, the decoration and furnishings a mismatch of colours and textures, its layout a maze of corridors and bewildering turnings. As new arrivals, we retreatants are given a tour by Cara, a young woman who exudes competence. She shows us the spacious sitting room, where we will meet for the morning sessions, and the library, with its carefully ordered sections of different areas of Christian thought. One closed door is forbidden to us, Bluebeard-style. 'Don't go in there – the boiler's broken,' Cara tells us firmly. Then we sit around the kitchen table, drinking tea and exchanging banalities with all the forced jollity of new acquaintance.

The time is approaching for the evening office. But I have been here barely two hours and am still taking in the new people and unfamiliar surroundings. There are plenty of other things to do with the golden hour that lies at afternoon's end. I could go for a walk. I could take a nap. I feel a rise of resistance to formal religious gatherings. It is easy to see the divine in clouds, trees and hills, an external force present in nature. But when I hear the standard line about the presence of God in people, the divine spark inhabiting the human, an inner voice sometimes replies in amazement: *Really? Are you sure?* Perhaps religious communities, with their self-conscious, flawed attempts at realising human goodness, bring out a latent misanthropy in me. My only other experience of alternative communities, a few days as a paying guest at a centre attempting to combine self-sufficiency with spiritual growth, had revealed the residents to be divided and depressed, the atmosphere of the communal kitchen heavy and cold. I and the other two guests, an impoverished couple miserably volunteering for their bed and board, holed up in another room with a bottle of wine and sang the 'The Lonely Goatherd' to cheer ourselves up. In short, I might not go to the first office.

But somehow, after a stroll down the lane to the bridge in the hollow, I find myself approaching the house at precisely the allotted time and walking towards the wooden chapel the community built for itself amid the trees. It is a quirky, triangular construction with a gabled porch and pointed windows and looks familiar, as if drawn from childhood story books or faded photos of refuges in faraway lands. I can't link it to any particular part of the world: it has no recognisable architectural style, being composed of whatever was cheap and ready-to-hand. The doors are open, and I step over the threshold. Inside, four telegraph poles serve as central cross beams, a piece of Perspex freckled with green mould forms the large upper window, while the floor is of inexpertly rippled concrete. Rows of chairs face each other; at their helm is an altar formed of slabs of dark wood. The overall effect is oddly alluring, calming ... it is a place you want to be.

I sit down on one of the chairs, trying to fathom the source of the charm. In part, it has to do with the melding of woodland location and timber interior, which creates a porosity as if the trees were in the chapel, the chapel in the trees. The sounds of the surrounding life pour in; the low cooing of the wood pigeons mingles with the higher strains of songbirds. Dappled light falls through the windows and open doors. People are trickling in in ones and twos, sitting down and composing themselves, closing their eyes and placing their hands at rest. I look around for the person who will lead the worship. There is no obvious candidate, no fussy preparations being made with books or worship accessories, although the middle-aged man dressed in beige nearest to the altar seems to be particularly deep in contemplation.

The silence settles and grows.

Then, as if rising organically out of the calm, the man in beige speaks, and a hymn swells out of the surrounding throats, rich and womanly, melody and descant merging and diverging.

The reading, he says, is from John.

'He must be greater. I must be lesser.' The female voice was one I vaguely recognise as belonging to the garrulous, kindly Welsh woman who had picked me up from the station, now speaking in lower, becalmed tones.

More silence. I wait for the reading to get underway, but the pause lengthens until finally I realise that the eight words *were* the reading, and are now the focus for a silent meditation. Then the leader takes up the thread of the service again, following an order of service the community had devised for itself composed of prayer, song, and readings. I feel an involuntary smile spreading as I listened to the main reading from the community's own liturgy: a simple passage about not being as important as we think we are, and how to deal with the pain of being pushed to the sidelines. That morning, the story of the MPs expenses had broken. Hearing the details on my portable radio in a chilly house miles from anywhere, I'd felt the unmistakeable stab of professional ego under threat: that was 'my' story, an area I'd been covering for years, and now someone else would be covering it. In a few measured paragraphs, the reading speaks straight to these concerns, offering challenge and consolation in equal measure. I feel my breathing deepen, and the last of my resistance to this particular community ebb away.

It takes me a while to piece together the make-up of the community. There are perhaps ten people who make their home at Nether Springs, while the other permanent members live in nearby villages. There is a woman in her forties who does the accounts from a caravan in the yard, a young married couple and Rob, a jovial, hairy biker of a man. Norman, the beige-clad man who had led the first office, hails from Gloucester; I enjoy the clipped burr of my hometown that accompanies his gentle smile. Many more people turn up at mealtimes, and the kitchen can go from empty to full in a flash. 'Sometimes we see them come in and we scrape food off our plates so there's enough,' confides my neighbour as we sit down to eat.

Several times, having decided to do something else, I find myself drawn last-minute to the chapel-in-the-trees for one of the four offices that punctuate the day. The midday office is short – 'just the time it took to boil a kettle,' according to community lore – and has a brisk, work-a-day quality. Compline, on the other hand, is an intimate, candlelit affair at nine-thirty, a little circle huddling together to petition for safe passage through the night. The services are part of the rhythm of the day, little pools of quiet between the sociability of the house. And it seems much easier in the hut, with the smell of the wood and the soughing of the trees mingling with human voices, to slip into the calm than in a more conventional church. I feel able, to some extent, to enter into the experience of the community.

On one occasion, I feel sufficiently outside the proceedings to observe them with complete coolness. I look round and study my companions. Every heavy-lidded face suggests a person immersed in an inner place, while keeping a part of themselves attuned to the external event. The sense of peace, I conclude, comes partly out of the rhythm of the liturgy, with its gentle interchange of sound and silence, and the texture of different voices: each service is led by several people, each picking a slip of paper with the references for that day's readings just beforehand. The result is a dynamic harmony that couldn't be further from the jump-up-and-down routine that usually characterises Anglican services.

It is hard to believe that the liturgy which formed the backbone of this experience was a homespun creation, originally scribbled into a Filofax in the 1980s. The embryonic community had wanted a book of common prayer that reflected their particular struggles and needs, an authentic expression of faith that was suited to the time and place in which they lived. Gradually, its founders built up a series of reflections and prayers that became *Celtic Daily Prayer*, a book first published in 1994. It has become a publishing phenomenon, and is now widely used by Christians with no connection to Northumbria. I like the modest-yet-hopeful tone of the claims that made part of the Evening Prayer:

> Lord, You have always marked
> the road for the coming day;
> and though it may be hidden,
> today I believe.
>
> Lord, You have always lightened
> this darkness of mine;
> and though the night is here,
> *today I believe.*[53]

I am scared of the dark. I don't mean the ordinary darkness, the restfulness of the bedroom after a long, wearisome day, or the thrill of a country lane where the lack of light brings forth nocturnal sounds and smells. I mean that absolute blackness that springs from a determined bid to seal out the light: heavy velvet curtains carefully arranged to close out every chink, or the pitch-black enclosure of a windowless cell. Only twice in my life have I really felt its claw-like, suffocating grasp, but these experiences were enough to ensure that I am never entirely without light. Once as a small child, staying with my godmother and sleeping in an unfamiliar bedroom, I awoke unable to see or breathe. Hearing my screams, she came fast; a simple adjustment of the curtains put things right. Decades later, on a press trip in the Brazilian Amazon, I awoke once more to find myself paralysed with terror. Somehow, my all-in-one hammock and mosquito net – much admired in jungle circles for the protection it offered against insects and falling spiders – had conspired to put me into utter darkness. While my body failed to move, my mind filled with the thought that I would do anything – *anything* – to put an end to the anguish. Eventually, I managed to struggle free of the grip of the dark and unzip the net, spending the rest of the night straining towards the bit of light just within eyeshot. The next day, I swopped the hammock for the old-fashioned, open variety. Spiders, malaria-carrying mosquitos would be as nothing compared to that feeling of all-enveloping suffocation.

So it is with caution that I approach the Northumbria Community's *poustinia*, a windowless wooden cabin behind the chapel amid a patch of wild garlic. '*Poustinia*' – from the Russian meaning 'desert' – is designed to replicate, through isolation and the removal of sensory stimulation, a spiritual setting similar to that experienced by the desert fathers. In recent decades, the practice of becoming a '*poustinik*' – one who withdraws to commune with God while remaining part of a community – has crossed from the Russian Orthodox to the Roman Catholicism.

And here it is again, popping up in the Protestant contemplative tradition.

I step inside the cabin and close the door cautiously, my inner radar alert for signs of panic. Nothing. Normality. The darkness isn't bad, after all; it even has a furry, cosy quality. And anyway, if I look down to where the floor and wall fail to join I can see a beautiful yellow strip of light.

There are a dozen of us on the retreat: several Baptists, a young Anglican minister, a Celtic Christian, a few bearing hybrid labels and me, the self-confessed writer–observer. Every morning after the first office, the group gather for a talk given by Trevor Miller, one of the leaders of the community. A Baptist minister from Jarrow, he has an upbeat, fluid style well-suited to explaining the relevance of Bonhoeffer to a twenty-first-century audience. He unpacks the thinker's oxymoronic formulations – alone and togetherness, solitude and sociability – with a jaunty ease, making it clear how they have informed the Northumbria Community. Vulnerability and availability, involvement and withdrawal – these are the paradoxical mantras the community has developed to express a life that was both engaged and apart, with all its messiness and conflicting imperatives. He shares his material exuberantly, concluding one riff: 'A smell of monastic eros and pathos.' He pauses, triumphantly. 'Wouldn't that be a good quote for your book, eh, Alex?' Only once did his cheery demeanour desert him as he alluded to a rupture that had struck the heart of the community over a decade before. 'I will never forget it,' he says, with something close to a shudder. Almost immediately he is back in his role of theological entertainer, a kindly comedian who seasons his exposition with self-parody. He avoids resolving marital disputes, he tells us, through the simple ruse of retiring to his monastic 'cell', a place that I took to be either metaphorical or the garden shed. Then his gaze rotates back to the whole group, his tone paternal. 'Now, you have a bit of time to go to the toilet and get a cup of tea. Because life consists of wees and teas. Have you noticed that?'

After the session, we split into small groups, having been encouraged, as 'travelling companions', to share our responses to what we had heard. I am with Angela, a novitiate companion of the community in her sixties who exudes common sense and Jan, a wide-eyed Scot who jubilantly introduced herself to the group as having 'no religion – just Jesus Christ!' 'That's evangelical, that is,' Trevor responded sagely. Jan looked puzzled. Of everyone staying at the house, she is the most open and affectionate, her need for contact with others bubbling over painfully into the periods of designated quiet. While everyone else slips away to read, rest or reflect, she loiters in the common areas in search of company.

Huddled around the fire, the three of us forget about Bonhoeffer and trade stories of why we are there. Jan, after a difficult youth involving drugs, had her first adult experience of religion in a charismatic Baptist church. Disillusion had set in after a dozen years: the church was big on sects and divisions but short on compassion and care, quick to reject those who didn't stick to its strict rules about lifestyle. She was struggling as a single parent, her mental health breaking down; suicidal, she made a last-ditch plea to the pastor. This time, she got the help she needed: a recommendation to spend time at the Northumbria Community. She'd been coming regularly for a year, for periods of up to a month. A spiritual adviser provided her with regular support, and each time she came away feeling different. 'I feel this is a place of preparation. I feel I'm in a period of transition, getting ready to go back out,' she says, leaning forward eagerly. Her words have a familiar ring, and after a moment I realise they echo Trevor's.

Angela tells of her disaffection with the denominations that had formed the mainstay of her religious life. Writing a history of the new Anglican parish in which she lived in southern England, excavating its first fifty years, had revealed so many faultlines that she no longer went to church. Meanwhile the Quakers, to which she was also drawn, hardly seemed to talk about God any more. But the Northumbria Community felt right. She had joined the previous summer as a dispersed member, and had a spiritual mentor with whom she maintained regular contact; other support came from meetings in her area. Since joining the community she felt less self-conscious about taking the time she needed for prayer, reading and solitude, despite the demands of married life and the outside world.

'Do you go to church, Alex?'

Jan is looking at me intently, and I feel that peculiar rush of energy that often accompanies a conversion attempt. I didn't sign up to a particular church, as I feel all faiths potentially had something of the truth, I tell her.

'I'm with Jesus! I don't think I'm a church person, I think I'm across faiths,' she rejoins enthusiastically, willing us both into the same camp. God's army would soon triumph, she goes on, and bring about the collapse of traditional religion; in its place will come a new spirituality that will unite all the peoples of the world.

'That sounds like a kind of last days' theory,' I remark, puzzled by the sudden leap from pluralist sentiments to the apocalypticism of evangelical Christianity.

Jan nods happily. 'Oh yes, I think something like that is coming.'

The next day, after the midday office, she catches me on the stairs.

'You know what I said yesterday about God's army, and the last days? I didn't really mean it like that. I meant what Trevor was saying this morning.'

That morning's session had dealt with Bonhoeffer's notion of a religionless Christianity, in which relationships and their difficulties lay at the heart of faith. 'You know, spirituality and relationship. Organic.' Jan canters on eagerly. 'I'm not good with words, you see, and I often come away and say, "I didn't mean that, I meant this".' The blue eyes look up entreatingly from their place further down the staircase. 'What Trevor said,' she repeats.

We stand there awhile, gently tussling with the question of how she married two radically different religious worlds – a cataclysmic, absolutist vision of the Day of Judgement with the gentle, steady-as-you-seek version of Christianity being proffered in latter-day Northumbria. But the more we talk, the further the mutual understanding we seek seems to recede. She is bewildered by her own confusion; I am desperate to let us both off the hook.

'Don't worry, have a think about it,' I say, modulating my voice into a reassuring tone. It is a while before she accepts my face-saving fiction that tomorrow, clarity will come. But eventually she descends the stairs with an 'I'll get back to you,' her face still crossed with perplexity.

Some light on the incident comes during my interview with Trevor in his hideaway study. Its location is a product of the changes the building has undergone over the centuries; the only way to get there is via a narrow stone passage that runs through the centre of the house, with an entrance concealed behind a door in the library you could easily mistake for a cupboard. But once inside, it is a gracious room with generous windows overlooking the grounds. Trevor has made it his own, filling it with books and religious knick-knacks including a smirking monk doll of rubber. The meeting is my one chance to talk to him in any depth, as he always makes a swift exit after the morning sessions and, apart from maintaining a silent presence at offices, is never in evidence at any other time. Elusiveness seems to be a characteristic of the community's leaders; when making arrangements for an interview with founder Roy Searle, it had been made very clear to me that his time was limited.

In the hour he can spare, Trevor talks with his customary fluency about how, without any advertising, the community has become increasingly popular as a refuge with those in the process of breaking away from the narrow, dogmatic faith of the evangelical churches. Instinctively, these new seekers are reaching out for support as they take their first steps towards a faith which accepts mystery at its core, and sees the acquisition of truth as an ongoing process.

'We get hosts of people here who are looking for a halfway house – a safe place where they can voice, without condemnation, the doubts and uncertainties they have,' he explains. 'It's not unbelief. People mistake doubt for unbelief. It's more about a revival of spirituality – people having their own experience of God.'

I notice he refrains from giving the hard, doctrinaire faith from which its adherents are trying to free themselves its obvious name. Recovering fundamentalists must be a tough client-group, I think, resistant and fearful of the light of uncertainty breaking out around them.

Out loud, I say: 'Is it difficult working with people in that state?'

Trevor considers for a moment. 'It's easier now. People come here already knowing that part of our hospitality is to welcome people on their journey of faith, whatever stage they're at.'

Yet the community espouses a resolutely Christian viewpoint, a position which would exclude me, with my pluralist, trans-Christian perspective, from joining, he went on: '"We shall sing the Lord's song in a strange land", that's what we say. We've found God and Jesus, and we're not looking anywhere else.'

In practical terms, everything about the community had to be created, from its liturgy to the chapel which had been constructed with what came to hand in the early nineties by entirely inexperienced builders. Trevor recalls laughingly the day the novices were surprised by the arrival of the ready mix concrete they had ordered, not having realised they would need to stop what they were doing and lay the base of the building before the concrete dried. The result, I tell him, is strangely beautiful. 'Aye, it's a thin place,' he agrees.

As I rise to leave, I express my envy of his secret study in the womb of the house. 'I'll make you even more jealous,' he smiles. 'I've even got my own chapel.' Beckoning me to follow, he leads me back down the passageway to the library, stopping halfway to pull back a red velvet curtain which reveals a narrow opening in the wall. We squeeze our way along a rib-bracing passage, duck under a low-hanging beam of concrete and emerge into a narrow, low-ceilinged chamber of red-brown stone. A desk-cum-altar displays candles and icons, and a brown carpet swirls, seventies-style, on the floor. I pause to examine a palm-sized book on a little table. 'The Hidden Life of the Soul by Jean Nicolas Grou' reads the lettering across its pale green cover. 'I used to keep that in my pocket when I did prison work,' says Trevor, picking it up and stroking it affectionately.

But with the ceiling and walls pressing in on me, I feel the familiar rise of claustrophobia. The little chamber, formerly used as a storage space, is windowless, soundproof and damp. After the cosy darkness of the *poustinia*, it strikes me as a place of incarceration: suffocating and oppressive. I feel deeply uncomfortable, and say so.

'I've never even thought of that, until you said it,' responds Trevor thoughtfully. 'Perhaps it's because, having worked in prisons, I don't notice it.'

Happy to leave this particular monastic cell, I say my thanks and make my way back down the passage and out into the library. The door closes behind me, and I hear the chain being put across. Like Cuthbert before them, it seems that the latter-day monastics of Northumbria struggle to protect their solitude from the demands of a busy world.

Pheasants zig-zag crazily out of our path as Norman drives along the high-hedged lanes. We are going to Wooler for my appointment with Roy. Like many others in the community, both men are Baptists: a result, Norman thinks, of a lack within the denomination. 'If you're a Catholic, or an Anglican, there are plenty of orders. But if you're a Baptist, and you want something more contemplative, where do you go?'

Terraced houses of the local red stone line the sloping streets of Wooler. Roy's is on the high street, its front door opening directly onto the pavement. At our knock it flies open almost immediately to reveal a balding, merry-eyed man in his fifties and two women – wife and secretary – hovering helpfully in the background. I have little more than an hour with him, and a lot of questions: Roy is going away the next day and needs to prepare. It is one of the many trips demanded by his role as community ambassador, a one-man roadshow taking the new monasticism to churches and conferences.

In the conservatory at the back of the house, Roy begins to tell me of the community's beginnings in the 1980s. As a young Baptist minister, he had become disenchanted with the churches around him, disillusioned by the mismatch between their dogmas and the realities of life in the economically deprived north-east. The Christianity he knew seemed to require constant activity, yet to offer little that was meaningful. Longing for something deeper, he found himself drawn to two local spiritual pioneers: John Skinner, an Anglo-Catholic with a charismatic personality, and Andy Raine, an eccentric creative based on Lindisfarne who was developing a ministry involving walking and dancing. John and Roy became spiritual companions, meeting midwinter in an old chapel, hot water bottles clasped to their bellies, and taking long walks across the fields as they talked. Gradually, a different approach to religion started to emerge, one that was loosely based on the Celtic tradition that had flourished centuries before in the north-east. Roy had never been particularly interested in nature, or impressed by claims about the 'spirituality of place', but walking his native Northumberland engendered a new relationship with the place. He became curious about its saints and their deep connection to their surroundings.

'It was something about Northumbria,' he says simply. 'We were engaged by the stories of the saints – not in a romantic way – but something in them inspired us. We learnt from the Celtic tradition about rediscovering hospitality as part of our humanness, and recognising the presence of Christ.'

With John, he had established the Northumbria Community in stages in the early 1990s. The Rule was introduced by Trevor five years later, but its application was lax by traditional standards, the result of a conscious decision to allow room for the failings and messiness of life. The dispersed community grew quietly, and now had two hundred and eighty companions, and two and a half thousand friends in various parts of the world.

'I would say almost half our people would be unchurched, or de-churched,' he goes on. 'The Northumbria Community would be their church, their only one. Most are believers, but some are not sure. We have an awful lot of people who are disillusioned. Some are weary of the activism of the church; there are lots of burnt-out charismatic evangelicals. After all, there's been a lot of prophecies about change, the coming of the kingdom of God on earth and' – a wry smile accompanies the shrug – 'It hasn't happened.'

It was part of the outflow of people from the evangelical churches which, contrary to received opinion, research showed to be on the decline. 'The theology doesn't allow for failure. Some people have been incredibly hurt by power. I think they are looking for places where people are not trying to control them. That sounds stark, but I hope you understand what I mean.'

'So what can you do to counter that?'

'Well, there's community, and the inner thing,' he replies. 'That means there's more humility, and we're less liable to power-plays, control. Hospitality is a core value – you're less likely to use people to achieve your own ends.'

'Why?' I ask, not quite seeing the connection.

'Because you're honouring them, and you're not expecting them to be an adherent of your movement.' He gives me a quizzical look to see if I have got the point. 'It's about saying we haven't got a monopoly on truth.'

I wonder whether there had been trouble along the way.

'Oh, yes, we've had Trouble.' A rueful smile spreads across his face.

He describes how, in 1998, John had upped and left without explanation, leaving his sister – Trevor's wife – and the rest of them in a state of shock, feeling emotionally and spiritually abandoned.

'It was very painful. He was one of the key figures – without him we would never have got off the ground – one of those prophetic types. A genius. But always restless, restless.' His eyes darken. 'We were rocked to the very core. It was like a fog coming down, as if everything we had believed in disappeared, because we were strong on relationship.'

In the collective soul-searching that followed, the community considered whether it should disband. But eventually it took heart once more, having learnt a hard truth: no community, if it was to be sustainable, could depend so heavily on the charismatic personalities of its founders.

Other, more worldly lessons came from the business side of keeping the community afloat: the group started loss-making ventures, failed to ask for their due in partnership projects, lost money, wasted time. 'Most of our problems have occurred not through relationship problems, but partly through naivety and stupidity,' confesses Roy. The tone is self-deprecating, but the dancing smile is back. I get the impression these were mere details after the challenges of Relationship.

Is it possible to live with others without conflict? The secular world has a black-and-white clarity about the issue. Rows and rifts, changes and departures are par for the course: unavoidable in politics, common at work, and unfortunate in families. We shrug and move on. Christian communities want to do better, and traditional monasticism, with its emphasis on commitment to a single place and set of relationship, takes the aspiration to its extreme. Who is right? When things go wrong, whether in an orphanage run by Mother Teresa or a monastery in modern Britain, it's easy to conclude 'QED! Religion is broken!' Yet it's possible to detect a certain smugness in the pitying gaze with which the secular look on the world. In the gap between the two views comes the voice of Bonhoeffer, the sage who never lived long enough to acquire the physical signs of wisdom:

> By sheer grace, God will not permit us to live even for a brief period in a dream world. He does not abandon us to those rapturous experiences and lofty moods that come over us like a dream. God is not a God of the emotions but the God of truth. Only that fellowship which faces such disillusionment, with all its unhappy and ugly aspects, begins to be what it should be in God's sight, begins to grasp in faith the promise that is given to it.[54]

I am reading a copy of Bonhoeffer's *Life Together* in the Nether Springs library. The evening light is turning golden, but the need for research has trumped the desire for a walk. 'Roy Searle 1978' uncoiled over the flyleaf in the neat handwriting of youth. Bonhoeffer writes:

The sooner this shock of disillusionment comes to an individual and to a community, the better for both. A community which cannot bear and cannot survive such a crisis, which insists upon keeping its illusion when it should be shattered, permanently loses in that moment the promise of Christian community.[55]

I spend my last afternoon talking to Cara in the room behind the Bluebeard door, which turns out to contain only ugly brown furniture, a TV and some toys for visiting children. It also houses a faulty boiler – the reason for the room's closure – and the acrid smell of spilled kerosene fills the air. I am keen to hear why Cara, of all people, joined the community: her youth and vivacity hardly suit her for a life in the middle of nowhere without any career prospects. She had moved to Nether Springs a few months before, after two years as a companion, and become a full member of the community. Her wide, smooth face belies her age and experience: she is in her mid-thirties, with years of teaching and overseas development work behind her, and much of her adult life has been spent in the Middle East.

Her experiences there had rocked the certainties of her upbringing on the English–Welsh borders in a conservative family of Baptists. Living in Jerusalem and Ramallah, amid opposing groups who all claimed that God was on their side, had brought her hard up against the reality of other faiths. The traditional beliefs of her youth required her to take sides; instead she responded by uncompromisingly applying the logic of the Christian emphasis on equality to the claims and counter-claims flying around her.

'If Christianity says that all are made in the image of God, then it's open to everybody.' She speaks emphatically. 'You can't say, "God wants the Jews back in Israel and therefore I'm going to act against Arabs". Equally, you can't say, "I despise Israelis". That is not godly either. I am a traditional Christian. I have found nothing in this life that would change that. But I have also found that God is working in people's lives in other ways.'

Her years in north Africa had represented a turning point in her attitude to other ways of believing. She and her closest friend, a local Muslim woman, were spending the afternoon together as they so often did, when her friend suddenly burst into tears.

'She started weeping because, in her understanding, I was going to hell because I didn't believe in Mohammed. I wouldn't be with her in paradise; she wouldn't be with me. I started crying too: that was how I felt about her.'

She pauses. I can clearly picture the scene: two young women, bound by the love of friendship and knowing their paths would soon separate, weeping together under the African sun.

'So we agreed to pray,' Cara goes on. 'She would pray to Allah that he would help me to recognise the God of Islam and Mohammed, and I would pray to God that she would come to recognise "the fullness of life". And we laughed about it.'

The episode represented neither a loss of faith nor a decisive step into another kind of Christianity. But internally, a profound shift had taken place. Back home, she re-examined her assumptions about identity and belonging and what it meant to be a Christian in Britain. Then she joined the Northumbria Community.

'The community is a gathering of true Christians, but at the same time it's an expression of Christianity I haven't found elsewhere.' Her brow furrows as she tries to fathom its distinctiveness. 'I think what I love most about this place is that it's very real. People say when they're having a crap day. It's a more honest, British expression. If I express a half-thought, they will have the grace to let me express it and work it out for myself. Initially, it was incredibly unsettling to be with a bunch of Christians who don't have expectations of you. There are far fewer places to hide. Here, people see you all the time, and quite quickly your fronts don't work. There will always be someone who does something that bothers you. Here, because you can't walk away, that helps you to develop as a person. You either develop patience, or the ability to say, "can I speak to you about that, because it really bothers me".'

She pauses and looks out of the window. 'We do have some sad stories. We're not shiny. It doesn't always work.'

'Do you know the Christian concept of *peregrinatio*?' The face she turns back is animated. Like the ancient Celtic wanderers, she is getting restless and making plans to leave the Northumbria Community. 'I'm getting to the point where now I need to be in a wider community, go back to a local church ... For me, this is not enough. I miss having neighbours, and a pub down the road.'

She has recently accepted a new job, and in a few months will be going back out into the secular world. And before long, the entire community will be on the move: Hetton Hall is up for sale, and a new base has to be found for Nether Springs.

In a modest way, I knew something about the loss of place. After more than thirty years in the same village, my parents were selling up and moving to a more manageable house some three miles away on the outskirts of Gloucester. Although I spent little time there as an adult, the Big House and its garden was a permanent place in the back of my mind where I kept a part of my self. It was impossible to imagine not being able to meander down to the gloomy brown river at the bottom of the paddock, to visit my favourite trees or take a peek into the dusty corners I had loved as a child.

The day of the move found me at my desk in London as usual, interviewing some housing professionals over the phone. As twelve o'clock approached – the hour at which the house would officially pass into other hands – I could hear my voice sounding increasingly shaky. At midday, trying to calm myself with carbs, I defrosted a bagel in the microwave. The plate underneath it cracked in two. For months afterwards, I felt unaccountably unsettled, almost as if a person I had relied on had died; it was some time before I realised that my feelings were nothing more or less than grief for the family home. Meanwhile I discovered that, if I closed my eyes and focused, I could transport myself back there, the distinctive panelling of the hall and rectangle of light that fell in through the heavy front door onto the Victorian tiles unfolding around me as vividly as if I were actually there. I would hover in certain places, enjoying the embrace of the walls I knew so well, suffused by a curious sense of floating about two feet above the floor. I hoped that the people who now lived there were not disturbed by my ghost.

My parents' new house, if rather less characterful, was modern and pleasant and called, in a nice reminder of my mother's dissenting forebears, Greenwood Lodge. The name of the close in which it sat, Ladywell, provided a link to the area's religious past. In one of the pastures that sloped gently down to the river stood the 'lady well', a gabled monument of limestone covering a natural spring. One tradition held that the Virgin Mary herself had set foot there and that the spring had sprung up to quench her thirst; another suggested that the monument was dedicated to her mother, Saint Anne. Whatever the case, the fourteenth-century construction was a residue of the network of sacred wells and shrines that had patterned the country before the English Reformation. Now overgrown and neglected, it supplied the adjoining drinking trough for cattle.

*

There is one more thing I want to do before leaving the Northumbria Community: visit St Cuthbert's Cave in the hills a couple of miles away. Legend has it that Cuthbert rested in its shelter when walking from Lindisfarne to Durham; it was said that monks fleeing the Danes with the saint's body a couple of hundred years later used the rocky enclave as a staging post. Cara gives me a lift part of the way, dropping me off at the track at the foot of the hill. I walk up through fields studded with stones, passing through some pine woods until I reach the cave. It is a wide-mouthed, shallow opening in the rock beneath a sandstone overhang topped with firs. A couple are lying side-by-side in front of it, face down on the grass. Not wanting to disturb them, I carry on to the cairn at the top of the ridge, and look east.

The surrounding landscape falls away towards a glittering sea. Across a strip of blue lies Lindisfarne, golden in the afternoon sun. I stand awhile, watching. There is plenty going on: a vigorous wind is propelling the clouds fast across the sky, while in the mid-distance a neat white column of vapour puff-puffs from behind a ridge, as if someone just out of sight is cranking a cloud machine. Over a nearby field, a lark is ascending and descending, levering itself methodically up and down the air currents, each stage accompanied by a burst of song.

Then, sheep scattering in my path, I make my way back down to the cave. The couple have gone, but at its entrance a freshly lit orange candle is burning on a rocky ledge. Someone has tied a bow of red ribbon and a silver tassel around the slender stems of some nearby grasses. I had seen plenty such offerings in Lebanon, in the shrines to prophets and saints that dotted its mountains: physical petitions for the healing of a sick child or a much-wanted pregnancy in the form of a lock of hair or a tiny garment. But in

Britain such residues of religious practices that pre-dated monotheism are rare. The presence of votive offerings amid all this natural beauty is strangely reassuring, testifying to a continuity between ancient and modern and an impulse that came from before organised religion and which would endure through the period of its fragmentation into ...

It's too early to say.

Some boulders stand a few yards from the cave's entrance. Their faces bear the inscriptions of the births and deaths of a local family that go back a century; the Leathers had used the stones as a natural alternative to a graveyard. I study the biggest rock; its slanted face makes a convenient tabula, and the names and dates sit lightly on its smooth grey surface: there is no trace of the long-running battle between pagan and Christian ways here.

Perhaps the Northumbria Community was enacting similar continuities and repetitions between the past and present, religion and its other. It was clear that the new monasticism brought no leap into a future untainted by the problems that had always beset communities. Neither did it offer an easy passage to a place beyond orthodoxy: adopting a more realistic kind of faith wasn't simply a matter of revising your theology, it was a process that involved pain and difficulty. The glimpses that Trevor, Ray and Jan had given me of their lives revealed confusion, break-up, even breakdown. In the end, the security they sought came not from continuity of circumstance, but an inner stability of purpose strong enough to accommodate difficulty and change.

But was community, with its inevitable compromise and conformity, always necessary to faith? There was an aspect of the contemplative tradition, as yet unexplored, that promised a path free of such limitations. If I really wanted to get a full picture of the changing spiritual life of my country, it was its solitary outriders that I now needed to find.

HIDDEN HERMITS

There have probably always been hermits-in-disguise: the old woman living alone at the edge of the village, the family man who, as the years went by, gradually retreated into a place inside himself where his wife and children couldn't follow. Maybe these people were quietly living a life of inner solitude, a wordless faith that remained unexpressed even to themselves. Perhaps they were unsung spiritual heroes and heroines on the way to the life of being rather than doing that so many religious traditions consider the peak of spiritual development. Or perhaps they weren't. Maybe they were just grumpy misanthropes or dysfunctional types who couldn't cope with the demands of relating to others. God only knows.

It's often forgotten that monastic communities began as groups of hermits who gathered to support each other in what was a fundamentally solitary enterprise. ('Monastic' comes from the Greek *monos*, alone.) Even once monasteries were established, the bigger fish were still impelled to go it alone: St Cuthbert, St Teresa and St John of the Cross petitioned their superiors for years for permission to 'go apart'. Solitude seems to represent a further stage of development craved by the spiritually ambitious, and the experiences reported from its frontline seem to confirm Thomas Merton's claim that hermits are the real McCoy, more serious about getting close to God than their community-minded counterparts.[56] It's a view that transforms them from anti-social creatures to explorers of a realm beyond the frontiers of known religious experience, prepared to take greater risks and endure more hardship than the average person.

This goes some way to explaining the undeniable oddness of some hermits. The fifth-century Christian Simon the Stylites spent nearly forty years atop a column in Syria, inspiring a movement of pillar saints perching across the Levant. This ascetic practice turned out to be a fad, another experiment in the many possible ways of subduing body to spirit. As Christianity spread, the fundamentals of eremitic life – solitude, austerity and prayer – lived on, becoming an essential part of religious life. Solitaries flourished in medieval Britain, with hermits attached to churches, monasteries and even the homes of the wealthy; fourteenth-century Yorkshire alone had around a hundred. A hermit gave a community cachet, but better yet was to have an anchorite, a solitary authorised by the ecclesiastical authorities who lived in quarters adjoining the church. ('Anchorite' derives from the Greek *anachorein*, meaning 'to go apart'.) Becoming an anchoress was popular among women, a socially acceptable alternative to marriage and childbearing and a spiritual path free of the male-dominated institutions of the Church. Mysticism offered an unmediated experience so personal that it was hard to discredit, although male spiritual directors sometimes sought to control the women under their jurisdiction.

The father of English mysticism Richard Rolle embarked on his solitary path in around 1319. Jettisoning his place at Oxford, he ran away from home, having cobbled together a hermit's outfit out of his father's rain hood and sisters' frocks.[57] ('My brother is mad! My brother is mad!' cried his favourite sister, understandably.) He took refuge in a series of hermitages around Yorkshire before settling in a cell in the village of Hampole and becoming spiritual director to a Cistercian nunnery. He went on to become one of the most prolific religious writers of his age, documenting how, after years of spiritual discipline, he experienced enlightenment in the most physical terms:

> I was sitting in a particular chapel, greatly delighting in the smooth flow of my prayer or mediation, when I suddenly experienced within myself an unaccustomed and joyous burning ardour. Although I first doubted where this might be coming from, I have since proved, over a long period of time, that it comes not from any creature but from the Creator, since it is more burning and more agreeable.[58] It was a rare reminder, in the cerebral Christianity of the west, that body, as well as mind, could know God.

The music came later:

> Suddenly, the sound of, as it were, ringing or rather playing of stringed instruments, above me, made me jump. Then, when I strained towards these heavenly sounds by praying with all my heart, I experienced – I do not know how soon – the blending of melodies within myself and drew forth the most delightful harmony from heaven, which stayed with me, in my spirit.[59]

The testimony of England's best-known mystic, Julian of Norwich, furnishes the material for the first book written in English by a woman. Little is known about St Julian's life, but she seems to have had a sense of her spiritual destiny from the outset, praying in her youth for both an understanding of Christ's passion and a physical sickness. Her wish was granted at the age of thirty-one and, on the point of death after a severe illness, she had a series of sixteen visions which she later recorded in *The Revelations of Divine Love*:

I saw on the face of the crucifix that hung before me part of his Passion unfolding before my very eyes: men showing their contempt, spitting on him, sullying and buffeting him. I saw his many exhausting pains – more than I can tell – and how his face often changed colour. At one moment I saw half his face, beginning with the ear, redden over with dried blood until this covered up to the middle of his face ... At one point, I was led in my mind down to the seashore. There I saw hills and valleys, green as though covered in moss, together with seaweed and shingle. I took this to mean that if someone were there under the wide water and given sight of God as God is continuously with us, he would be safe in soul and body and come to no harm. Furthermore, he would receive more comfort or solace than any this world may or can describe.[60]

The faith she derived from this experience was lasting, and Mother Julian lived for another forty years, dispensing spiritual counsel from her anchorite's cell in a Norwich church.

But where were the hermits of contemporary Britain? What form did the impulse to go apart now take? It was impossible to get numbers of solitaries accredited by the churches. I rang the Anglican and Catholic press offices, and got bemused 'don't know's: the few official hermits in the country tended not to feature in national data because they were attached to particular orders or accredited by individual dioceses.

Yet I had a hunch that the solitary still existed, albeit without the label or recognisable way of life that had marked them out in times gone by. Perhaps there was a contemporary version quietly embarked on a quest for the divine in the everyday, while living an unremarkable life? Every now and then, a sign of this subterranean spiritual life came to the surface. The loquacious writer and mother Sara Maitland published a book about her decision to live alone in the wilds of Scotland.[61] Soon afterwards, in a bizarre echo of Simon the Stylites, a professed Catholic hermit mounted a plinth in Trafalgar Square as part of a public art project run by Antony Gormley. Rachel Denton had given up her career as a science teacher to live in solitude, naming her council house after St Cuthbert.[62] Such cases struck me as indications that the age-old impulse for solitude lived on, but was taking a new form.

So I wasn't surprised when, opportunistically plugging likely keywords into Google, I happened on the website of the Fellowship of Solitaries. The Fellowship described itself as a loose network of people answering their individual calls to solitude in the midst of busy, ordinary lives. They had no institutional affiliation, were unrecognised by the communities in which they lived and did not follow any kind of Rule. The website explained:

The solitary life is essentially hidden; there is no badge or habit, no special title, nothing to suggest a corporate identity. The Fellowship has none – it is not a community or a society, just a fellowship of people each pursuing his or her own path but banded together for support and encouragement. Our witness is the way we live, and is thus a prophetic sign in its solitude, simple unobtrusiveness and silence ... Because the life is solitary, it is personal to each; no two follow the same path. For that reason the

Fellowship has no rule of life; it is most unlikely that it ever will. How we can pray best is for each to discover for her or himself.[63]

Eureka. I had found my contemporary hermits. Formed with just a handful of people in 1990, the Fellowship had soon acquired, without the help of advertising, over three hundred members, and a leading voice to articulate their distinctive condition. A writer and former bookseller, Eve Baker had been one of its first members, taking over the role of coordinator after founder Peter Edwards resigned due to ill health. Solitude, she wrote, in a slim, simply written volume, was necessarily a state which went against the grain of society, just like monasticism before it became institutionalised. These days, the path of solitude offered a counterpoint to the 'constant verbalisation' of modern society and a contemplative alternative to the relentless activity of the Christian church.[64]

My initial contact with the Fellowship was discouraging. The website gave only a postal address in Northumberland for the current coordinator, and it was a month before I had a reply to my letter. It came in the form of an email, popping up incongruously on the news desk on press day. Its tone confirmed my stereotype of the kind of person who would fulfil such a role: a quintessential Englishman, retired and retiring, probably with a lot of facial hair. He did not normally correspond by email, wrote John Mullins, and was only doing so now because his printer was broken. As for my request to be put in touch with members, the Fellowship had received a similar enquiry once before, from a television company. But no one had wanted to talk to the media, and it had come to nothing. He himself did not want to be interviewed. 'After all,' he pointed out, 'Solitude and publicity of any form seem a contradiction in terms.' He was, he added, a 'transient caretaker' of the society, limited by his inadequacies in theology and IT, and was doing it only until someone better came along.

This off-putting response was belied by a generous supply of information about the Fellowship, along with a half-invitation to get back in touch. I took heart from eastern tales of the true seeker having to knock repeatedly on the door of the master, and wrote back carefully, amplifying my request and asking he suspend any decision about an interview. Over the following months, an intermittent correspondence developed, and one day I was rewarded by the arrival of a fat envelope on the doormat. It contained the list of the Fellowship's members and their descriptions of their spiritual positions, accompanied by a strict injunction against contacting anyone directly.

'It is to help you understand both the amazing variety of people who are called to this "other God", yet at the same time it reveals that this "other God" is mostly discovered within the hidden depths of organised religious church', wrote John. 'Which begs the question: why do the churches so habitually misunderstand, distort and bury the reality of this "other God"? ... It is a shame that so many genuine people have had much of their lives seemingly wasted trying to conform to the ... God of church authority, rather than nurtured through prayer towards spiritual "fullness of life" within one's heart and through relationships'.

I studied the list. It was certainly varied: there were Anglicans, Quakers, Catholics, Methodists and someone from the Orthodox tradition. A couple of people described themselves as influenced by Buddhism, and there was a Druid living in Islington. There were a few monks, nuns and ministers, and a full-time hermit with impressive spiritual credentials. But the majority were ordinary people pursuing ordinary British lives. 'Practising a "monastic" life in the cell of my council flat. Seeking God in the everyday moment', wrote one. A family man declared himself to be an itinerant, married hermit. How did his wife feel, I wondered?

The jobs of these undercover hermits suggested there was indeed a connection between spiritual life and 'right livelihood'. Overwhelmingly, the occupations were teaching, caring for others or doing something creative; many worked in education, health or social care; a few were counsellors and postal workers. One sounded particularly good company: 'Gardener and clown. Happiest when tilling the soil. Increasingly seeing the funny side of life'. Politicians, estate agents and journalists, on the other hand, were nowhere to be seen and, of the two business folk listed, one was apologetic about the venality of his occupation. Some entries afforded glimpses into the inner worlds of their authors in a few economical words. 'Still seeking', said one simply.

Another had got it down to a single word: 'Seeking ...'.

Six months after my first letter, John Mullins picked me up from Nether Springs. My second, last-minute request to see him, tentatively made as I was preparing to visit the Northumbria Community, had met with ready assent. He lived nearby, and would be happy to help with transport as there were few local buses. He mentioned in passing a hermit friend who had been living in seclusion for thirty-seven years, on a hill just up the road from his house. A visit could be easily arranged. The door to the world of the solitaries was suddenly open.

The hippyish American who turns up in place of the ageing English fogey I had been expecting has a mellifluous, east coast accent that often bubbles over into laughter. It is easy to see, in his wide blue eyes and floppy fair-grey hair, traces of the idealistic young man who had moved from the States to marry an Englishwoman thirty years before and become a social worker. We are not due at the hermit's until three, so we stop first at John's house, a long stone cottage set against the hills on the edge of Wooler. Inside, a boisterous black Labrador springs about, while an elderly lady-cat sits, paws drawn neatly together, blinking in genteel distaste. John opens a side door and two large-grown kittens shoot into the kitchen as if fired from a cannon, jump onto the table and climb into snugly fitting cardboard boxes. The table is stacked with correspondence, bills mingling with unopened envelopes, and John fishes around in the piles, pulling out titbits from his correspondence with solitaries for me to read. Then he sets about getting us some lunch, hopping around the kitchen collecting bits of bread, cheese and salad, and slicing and buttering in the manner of someone who is only just coping.

Over lunch, he talks of the difficulties of running a network of people who, by definition, don't want much contact. A national event bringing members of the Fellowship together, face-to-face? Out of the question. The quarterly newsletter is the main channel of communication, so he tries to use it to get people to share their experiences, questions and problems. But it is difficult getting contributions, and some of what he printed drew complaints. There is a lot of work, but when Eve Baker had stepped down there had been no one else willing to do it.

Afterwards, we repair to the sitting room where a fourth, tortoiseshell cat clambers onto my lap. John brings me some of the letters that had come in response to his request for contributions to the newsletter. 'They tend to be straight from the heart. There's no social aspect to it: it's purely about their interior life, and it just jumps off the page.'

I leaf through the pile, dipping in and out of the letters. One correspondent describes herself as very much 'in the world', with a family, close friends and a job. But, she goes on, 'in another sense, I have always been solitary. From a child, I can say that I have always been aware of God, or the Other, deep within my being.

'The overwhelming need is to simplify life, to attempt to cut out distractedness so that the voice may be heard', she continues. 'However, I do find the Christian church to be one of the hardest places to pursue spirituality and I have had, for years, a love-hate relationship with it. The biggest difficulty is that to be just praying is to be seen as not pulling one's weight'.

I linger over another short note, uncertain what to make of its contents. It is just a few lines scrawled across a grey page. 'I'm afraid I don't really have anything to contribute at the moment as this past year my vocation has been smashed to bits and I'm desperately clinging onto the pieces', their author has written. 'Nothing much has given me solace. I'm in a spiritual wasteland, the newsletter has been my lifeline. Thanks for all you do'.

They are just a sample of the many letters he received each year, John tells me; a correspondence so big he couldn't always reply, although he tried to answer those that called, directly or indirectly, for a response. As the tortoiseshell crossly attempts to assert her dominance over the papers spreading out over my legs, I wonder about this unrecognised need for spiritual support and what it says about religious institutions.

'If something like this was a lot more well-known, even within the churches, it would attract a lot more people,' he agrees. 'If you did the marketing and got it out there, I think the response would probably be overwhelming, at least for one person.'

He tells me about a professional visit he had made to a fourteen-year-old-boy who refused to go to school, and who barely spoke. Social worker and client had sat through an almost wordless interview in which only a few questions and the odd laugh punctuated the silence. 'I've no doubt that there was some sort of experience of solitude,' he concludes. 'From a professional point of view, there was something: schools and social workers would try to fix the boy and his behaviour. But clearly he was experiencing something deeper. Churches and social services are missing something when they do this; looking in on someone's interior life from the outside, it's almost making a negative diagnosis of someone's experience.' He pauses. 'I tell you this because, from the beginning, people have written in and told me that they didn't fit in, that there was something wrong with them. I think there are a lot of people who wouldn't be able to recognise this experience, or label it, and yet it's there in them.'

'So is it hard to reply?' I ask. Responding to such confidences and cries for help seems a daunting task.

'I don't find it hard to reply. Maybe I should,' he returns simply.

To the man asking for advice on how to approach his first Buddhist retreat, he warns of the pitfalls, such as expecting too much too quickly, or mistaking the first fruits of silence for true enlightenment. I notice that, as he talks, a quiet assurance has replaced his former diffidence. Unfazed by the spectre of unbelief that frightened so many, he has a gift for dealing with the intimate correspondence that comes his way, and he has become a keeper of spiritual confidences, an unofficial confessor with whom people can deposit their doubts and difficulties.

'And the woman in crisis? What have you said to her?'

By way of reply, he moves swiftly to the desk at other end of the room, returning with a large hardback which he deposits into my hands. Its yellowing pages fan out from its black fabric covers, spilling extra letters and papers into my lap. It is the complete works of St John of the Cross, the book which, along with influences from Buddhism, has been his personal resource for the past thirty years.

He sits back down. 'A lot of people understand faith as a set of beliefs rather than a way of living. Just because someone is having a desolate experience doesn't mean they are moving away from God. People tend to grasp onto the sweetness and joy of life, and feel that they are moving closer to God, when it's completely irrelevant how you're feeling. But in fact, the "abyss of faith" highlighted by St John of the Cross is a sign that real engagement is taking place.' He hands me a slim leaflet with a self-deprecatory laugh. 'If you want to hold a mirror up to your failings, just write some poetry.'

It is the Fellowship's Advent newsletter. The poem on the cover evokes the experience of believers who find, instead of the reassuring presence of God, nothing but 'collapsed plans' and 'crumbling illusions'. It is the kind of thing that would upset the most conventional believers, and in my mind's eye I can see a host of tutting Anglican ladies, exchanging looks of baffled disapprobation. *We don't want this sort of thing, and so close to Christmas too!*

John laughs when I share this mental image. 'It's the reality! It's less about holding on, more about letting go.' He pauses.

'Groundlessness – that's the only place where one can have genuine experience of God, unmediated by one's memory, intellect and desire. Coming back to the choice of solitude, one doesn't need to go through any ascetic practices, because life throws stuff at you and eventually you are in a place where everything is stripped away, and you have nothing to hold onto. A lot of people get caught up in treating spiritual practices in an almost mathematical way – "if I do these things, I can achieve that".'

'So how do you make time for solitude?'

'I don't. I have no time at all. I just fit it in when I can,' he replies. 'If you don't have generosity and charity, if you're holding onto "my solitude", it almost becomes the modern me-time. If circumstances arise where you need to give up your prayer time, just go ahead and drop it, and come back to it later. It's a minor miracle that the newsletter gets produced at all. There are lots of people out there who could be doing it better, and you have to ask yourself why. If your solitude is me-time, the last thing you need is to put out a newsletter for two hundred people. I think that's why no one came forward to be the coordinator.'

It is time to go and see the hermit. But before the discussion ends, I want somehow to bring out into the open the strange little journey I had been on to meet him.

'Your first letter was very negative,' I venture.

He smiles gently, making no attempt to justify himself. 'Yeah, yeah, there you go.'

Then a broad grin spreads across his face. 'Well, it's worked out just fine.'

'Oh, you're going to see Brother Harold,' members of the Northumbria Community had said casually, when they heard what else I planned to do in the area. It was quickly becoming apparent that the locals found it entirely normal to have a hermit of nearly four decades' standing just up the road. Hairy biker Rob was a particularly good source of hermit gossip. Brother Harold, he said, possessed a quad bike, a bell called 'Resounding Thomas' to declare spiritual warfare against the forces of evil, and an endless supply of cake provided by local ladies.

It is raining hard as John drives through the winding lanes towards the hermitage. The road peters out at the bottom of the hill, and we continue up along a dirt track bounded by fields. At the top, the landscape opens up into a vast, panoramic horizon. But it is hard to see much; it is as if a grey net has been cast over the entire landscape, and the coats of the sheep grazing nearby are visibly sodden. As the car swings round into a parking position, I hear myself exclaim in surprise: 'It's a little monastery!'

Instead of the single dwelling I had expected, a set of low, red-roofed buildings in the Romanesque style spread over the summit. Solid and square, with arched doors and rooftop crosses, they are redolent of monasteries I have visited in the Lebanese mountains. But in place of the smooth stone flagging that would normally dignify a religious establishment is the muddy terrain of a farmyard. Bits of equipment and log-piles litter the ground. At one side stands an old caravan which looks as if it has seen better days. We make our way through the gate, and John gives me a tour. The retreat house contains four self-contained flats set out along a wide, light-filled corridor, and we step inside one. It is a little one-up, one-down, with a bedroom, study area, wood stove and prayer rail: everything you need for a spiritual get-away. Then we cross the yard to see the chapel the hermit had built to replace the makeshift arrangement in his loft. It is a substantial, elegant building, the terracotta of its tiled roof bright against the pastel masonry. Inside is an interplay of stone and light, a harmony of square and curve that is breathtaking. I move around, examining details, while John looks on, smiling at how awe-struck I am. No thought or expense has been spared in the detailing of the stained glass windows, with their abstract play of colour and light, or on the high-spec, contemporary church furniture ... Where, I wonder, my hand on the solid, glossy wood of the lectern, did the will and the money come from to create this beautiful little church in the middle of nowhere?

The hermitage has come a long way from its beginnings in 1971, when Brother Harold Palmer had taken up residence on the desolate moorland in a borrowed caravan. As a young Franciscan monk, Brother Harold had visited enclosed orders in Europe, and been impressed by the zeal with which the monks pursued the life of contemplation. Despite his own order's refusal to allow him to live apart, he was determined to fulfil his dream of becoming a hermit, and persisted until permission was granted. There followed several years' search across England for a place suitable for withdrawal. The hilltop site known as Shepherd's Law seemed uninhabitable at first: ruins were all that remained of the eighteenth-century folly farm. But seven years of toil, with support from friends and the local community, had brought the house into being, complete with a library and a chapel in the loft. In 1989, the four-celled annex was added so that others could enjoy the solitude. Maybe, in time, like-minded souls will join Brother Harold permanently and form a modern-day community of hermits. There is just one thing missing. In 1996, work began on the outside chapel, funded by a legacy from Brother Harold's mother, and had only recently been completed. The decades of human endeavour that have gone into the little settlement make Grand Designs look like a walk in the park.

Finally I am to meet the hermit himself. The voice that answers John's knock is cheery, but the dimness inside makes it hard to see its owner. First to emerge out of the gloom is Brother Harold's smile, a twinkle-eyed, mischievous look compounded by the absence of his two front teeth. His face follows, framed by a beard and a woollen *chullo* with ear flaps and dangling tassels. His outfit is a funky affair made up of various lines of defence against the cold: grey jogging pants, navy socks with sandals, and a fleece of the deepest rose. There is no electricity in the hermitage – artificial light, when needed, comes from the paraffin lamps hanging from the ceiling – and the unadorned breeze blocks of the walls add to the obscurity. But with its dark wood furniture and crackling fire, the place has a homely air which makes it a cosy retreat from the wind and rain.

We pull up chairs around the wood stove and the hermit invites me to ask him questions. But he fast proves not to be the easiest of interviewees. Something between an English evasiveness and a scholarly diffidence seems to get in the way of direct responses. 'Oh, I'm sure writer X can tell you much better about this than I can,' he will reply; other answers take the form of references to events in religious history. He elides points, mingles past and present and slips in quotations without attributing them. Some of my questions trigger bouts of laughter or an enigmatic smile; others provoke a mirthful, sideways glance to see how serious I am about getting an answer, sometimes looking to John to share the joke. In the sober moments, it is as if his remarks are driftwood surfacing from a vast ocean of experience that remains untranslatably Other, a fragment from a world operating on other terms. Trying to get a real sense of the life that is being lived underneath is tricky.

'So you have always remained quite certain that you wanted a life withdrawn from the world?' I venture.

'I'm not sure you can say that. You must carry on – it's not me. I must decrease, He must increase,' he replies. I vaguely recognise the quotation from the Gospel of St John. 'In my case, on the journey of the faith only very occasionally do you get to the brow of the hill. Most of the time we're simply struggling on, in the jungle at the bottom. It's a very interesting journey, because you're not shown everything to begin with. You only find out things on the way, if you see what I mean. I'm in the jungle at the moment. You have to live day to day.'

'Do you ever think of leaving the life of solitude?'

'Oh, most of the time.' He laughs gently to himself, whether at the irony of his situation or naivety of my question, I can't tell. 'Oh dear me. It's like that saying of St Teresa's – "no wonder you have so few friends, Lord, the way you treat them".' Gradually, he rocks himself back to sobriety. 'But it's not real, it's fantasy. You have to stay with reality.'

The fire crackles and spits. 'So what is it about this way of life that makes you stay?'

'Well, it's not the silence, is it,' he muses. 'It's what the silence is for. The silence allows that part of us which is deep inside of us, which you call the heart, to come to the surface. It's what happens in the silence – being aware of presence.'

He takes off his hat and clasps it against the side of his head as he considers further.

'I don't have a radio here. I'm pretty certain that, if I had one, I'd have it on all day long, and I'd want to hear the news. When people hear the news that bit of them that wants to be open and attentive is covered up.'

There is a lengthening silence. It is clear that the best way to get the hermit to talk is to say as little as possible. Outside, the wind and rain lash at the long, narrow windows; the landscape is a blur of grey. Inside, the gathering gloom has a deep, browny quality. Eventually, the hermit resumes his thread.

'One of the major things when I first came here was that I became aware of those people who have lived this sort of life in the past. I didn't know what was happening. It was as though I was in a cardboard box, with the Community outside, and suddenly the bottom fell out of the box. I was like Alice going down the rabbit hole, and I was in Wonderland.'

He pauses to giggle as I scribble frantically. 'I hope you're not putting all this down.'

Hoping he will continue, I say nothing.

'The Wonderland was communion with the saints – the saints of Northumbria, the holy people who lived here in the past,' he goes on. 'The comfort of it was that there are plenty of people who have done what I've done before, and I was just following in their footsteps. It's not a solitary life from that point of view, because you are in communion with the angels and the saints.'

There is another long silence, and the hermit slides me one of his sideways smiles. 'For me, it's all – I mean, I don't have to talk about it – it's all part of the world.'

'Is it possible to communicate something of this experience?'

'Yes,' he replies. 'It's certainly communicable in the sense that you come here. If I had a gift for writing, it would be communicated through that. The other side of the question is do people want to receive what is communicable?' There is vigorous agreement from John, sitting to my left. Brother Harold leans back in his chair and pronounces: 'There is a unity in humanity, and the effects of it go all over the place.'

'Are you talking about the influence of prayer?'

'Yes, but it's more than just that,' he replies. 'It's not what we do, it's what is done to us. Yes, we are bound to pray, and ask for our bread, forgiveness, and so on. But in the end, we are vessels into which God's breath may come. So yes, we know that prayer is not limited by space: "Angels and archangels and all the company of heaven".'

This time, the quotation he slips in, so often heard during my Anglican childhood, is alive and resonant. I have a sense that, far from being alone, the hermit feels truly accompanied. He concludes with quiet emphasis: 'All I can say is that it *is* so, it *is* true.'

The testimony is enough; I don't need to probe the hermit about his inner life any further. But one, more worldly, question remains. As an ecumenical Anglican, he had long believed he could exercise his Catholic sensibilities within the tradition of his birth. But in 1996, he formally entered the Roman Catholic Church as a consecrated hermit. It was a shift of allegiance that took him over Christian Britain's historic faultline, a decision which had bemused and angered some of his more sectarian supporters. It puzzles me, too. Why, given his insistence that denomination doesn't matter, has he found the change so necessary?

'It's not a question of changing one's denomination. It's Christian tradition,' he explains, looking at me quizzically. 'Do you see what I mean? In this country, until the sixteenth century, we were all Catholics.'

The hermit's perspective challenges the version of history I have unthinkingly accepted since my schooldays. History, as someone once said, is told by the victors, and the tale I had learnt was undeniably Protestant, an account that painted recusant Catholics as over-emotional folk who insisted on hiding in cupboards because of a silly attachment to smells and bells. It was a view, according to the more sophisticated accounts of the English Reformation I was now reading, that masked the destruction that had accompanied the creation of the Anglican Church. Eamon Duffy writes movingly of the richness of late medieval English Catholicism, his historian's eye detailing the colourful images that adorned the churches, the saints' days that punctuated the year, and the local customs and shrines which gave each region its identity.[65] A brief period in the 1530s saw the churches stripped of their religious art, the monasteries that stood at the heart of communities denuded and shut down. The pilgrimages which led ordinary people from one holy place to another, marking out the songlines of their land, were banned. Any traces of the popular folk religion that had endowed place and time with spiritual significance that lingered were deemed 'Popish' and heretical, an expression of a hostility that British sinologist Martin Palmer compares to the iconoclastic frenzy of more recent regimes: the Chinese communists as they imposed the Cultural Revolution, or the Taliban as they smashed the ancient Buddhist statues in Afghanistan. The destruction of the English Reformation was, he argues, responsible for 'an extraordinary psychological traumatising of the soul' which remains unhealed to this day and partly accounts for the characteristically British uncertainty about the spiritual.[66] Listening to Brother Harold talk about his vocation, it becomes clear that he belonged to the world that had flourished before the Reformation, and that his life is an attempt to continue that tradition.

His connection with another tradition is less welcome. In eighteenth-century England it became fashionable for the rich to employ an aged man to inhabit a picturesque hermitage in a remote corner of the estate to impress visitors. Brother Harold's residence on Shepherd's Law is thanks to the generosity of an aristocratic landowner. The arrangement has given him an insight into the situation of his eighteenth-century predecessors; when invited to functions on the estate, he was seated with the butlers and gardeners.

'The pet hermit,' I supply.

'Yes,' he nods. 'That's how I was seen!'

He stretches his legs out towards the stove, adding comfortably, 'I'm used to it now. Now, would you like that cup of tea?'

His relief that the interview is over is evident. He bustles around his kitchen, a grandfatherly figure, setting the big kettle on the Rayburn and opening a packet of tea cakes which are, indeed, a gift from the local ladies. The three of us sit round the fire, discussing current affairs: Brother Harold is keen to discuss Broken Britain and the Middle East, and a sense of urbanity prevails. Now we are three well-informed people, putting the world to rights over a cuppa.

It is time for me to catch my train at Berwick, but John has one final request to make of his friend. 'Can Alex see the upstairs chapel before she goes?'

The hermit nods, and John and I climb the wooden stairs into the eaves, leaving him in the sitting room. Despite its low, rafted ceiling, the little chapel has an endearing formality, with rows of chairs set before an altar and several impressive icons. 'Holy, Holy,

Holy', embroidered in pale gold lettering on the red altar cloth, gleams through the gloom.

John sits down on one of the benches, while I remain standing, intending to look around and take in the place, like a proper church tourist. But it is difficult to move. A concentrated silence which holds me in its grasp seems to have taken hold of the place. The air has acquired a peculiarly dense quality, as if it has been rapidly constituted, rushing in from the sides and above. It is as much as I can do to adjust my position slightly to inspect an icon of St Cuthbert on a nearby stand: a simple depiction of the hooded saint in grey and yellow. A few moments later comes a feeling of relinquishment, and I turn to see Brother Harold standing behind us, just beyond the chapel doorway. He must have followed us up, after all.

Outside, the mist has descended further, covering the hill and most of the surrounding landscape with a thick grey blanket. As the car ploughs its way down into the fog, we discuss the hermit's uncertain future and possible legacy. It is unclear how long he can stay up on the hill alone, given his advancing years, the cold and the continual need to chop firewood. No one has, so far, come to populate the annex of cells or to join him for services in the exquisite outer chapel. But then, he has not made any particular effort to recruit anyone, and was dismissive when I asked about new blood, saying I was trying to measure spiritual success in the arithmetical manner of his bishop and the committee that governed the hermitage trust. Yet wasn't it in the hope of founding a new community to continue the tradition of Catholic contemplation that Brother Harold had been praying, fundraising and building all these years? I feel it would be a pity if his vision remains unfulfilled. But John, with his more Zen-like approach, says it doesn't matter: whatever happens, the chapel on the hill is like 'a beautiful orchid' which holds within itself the justification for its existence. Is Brother Harold's brave, beautiful world part of the past, or the future? There are no ready answers. I am late for my train, and the car speeds across the chill green desert of Northumberland.

Back in London, I am discovering an unexpected consolation for the increasingly rough corporate politics of recessionary journalism. With its buzzy markets and network of streets and passages, Farringdon provides diversion the minute I step out of the office. With more places of worship than any other area of London, it is peculiarly rich in churches. Their guardians know what riches they have in their stewardship, proffering lunchtime services and concerts to dispirited office workers with an air of quiet assurance. Even in the heart of the crime-ridden capital, they maintain an open door policy which allows casual visitors to drop in for a few minutes without sacrificing their sandwich or lunchtime errand.

For as long as I can remember, I have relished the visceral thrill of stepping over a threshold into a dark stone building, the dramatic shift from the bustle of street or country lane. Paying a church a visit when it's not putting on a show, empty save perhaps for a verger pottering in the shadows or a lone figure sitting quietly in a pew, is a peculiarly rewarding experience. There's an immediate, physical hit – the sudden drop in temperature, the unexpected space opening up in front and above. Move further into the nave and you feel the cool rising from the stone against your skin, and the mingled odours of wood, polish and flowers in your nose, while your eyes adjust to the altered quality of the light.

Every church is different, but they all share that atmosphere that comes from the deliberate creation of a place for that which is other than the daily run, a space for being rather than doing. Sometimes, on stepping over the threshold, I experience a palpable wave of relief, a sensation of something being lifted from my chest, followed by a subtle slowing that spreads through my limbs.

For spontaneous visits of this kind, Farringdon is paradise. There is treasure on every other corner, adding another layer to my developing picture of Britain's chequered spiritual history. St Sepulchre, the musicians' church, houses an elegant white chamber with pretty arched windows and a gold-domed ceiling. Its former vicar John Rogers, burned at nearby Smithfield for preaching against 'pestilent Popery', is commemorated by an unobtrusive plaque by the door.[67] Then there is St Andrew, a chunk of white classicism bestriding Holborn Viaduct, a guild church with a weekday ministry for city workers. It offers lunchtime counselling, the vicar sitting in the aisle beside a notice saying 'Listening Service', hands folded receptively over his cassock. I have no inclination to avail myself of it, but it is nice to know it is there. Further north, St Alban's, an Anglo-Catholic pile of Victorian brick with pastel murals, isn't to my taste, but its location just off Leather Lane market makes it a convenient stop-off between eating and shopping. St Bartholomew the Great behind Smithfield, which claims to be the most ancient church building in London, certainly looks picture-book old, with its chocolate, white-edged stonework and crenelated towers. But I find its take on the vexed issue of church admission charges – a pray-or-pay policy in which you pay to look, or pray for free – has uncomfortable spiritual ramifications. I can't promise the man on the door that I am definitely going to pray, and can I look too, if I do? Who decides what constitutes prayer anyway? The man seems sceptical about my spiritual sincerity, and I don't have time for a proper tourist visit at lunchtime, so I never get beyond its inviting exterior.

Never mind. There are plenty more churches. In the middle of a city where almost every inch has been gobbled up by businesses or property developers, here is a glut of gorgeous, gratuitous spaces where, for a few moments at least, the spirit can soar.

Betrayal. In the office, the crisis in journalism is eating into souls, and the effects of Economic Pressures and Corporate Politics are like an overflowing river, seeping between desks, subtly changing behaviour and relationships. The tight-knit editorial team, made up of people I have known for years, has so far resisted the corrupting influences that come from outside, and got on with the work while being pretty nice to each other. But as the recession bites, life in the office takes on an Animal Farm-like quality. It isn't the high-octane treachery of the movies, and doubtless similar acts of double-dealing are being replicated in a hundred nearby offices. But it still feels like betrayal, and it is happening to me.

The usual remedy for office politics – a trip to the loo for a few deep breaths or a spot of cloud-watching from the corporate balcony – doesn't work. There are no two ways about it: I have an irresistible urge to cry. I slip out of the building, and let the street enfold me. The walking cure doesn't quell the urge, nor does a visit to a shoe shop with a sale. Where to go? Then, glimpsing a wedding cake spire poised daintily over Fleet Street, I make a sudden decision to head for St Bride's. Despite its role as the journalists' church, I have never yet been inside.

It is certainly noisy enough to be a journalists' church, with the clattering and clanging of men clearing up after a lunchtime recital. But at least one other professional has a similar idea. In a pew near the entrance, a woman in a tailored cream jacket is collapsed in a right angle, the forehead beneath her blond bob pressing against the rail. I choose my own corner at the far end of the church and let the tears flow. It is only when I finish that I look up and start to take in my surroundings. The Baroque interior has columns of the deepest caramel and a voluptuous ceiling embellished with garlands of gold. I am sitting in front of the side altar that commemorates journalists who have recently died; it is covered with photos of correspondents and cameramen killed in action and newsreaders felled by cancer. A wooden memorial tablet on the wall lists those who have died covering Iraq, AD 2003, and some of the names are familiar. I am in a tiny shrine to the martyrs of current affairs.

But it is the writing engraved in the caramel altar that compels my attention. 'AND THE WORD WAS MADE FLESH AND DWELT AMONG US'. *Really? Are you sure?* Today, the core statement of Christianity, the claim of God-in-man seems more implausible than ever, the gap between divinity and humanity unbreachable ... But didn't the Bible have an account of the close-to-home variety of betrayal? Not Judas, the turncoat who handed Jesus to the enemy for cash, but Peter, the close friend who caved under pressure. A slim paperback of the gospels lies on the bench in front of the altar. I pick it up and flick through, comparing each gospel's account of Peter's denial. John contains a nice illustration of the body language of shifting allegiances: 'The servants and the police had made a charcoal fire, because it was cold, and were standing round it warming themselves. And Peter too was standing with them, sharing the warmth'.[68]

It is comforting that the uber-text of my inherited faith has such an acute understanding of the problem. Replacing the book on the table, I leave the church and head towards Westminster where, with two cabinet ministers in two select committees, the afternoon promises politics in its overt form.

It is hardly the Resurrection, but the following week some of my faith in people is restored. Conversations were had, and misunderstandings cleared up, although some Peteresque shadows lurk in the corner of the office. Meanwhile, John Mullin's efforts in publicising my request to members of the Fellowship has paid off. The following weekend, I set out to meet my first ordinary solitary.

INTO THE SILENCE

Joyce Nethersole lived in Canterbury. A former nun, her life was pretty much indistinguishable from that of the people around her, except for the praying she did on the quiet. I would be welcome to come and share a meal with her, she wrote in her email, and she didn't need much notice: she was usually free, and I must be much busier than her. She sounded open, friendly and down-to-earth, and I was intrigued by the course her life had taken. I was also curious to see Canterbury, once the market leader of Britain's religious cities, and a place I had never visited.

Canterbury's status as the administrative centre of the Christian church in England goes back to 597, when Augustine was sent by the Pope to prevent the British reverting to paganism after the departure of the Romans. The city became the seat of Britain's first archbishop Augustine, who built a cathedral and an abbey. But what really made the city's name was the assassination, in 1170, of the archbishop Thomas Becket by supporters of Henry II. The murder in the cathedral dramatised the clash between church and state, sanctity and power that would characterise English history for centuries to come. For the devout, Becket became an object of veneration, and the site of his murder a shrine. The cathedral became the destination for a new pilgrimage route between Southwark and Canterbury, putting the Canterbury pilgrimage at the heart of the movement which took huge numbers of British pilgrims all over Europe for the next three hundred years.

What is a pilgrimage? You could say that the network of pilgrimage routes that criss-crossed England in Anglo-Saxon times were a way of mapping out the landscape, connecting places with the human just as the songlines chronicled by Bruce Chatwin brought the land into being for the Aborigines. Pilgrimages were also good for business, helping the church to generate income and creating custom for the hostelries along the way. Just as holidays came from holy days, tourism was originally faith tourism, the first holiday souvenirs being the relics put up for sale by the ecclesiastical authorities. For the pilgrims themselves, the religious imperative provided a reason for a trip at a time when the expense made it hard to justify travel for its own sake. They were drawn, as the vivid portraits of *The Canterbury Tales* make clear, by motives as mixed as the characters themselves, from the pious nun to the man-eating Wife of Bath. (Chaucer describes her as 'gap-toothed' – an expression indicating a wandering nature in both senses.)

Above all, pilgrimages met the human need for a journey and all that it brings: new sights and people, unexpected events, all wrapped up in the irresistible promise that the outer journey will bring about an inner transformation, a permanent intangibility to take home. Because, whatever your theology or lack of it, travel always does something to the mind. Perhaps it has something to do with the personal investment it requires: you undertake a journey; it doesn't happen to you. 'Travel', deriving from 'travail' – toil, trouble, or suffering, is a physical business involving exertion and a degree of discomfort. The journalist and compulsive traveller Martha Gellhorn reveals in her bleakly hilarious accounts of her adventures in far-flung places the intrepid traveller's dirty little secret: an unnecessary journey is often disappointing and, from any sensible point of view, a waste of time and money.[69]

And yet ...

However you cast the motivation, pilgrimages provide the most splendid excuse for a trip, just as writing a book can form the pretext for exploring a country. Maybe that, too, is a form of pilgrimage.

'This coach is number eleven of eight,' announces a female voice in confident, cut-glass tones. The passenger across the aisle catches my eye, and rolls his own. We are bowling through Kent's golden-green landscape at the end of a changeable July. Huge granite clouds balloon out of the horizon, their edges gilt with the rays of the sun. The day could turn to rain or shine.

Outside the station, I ignore Joyce's instructions to take a bus, walking away from the city walls towards the outskirts of the city. The signs along the way catch my eye, but when I turn my gaze to follow them, Pilgrim's Way and Pilgrim's Lane turn out to be nondescript little access roads leading to clumps of cheap housing. Finally, as buildings gradually give way to woods and fields, I arrive at the right bungalow. It is a tiny, almost Tolkienesque dwelling, set in a garden crammed with ornaments and gardening tools, its two mini-lawns divided by a dainty path. The front door is open and sounds of rummaging come from within. I ring the tinkly little bell fastened to the wall. The rummaging continues, and I ring again.

A broad-beamed woman in a checked shirt and dark trousers lurches towards me. It's hard to tell her age; her ruddy cheeks and grey-blond hair suggest vigour, but her face has an askew look, with one blue eye wide-open, almost staring, the other half-closed. It's just a step across the lobby into her little sitting room, where a large black cat is sitting on the window sill. Every inch is filled with objects: photos jostle knick-knacks; books and DVDs cram the walls. Royal faces look regally out from plates and puppies stare winsomely from postcards. This is the home of someone who likes company and needs to be surrounded by reminders of the people and things she loves. My eye falls on a row of Georgette Heyer novels, the historical bodice-rippers which had been a staple of my adolescent reading.

'Oh, yes, I was reading one the other day. They're always fresh.' Her laugh is self-deprecating, and her low, gravelly voice makes it impossible to hear what she says as fanciful. 'Very silly. Now, what would you like to know?'

Living alone at nearly eighty, her life isn't very different from that of someone following vows of Poverty, Chastity and Obedience, she explains wryly. She is poor and has no sex life, so it is just the Obedience that has fallen by the wayside. She had spent twenty-eight years as an Anglican nun, having somehow fallen in love with the idea of the religious life as a teenager. She liked men of the cloth, too. Bicycling around her parish of Margate as a girl, she had been particularly taken with one young minister. 'Eric. He went on to become an archdeacon. I thought I would marry him.' Again, the low laugh. 'But he already had a girl.'

'The Archdeacon of Cheltenham?' I ask in astonishment. 'Married Linda?'

Joyce nods. A's father, the clergyman, provider of lifts and my foothold in the centre of Gloucester. Our gazes lock as we digest the coincidence; then she resumes her story. She hadn't much liked being a Companion of Jesus the Good Shepherd, an Anglican order devoted to education, but had cheered up when sent to Guyana to teach, enjoying the company of her primary school pupils. Recalled to the convent in England, she became increasingly unhappy and, fearing a breakdown, requested a sabbatical. The request was declined. In the end, she walked out of the convent, got on a bus and went to London, where she was taken in by another ex-nun. As the pent-up grief of years started to come out, Eric offered succour, and the two of them drove around the countryside, he looking for a pub, she sobbing in the passenger seat.

'Why were you so unhappy?'

'It's very difficult living in a convent when people are older than you, and think that you're grumbling about nothing, and they want to give you a Valium. The mother, she was hopeless, really. She was young, but she was very narrow. A cold fish.' She pauses. 'You're not supposed to have friendships, and that can be quite isolating.'

A picture of an affectionate young woman being frozen out is forming in my mind like a developing photo. 'I was told, on Obedience, to come back, but I couldn't stand it any more. I think I'd grown out of it, really. If you believe you're called to the religious life, everyone gives you a shove, because they want people. But I don't believe in vocation any more. In fact, you're not called, you choose. When you get there, if you don't like it, it's a job to get out.'

She pauses again. 'There are only three of them left now.' She takes a silver-framed photo from the mantelpiece and puts it into my hands, a finger resting on one of the subjects. 'She's taken over as Mother. Sister Ann Verena. Seventy-five.' A familiar figure looks out at me: red face, black habit, always laughing. It is the cheerful, popular nun who had taught us at school, relentlessly good-humoured in the face of the pranks played in the chemistry lab by the archdeacon's daughter.

We recover quickly from this second crossing of lives, and Joyce resumes her story. Life on Civvy Street proved manageable, although she'd missed the boat on the husband front. She found work as a housekeeper in retreat houses, becoming warden of the home for the elderly at the Eastbridge Hospital, posts which came with live-in accommodation. At retirement, she was rescued from the prospect of homelessness by cousins until she was housed by the council. All the while, her hidden life of prayer went on, undetectable to those around her. In 1990, she took formal vows as a solitary in the Anglican Church, and felt she'd found a way of life that suited her. But as time went on, even that loose affiliation felt too institutional, and seven years later, she applied to be released from her vows. She had finally made the transition from official religious to independent solitary.

As we decamp to the table for lunch, I turn this strange spiritual journey over in my mind. Joyce's style of narration is so down-to-earth, almost entirely focused on external events, that it's hard to get a sense of the seismic internal shifts that must have underlain them. While we eat, Joyce leafs through a little spiral notebook, sharing its contents with me. It's a kind of spiritual log book of key dates and life events, along with notes to make special prayers for people, recorded in the careful handwriting of an older generation.

A couple of entries in loopy biro read:

April 95 Still seeking
Sept 95 Still seeking

'Still seeking what?' I ask.

'Seeking an identity, I suppose.' She turns a few more pages. 'No spiritual reading since 2004, by the look of it.'

Outraged at the lack of attention, the cat leaps onto the table, knocking over a glass and flooding the plastic cloth with apple juice. Joyce mops it up phlegmatically and opens a second notebook. It's the intercession book of her convent days, a record of people to pray for and special days to observe. 'I still keep it up. You'll go in there somewhere.' She turns to the day's date. 'There's no one in there: you put yourself in.'

I write my name in, privately relishing the thought my visit will be remembered and on that day, a year's hence, I'll probably get a prayer. The day, the diary makes clear, is dedicated to St James, one of the inner circle of the Apostles. Since we are to share a page, I wonder out loud what the saint's special area of responsibility is, but Joyce can't remember off-hand.

Meanwhile, I have a more important question to ask. 'Here's the thing,' I tell her. 'I'm puzzled. You've had this long, interesting religious life' – she nods – 'but at the same time it's been very difficult, quite disappointing.'

'Oh, it's been terrible, at times,' she agrees, turning her half-gaze on me like a blue beam. 'Quite excruciating.'

'And yet you don't seem to have ever lost your faith.'

She nods. 'God's still there. He doesn't change. I still pray. He's my constant companion.' She leans back and laughs a little bleakly. 'Well, there isn't anyone else.'

'But you've never turned away?'

'I've never turned away, no.'

By way of further explanation, she gets up heavily and, beckoning me to follow, goes into the bedroom. Effectively, it's the same room, partitioned off from the living quarters by some judiciously placed wardrobes. The little mantelpiece above the bed bears an array of icons, while the adjoining shelves display a china nativity scene and the tortured figure of Christ on a wooden cross. She takes from the shelf a crumpled-looking piece of paper covered in plastic and shows it to me; it's an icon of Jesus in shades of grey, his head framed in a mist of yellow. We contemplate it, her aid to nightly prayer, for a while.

'So have you found the way of life, the identity, you were looking for?'

'Yes, I think so,' she replies. 'I pray on the hoof. I used to go to church more, but I can sit here and pray as well as I can go down the road and pray. I'm concerned about different people from the past, and those around me. If someone tells me about someone who's ill, I visit or pray, whatever.' She pauses. 'I've had a good life, and now I'm preparing for the end of it. I think I'm just happy being me now.'

'Why the solitary element?'

'I find people quite stressful,' she replies. 'I was in a tizzy about you coming: you don't know what people are like, or if they're going to be fussy about food. I was evacuated during the war at the age of ten. I had a bad billet, and was uprooted from friends at thirteen – never cried so much in my life. When you have to rely on yourself from an early age, you become very independent. I've got so used to doing my own thing that I continue to do it ... I think that's all I can say, really.'

'Thank you so much, for letting me in,' I tell her.

'Oh, that's all right,' she replies, gruffly. 'I've enjoyed having you. I needn't have worried.'

It's a blazing afternoon as I make my way back towards the city centre with the vague intention of taking in some of Canterbury's religious attractions. As I walk, I try to digest Joyce's life story. I like her understated responses, her willingness to accept the psychological explanations for the direction of her life rather than reach for grander theological interpretations. Yet at the same time, I am struck by the unconditionality of her faith – it didn't matter if she lost her ecclesiastical credentials, stopped going to church, or was lonely – it was there, like an underground stream that ran on regardless. The way she saw it, the failures and miseries of her life had to do with choices that hadn't suited her, or circumstances she couldn't control: despite her miserable time as a nun, she hadn't taken the obvious route of rejecting religion, even as a recovery phase. I once heard a Rwandan singer asked on the radio about how he had managed to create such beautiful music given that he had lost his entire extended family in the genocide of 1994. 'You have to love life unconditionally,' he had replied simply. In her down-to-earth way, Joyce seemed to have something of the same enviable ability to separate life's disappointments from its meaning. It was a working answer to religion's perennial bugbear: the problem of evil, and one that could not be taught but only lived.

I hesitate outside Augustine's ruined abbey, the sun burning on my neck. It has become a hot afternoon, and the cool green vista beyond the walls looks inviting. 'There is no charge to enter our shop,' states the sign shamelessly. I walk on, into the heart of the city. It is crammed with foreign tourists, its cobbled streets filled with people spending and snacking in boutique shops and chic little cafes. Britain might be in recession, but Canterbury seems to be booming. Butter Market Square seethes with teenagers, flirting in high-tempo Spanish and Italian. I recoil from one particularly boisterous-looking group, and bump smack into a woman who visibly stops herself from cursing me. I peer through the narrow portal leading into the cathedral. But the church authorities want a rapacious sum to enter its precincts, so I take to the shops in protest.

An hour later, buoyed up by a successful shoe purchase, I find myself outside an intriguing, dark entrance set low into the wall of the High Street. The cool stone interior, with its delicately lit arches, beckons seductively, and the gentle hum coming from inside promises a welcome contrast to the shoppers' rapid footfall. I am in front of Eastbridge Hospital, founded as a hostel for poor pilgrims visiting the shrine of St Thomas some twenty years after his death, and now a home for the elderly run by the Franciscans, with a chapel and exhibition open to the public. Since I am a poor pilgrim – poorer, anyhow, having bought the shoes – I step across the threshold.

It's hardly quiet in the upstairs chapel, with a babble of street-voices floating up through the lead-paned windows. But next door, the refectory is full of emptiness. A fading mural depicts Christ in delicate yellows and greys, his lower half disappearing into the ageing stone, while his head, surrounded by accompanying angels, is more clearly delineated in darker shades. The condition of the mural gives it an odd, liminal look, making it difficult to say whether it is coming into being or fading away.

Downstairs in the Undercroft, clusters of people are viewing an exhibition, loud, middle class voices correcting each other about the information presented on the panels. The exhibition is about pilgrimage and this, it turns out, is the special responsibility held by St James, my companion in Joyce's prayer diary. One display spells out, road signage-style, the acceptable forms of transport for a pilgrim – foot, bicycle or horse. A picture of a car gets a line through it and a big, black **NO**.

St James's career as patron saint of pilgrims began in the ninth century when a hermit, following a star that stopped over a field in north-west Spain, claimed to have discovered the apostle's remains. Legend has it that the disciple had gone to Spain to free the Iberian Peninsula from the Moors and that, after his execution in Rome, his followers took his remains back there. Whatever the case, the relics of such a senior saint promised a lot of intercessory leverage for sinners seeking absolution and the Santiago de Compostela became, along with Rome and Jerusalem, one of the three great pilgrimage routes of medieval Europe.

Recent decades have seen a resurgence in pilgrimage along The Way of St James. In 2013, the Cathedral at Santiago awarded 215,880 people the *'compostela'* – the pilgrim's certificate for completing at least 100 kilometres – a sharp rise on the few thousand pilgrims of the 1980s. The growing numbers generate concerns about the impact on the environment.[70] A former chairman of the Confraternity of Saint James describes behaviour worthy of a Canterbury Tale: pilgrims parading about in bikinis, binge drinking and relieving themselves on the camino.[71] The growing numbers testify to the rise of a new kind of spiritual traveller, one whose motives are fluid, various, hard to pin down. The Confraternity's website advises prospective walkers: 'You will in fact meet relatively few pilgrims with an expressly religious/catholic motivation, though you'll meet equally few who deny any interest in its spiritual side. Precisely because it is so broadly defined, it attracts seekers of many different kinds.'[72]

I had never been on a pilgrimage myself, but it occurred to me that I had already witnessed an unofficial, secular version close-up. For several years, I worked as a volunteer-organiser on an ultra-marathon across the Sahara: a gruelling, week-long event in which amateur runners, carrying their own food and equipment on their backs, ran a hundred and fifty miles across the burning sands. By day three, most of the seven hundred runners on the Marathon des Sables were visibly the worse for wear, debilitated by dehydration, their feet a mess of weeping blisters. At night, after each stage of the race, the bivouac evoked the scene of some humanitarian disaster, with the smart, fit-looking people of a few days earlier haggard and filthy as they limped to their tents. Yet the suffering was self-induced, and the competitors paid handsomely for the privilege. Almost everyone bought into the race orthodoxy, which stated that the marathon was all about 'overcoming your limits' and that 'anyone could do it' despite the fact that, every year, a sizeable proportion of people dropped out or were forced to withdraw on health grounds.

As a checkpoint monitor, I was in a position to observe the runners closely, while writing about the race for newspapers and magazines gave me the chance to probe their motivations. The motives of the elite athletes, a tiny minority who skipped cheerily through the checkpoints, their muscular flesh barely moist, were straightforward: like ultra-fit dogs, they needed the exercise. For military entrants, the race presented a more interesting form of training than their usual exercises. But the reasons of the large number of amateur runners were harder to fathom. A surprising number cited bereavement, often through cancer, saying they were doing the race 'for' a departed mother, spouse, or best friend. For others, it was something in their own life that had to be expiated: one novice I interviewed said the marathon was her way of 'overcoming' bulimia. Sometimes the runners exuded a penitential demeanour so strong that you didn't need to know anything about their story to see it. 'Chemin de croix,' a colleague muttered darkly as we watched some poor soul hobble past, back bowed under the weight of his pack, eyes cast to the desert floor. One middle-aged Frenchman made me feel sad every time I saw him, pushing his disabled son from checkpoint to checkpoint in a specially altered wheelchair complete with sun canopy. I can't remember what he said, but his tone was always apologetic, the look in his eyes hauntingly guilty.

Yet whatever the motive, for some the journey across the desert clearly brought about an important inner change. You could see it in the stripped-down look in their eyes as they sat at the end of the day, encrusted with sand, surrounded by everything and nothing: a water bottle, a few fellow travellers and the vast, empty horizon. The bulimic I followed for the week, convinced she wouldn't make it, finished the race radiant, claiming that the experience had been life-changing. Who's to say what constitutes a successful transformation?

A month later, I had an appointment with another freelance solitary on the other side of the country. Stephen North was a family man in his forties, a former social worker who lived in Monmouth, just over the English/Welsh border. I could go while visiting my mother in Gloucestershire and borrow her car to get there.

The drive would take me through a borderland of shifting boundaries. Road signs in Welsh indicated you had entered another country; a few turns of the road later, you were back in England again. Until it was finally deemed Welsh under the Local Government Act of 1972, Monmouthshire – deriving from the Welsh Myn-wy, meaning 'swift water' – had been geographically ambiguous for centuries, belonging at times to England and at others to Wales. The name of the English village where I grew up bore a linguistic trace of this fluidity: Maisemore means 'big field' in Welsh.

The Forest of Dean formed a natural boundary between Monmouthshire and the Severn Vale. The twenty-four thousand acres of ancient woodland was a landscape of plunging valleys and conifer-covered crests; you could be among densely wooded tracks, inhaling the steamy greenness that arose from the ferns and, ten minutes later, standing on a peak staring at a distant horizon. We had picnicked as a family on May Hill in the 1970s, an upturned bowl of land topped by a caterpillar of trees that could be seen from miles around. A photo of my brother and I running up that hill, he in an elasticated tie and shirt set, me in a home-sewn dress trimmed with bric-a-brac, stood in the dining room ever after. The Forest's geographical distinctiveness had always nurtured different ways of living: ancient rights allowed its people to graze their livestock amid the trees, while those born in St Briavels could become free miners if they mined its coal-rich rock for a year and a day. My own experience of its uniqueness came courtesy of the bikers of my youth who roared out its depths on their powerful engines, bringing their strange, almost incomprehensible dialect to the streets of Gloucester.

Wanting to see the Forest in its late summer colours, I took the scenic route to Monmouth. The trees were dark green tinged with gold, but the road was as hair-raising as ever, perilously close to arboreal precipices, a roller-coaster carrying the car like a raft on fast-moving waters. It was with some relief that I exited the canopy to follow the Wye, a wide belt of shallow water tumbling through steep, wooded cliffs, and found myself in a majestic landscape. Square houses squatted against the hillsides, the red of the local stone bright against granite. Tintern Abbey was a short detour away: I had never been and, after my sortie into Brother Harold's world, I was curious about Britain's Catholic past. The thirteenth-century abbey was one of the first to be shut down under the dissolution of the monasteries: 1536 saw its windows smashed and its roof stripped of lead. Its monks, a contemplative order of Cistercians who sought to follow St Benedict's Rule in its original, sixth century form, were evicted. For two centuries, Tintern stood abandoned. Then Romanticism brought remote, wild places into vogue, and the tourists began to come. In the twenty-first century, the ruins fed the contemporary love of heritage and had found a doting steward in Cadw, the conservation arm of the Welsh Assembly Government.

The abbey car park is nearly full when I arrive, with parents busy putting up pushchairs and ushering their offspring towards the toilets. Weaving through vehicles and people, I make my way towards the red ruins. They are certainly impressive, their huge, bare outlines cutting into the sky. But, with its manicured grass, carefully placed benches and scrubbed-clean stones, the monument betrays little of the violence that makes up its history. It is surrounded by admirers, searching for the right camera angle as they look adoringly up at the smooth sandstone pillars. Within minutes, my inner eye etched with cameras and pushchairs, I return to the car and head back to Monmouth.

Stephen's house is a modern semi; Stephen himself a softly spoken Yorkshireman who immediately puts me at my ease. But we are not staying in: so that we can talk without interruption from his family, he has booked a room at nearby Tymawr, a contemplative order of the Anglican Church in Wales where he is an associate. As he drives through the winding lanes towards the uplands of the convent, I soon abandon any attempt at small talk. It isn't necessary; he is clearly at ease with himself, the situation, and with silence.

The convent is a large Victorian house set in generous gardens amid rolling farmland. As we walk through the grounds, Stephen slides me a sidelong look. 'I'm nervous!' he confesses laughingly. 'I'm not a great discloser.' He leads the way to the modern bungalow that serves as convent annex and, taking the key from his pocket, unlocks the door. Inside, the atmosphere has the chill of a place used only intermittently. It is furnished hotch-potch style, with a sofa of orange wide-ribbed corduroy and tables piled with books and pots of paint. Stephen makes coffee in the open-plan kitchen, while I leaf through a book by Sister Wendy, smiling at the characteristic commentary that brings out the humour and sensuality of religious icons.

Once we are settled on the orange sofa, Stephen talks freely. Having grown up in a cold family without any religious beliefs, at university he had undergone a lukewarm conversion to Christianity and married his student sweetheart Wendy. His solitary journey began much later, triggered by a life crisis. His young son had been bullied for some time and, one Sunday morning, seeing the culprits on the climbing frame outside, he went out and confronted them. In the ensuing scuffle, the chief bully fell and broke his arm, and Stephen was charged with assault. He was convicted and given a small fine. It was hardly the worst crime in the world – a momentary lapse of control in defence of his own child. But the incident, and the criminal record it brought him – a social worker specialising in child protection – shook him to the core.

'It was that whole explosion of my sense of identity, of self-worth. It was like a clattering, clashing of it all, into fragments.' He stares out of the window. 'I remember being in the police station and having a really strong sensation that Christ was there with me, reassuring me and saying that he too had been arrested and shared some of this experience. It was so powerful you just couldn't ignore it.'

During the years that followed, he explored the contemplative side of the Anglican tradition. Guidance came from three local figures: Rowan Williams, the then Bishop of Monmouth; Brother Ramon, a Franciscan hermit who was giving a series of talks at the convent; and Stephen's parish priest James Coutts. In 1995, inspired by Eve Baker's book *Paths in Solitude*, he joined the Fellowship of Solitaries.

'She just spoke to my heart. You know that Bob Dylan song about Italian poetry that speaks straight to your soul? That was exactly how it felt when I read that last part of Eve's book: it took me away from that kind of religious busyness and to the depths of solitude and prayer.'

For a few years, he found a home in Franciscan spirituality, a contemplative Anglican order that stressed simplicity, and joined the order as a tertiary. A form of lay membership open to those married and living in the community, it seemed to offer the perfect balance. But in practice, the role carried so many pastoral and administrative responsibilities that he found himself caught up in precisely the busyness he had been trying to avoid. Worse still, all this religious activity was taking him away from Wendy. 'I became aware that the choice was between being a third order Franciscan and being married. It was a bit like having an affair. It's the nearest I've ever come to having an affair. I was being unfair, and I was being unfaithful.'

His face broadens into a smile. 'There was really no contest. Wendy was going through a difficult time because her mother was dying, and I don't think I was really there for her. So I came to the decision that I should ask to be released from my vows, and I was.'

But the craving for solitude persisted. He was drawn to a job as a care manager in Yorkshire, but rejected the idea of working away from home until the ever-understanding Wendy picked the job advert out of the bin. Living alone in Yorkshire, he had finally found some solitude. The couple were still married, but were now 'LATs' – people Living Apart Together. By dint of driving up and down the country, they saw each other one weekend in three.

'It was an understandable mistake,' he says. 'What I found was that doing the full-time job, also having to cook, clean, wash, do the garden: there was actually less space then.' *Dog bites man! Housework Takes Time, Man Discovers!* Listening to this part of his story, I have to suppress a rise of uncharitable female smugness. So after a couple of years, he rejoined his wife on the Welsh borders, leaving social work for gardening and maintenance work and finding a loose framework for his spiritual life within the Tymawr community.

'So how do you do the solitary thing now?'

'Mmm. How do I?' Leaning forward, he pauses to think. 'It's really hard to know how to answer that. I think there is my inner cell, and I always carry that around with me. It's important to go fully back into it regularly, and I do that at points during the day.' Morning prayer is said in the children's room, as they have now left home. He holds a solitary evensong on Saturday evenings, and joins the nuns at the convent chapel on a Sunday.

Yet he is conscious of a growing sense of apartness, a need to work things out without the constraints of institutional frameworks. And the more he reads and observes, the more he feels that this approach is in tune with the times.

'I sense that, increasingly, numbers of people are finding their relationships with religious institutions less and less nourishing and, as a result, we are finding our nourishment in these sorts of secret places. There will possibly be some very exceptional individuals who will carry the burden of a more public experience. But perhaps for a long time yet, the majority will be hidden individuals, living their quiet lives almost unnoticed.'

A Yorkshireman suspended between England and Wales, he has come to accept a state of geographical not-belonging. 'We are on the border here; it's very much a borderland. That seems to be appropriate for me – I don't really feel I belong anywhere now.'

Unwittingly, I had been meeting the Other Anglicans, those disaffected with a religion that defined commitment in terms of good deeds and involvement in church affairs who were trying to put the tradition back in touch with its contemplative side. Unlike their fourteenth-century predecessors, these modern solitaries got no support from the wider culture. Without roadmaps or spiritual advisers to guide them, forging their own path was a lonely, uncertain business. The spirituality they were evolving didn't entail rejecting religious institutions. It was more about working out a different relationship with them, one that was looser, more oblique, and left plenty of space for ordinary life. And it seemed that more and more people were quietly embarking on this path: behind the story of the declining numbers entering religious orders lay the signs of a counter-trend: convents and monasteries were now attracting growing numbers of associates, apparently meeting a need for people who wanted a religious focus while living everyday lives. The press offices of the Anglican and Catholic churches confirmed the upward trend in associates, oblates and tertiaries. 'There's a huge rise, from anecdotal evidence, over the last ten years,' a spokeswoman for the Catholic Bishops Conference of England and Wales told me. 'The statistics aren't available.' Noticing the same phenomenon, the Church of England had started collecting data, and found to its surprise that at the end of 2009 there were over three thousand Anglican associates. 'We are aware that this is an emerging way of life and intend to make this an annual exercise,' one of its researchers told me. Tymawr was a case in point: a tiny convent, it had just ten nuns and a single novice. But with a hundred and eleven associates and forty-nine oblates, its influence rippled out into the wider community.

It was clear that the Fellowship of Solitaries – hardly a network, much less an organisation – was answering a need that was not being met by either religious institutions or the secular world. Its members' demands were modest: they didn't want to meet each other, or even to communicate directly. They just wanted to know that there were others out there like them who felt the inner compulsion to go apart, a pull so strong that it trumped the need for love and success. As in life, their chosen path brought its own twists and turns: often a solution that had worked for one phase didn't work for another, and then the search had to take off in a new direction. The contributions to the newsletters suggested that, for some members, the Fellowship had also been a staging post.

One solitary wrote: 'I am departing from the Fellowship but will remain with it in my heart. It was not disquiet re the Letter— read with humility—such remarkable people sharing their inner life. I feel I must (need) to let it go. I am listening to me ... Starting with me—not aspiring to or attempting anything else. "Me" knowing that I am in the palm of the hand of God—but not "doing"— just "being".'

Another confided: 'I've pondered long and hard and have finally decided that I can go on my way out of the Fellowship of Solitaries. It was such a relief to find out that there were others "out there" who did not fit into the expected religious patterns, that I was not some sort of loner or misfit but had truly discerned the solitary in my own heart. And now, ten years on, it no longer matters, and I can just accept the inner hermit with happiness.'

Now they had the strength to go on alone, deeper into the silence.

SUFI WAYS

Christianity, I reminded myself, was not the only form of mysticism going. Perhaps it was time to get out of my sectarian comfort zone and see things from another perspective. After all, St James may have been the patron saint of pilgrims, but he was also known as the Moorslayer after the legend that he had miraculously reappeared in the ninth century to help the Catholics with the Reconquest of Spain. After decades of immigration, Muslims were now Britain's second-largest faith group, and Islam included the mystical tradition of Sufism.

The first Sufis emerged in the caliphates of the early Muslim world, wanderers seeking a knowledge of God beyond the constraints of formal religion, an all-consuming relationship with the divine which ultimately brought about the annihilation of the self. Legend has it that one of the earliest Sufi masters went into an Iraqi marketplace and made a public statement of the unity he had achieved with the divine: 'Ana al Haqq—I am the truth!'[73] Al Hallaj was publicising a condition potentially available to all, but in the eyes of orthodox Islam, in identifying himself with one of the ninety-nine names of Allah, he was committing blasphemy. After a long imprisonment, he was brutally executed. It was one example of the persecution Sufis often suffered, making them reluctant to worship in mosques. But gradually the roving mystics settled into orders and developed their own rituals; the practice of 'remembering' God in the form of a zikr or circle for prayer or recitation was central.

Impelled by the need to share their mystical insights, they remained part of society. Combined with the need to protect themselves from persecution, this meant that anyone could turn out to be a Sufi. 'The Sufi is hidden, could be your neighbour', wrote Idries Shah, the author who popularised the tradition in late twentieth-century Britain.[74] Far from being a branch of Islam, Sufism was 'the inner, "secret" teaching that is concealed within every religion'.[75] Its practices brought together disparate strands of the deeper wisdom that had preceded Islam, evolving into new forms that adapted themselves to their times. Its fluidity, as contemporary scholar Reza Aslan puts it, made Sufism:

> ... a medley of divergent philosophical and religious trends, as it were an empty cauldron in which have been poured the principles of Christian monasticism and Hindu asceticism, along with a sprinkling of Buddhist and Tantric thought, a touch of Islamic Gnosticism and Neoplatonism, and finally, a few elements of Shi'ism, Manichaeism and Central Asian Shamanism thrown in for good measure.[76]

SOLD to the woman on the spiritual quest. My first step would be to read Rumi, the thirteenth-century mystic whose exuberant poetry had become the best-known expression of Sufism in the west. Jalal ad-Din Muhammad Balkh – whose more popular name derives from Rum, meaning Anatolia, where he spent most of his life – was also the father of spiritual whirling. The Mevlevi Sufi Order founded by his son practised the *sama*, or ritual of 'turning' to music which had reportedly come about when Rumi, hearing in the rhythm of the market goldbeaters the beat of the words 'there is no god but Allah', held out his arms and began to spin in ecstasy.

The Penguin edition of Rumi's *Selected Poems* sat around the flat, ignored, for months: I had enough on my plate without the musings of a medieval Persian. I suspected myself of avoidance: the spiritual ambitions of Mother Teresa and Teresa d'Avila, with all their trials and privations, had made for rather joyless reading. But finally, while I hurriedly packed to share a holiday with B and family on the Pembrokeshire coast, the volume went into my bag. My friends were renting a cottage near St David's owned by an eccentric old lady: a longhouse just off the coastal path, accessible only by driving across fields. The house was set in a dip just behind the cliff edge and was separated from the path by a dense tangle of gorse and bramble through which a narrow track had been hacked. It was a surprise to emerge from the undergrowth and find yourself above a heaving, glittering sea.

And so it was, having travelled across country to the most westerly point of Wales, got soaked to the skin on our first coastal walk and eaten a late, boozy dinner, I fell into bed in a Pembrokeshire longhouse and, in a drunken, exhausted haze, opened Rumi for the first time. After three randomly chosen poems, I was laughing with recognition. The voice that spoke from the page was friendly, wise and very funny. The poems were populated with ancient figures – there were Arabian archetypes and stars of the Scriptures such as Moses, Joseph, Jesus – but the tone was resonant, contemporary. Across eight centuries, Rumi advised:

> Today, like every other day, we wake up empty
> and frightened. Don't open the door to the study
> and begin reading. Take down a musical instrument,
> Let the beauty we love be what we do.

There are hundreds of ways to kneel and kiss the ground.[77]

In the days that followed, the voice of Rumi blended perfectly with my cliff top existence. There was no internet connection and, except on a very particular part of the cliff, it was impossible to get a mobile signal. We simply forgot about such things and went back to the world in which we'd grown up, a return made easier by the plastic gadgets of the 1970s that filled the kitchen. In between walks and meals, I'd make my way through the thicket to sit above the sea, dip into a poem and then take time to absorb my surroundings. The cliffs were marked by bands of colour: above the black stripe of the water-mark was the mustard-yellow of the lichen; then came the grey-white stone. Even the view from the longhouse was constantly changing. When the sun shone, it opened up a rolling green Sahara that made me want to dance into the horizon; at other times great rolls of cloud were pushed across the sky by the Atlantic winds. Sensing this was a special place and time, I was sad to leave. And sure enough, not long afterwards, my friends' aged landlady died, and the house was no longer available.

'Don't grieve', advised Rumi. 'Everything you lose comes around again in another form'.[78]

Back in London my task was to find, among the myriad versions of Sufism, an order that bridged the gap between east and west. The UK branch of the Sufi Order International seemed to fit the bill. Founded by Hazrat Inayat Khan, a musician who had come from India in the early twentieth century, the order's approach was in keeping with Rumi's message that '*tawhid*' – the oneness of God –

issued in a universal wisdom that underlay all faiths. Sufism, Khan declared:

> ... is not a religion or a philosophy. It is neither deism nor atheism, nor is it a moral, nor a special kind of mysticism, being free from the usual religious sectarianism. If ever it could be called a religion, it would only be as a religion of love, harmony, and beauty.[79]

In practical terms, the Sufi path he counselled was less of a free-for-all. Spiritual development was organised through a system of *murshids* and *murids* – teachers and students – *murid* is Arabic for 'committed one'. The spiritual masters passed their knowledge down through the generations, creating a continuous spiritual link; sheikhs and pirs ('pir' is Persian for elder or saint) formed the links of the chain of transmission. In the Sufi Order, Inayat Khan had passed the baton to his son Pir Vilayat, who in turn had passed it to his grandson Pir Zia, the current head of the Order, who lived in the States, where he had founded an organisation called The Seven Pillars House of Wisdom. He was soon to visit London and would be speaking at one of the regular talks that took place at St James's Church in Piccadilly on Monday evenings.

The church was a walk away from where I had spent the afternoon covering a select committee on the financial management of the Home Office. In the Gothic corridor, MPs and journalists were gathering for a political showdown. The Parliamentary Labour Party was meeting to decide whether to mount a leadership challenge against Prime Minister Gordon Brown; led by a group of influential women MPs, the meeting had already been dubbed 'The Night of the Long Stilettos' by *The*

Mail.[80] The throng was as animated as a pre-match crowd. 'She's clutching what looks like a speech,' a TV journalist was telling his phone with satisfaction. I slipped into the Ladies' and the heavy wooden door shut out the sound. Behind me, in the mirror, hovered a familiar figure, an MP carrying out a pleasureless check of her face. She looked exhausted. I had known her a dozen years before in the optimistic dawn of New Labour; I could easily have said hello. But a whole political era had passed since then and the gap between then and now seemed unbreachable.

Security helicopters hover overhead as I make my way across St James's and Green Park. I feel an enormous sense of weariness. The Tories are coming, and I can already see ahead to the time when they, in their turn, will be imploding, ousting their once-lauded leader. Then the whole cycle will begin again, with its rows and proposed reforms ... I turn into Piccadilly and step into the Baroque loveliness of St James's Church. A crowd clothed in pink, orange and turquoise fills the pews, and the air bubbles with excitement. But the audience quietens as a diminutive figure in a black Nehru jacket and Moroccan slippers moves slowly towards a seat in front of the altar. Pir Zia's catlike features, carefully clipped beard and sleek black ponytail look incongruous against the sculpted flowers and fruit behind him. As he begins to talk about the ideas underpinning The Seven Pillars House of Wisdom he had founded, I'm aware of a further dissonance: his diction has the crispness of the English upper elite.

'It seems to me that religion today is in crisis.' He speaks with quiet assurance. 'On one side, there is the rejection of exclusivist truth claims, airtight dogmatic systems, ecclesiastical power structures. There is a widespread scepticism regarding these aspects of religion. At the same time, there is a resurgent zealousness, a fundamentalism which is all the more adamant and aggressive in its attachment to secularism. So there is a conflict, and all of us are trying to find our way in this dilemma. What The Seven Pillars is trying to articulate is some kind of middle ground, an alternative to these extremes. It's got to be – it's *got* to be – pluralistic. And yet the relativism that constitutes the common denominator of contemporary pluralistic society is one that has no appreciation of the value of the sacred, no regard for the mystery that transcends our human understanding. And recognition that that grand mystery is a crucial force in history and in our lives.' With its light American inflexion and ordered academic style, his speech has the placeless precision of the internationally educated.

'So how do we reconcile the need not to go back to a relativistic, narrowly circumscribed, tribalistic, nationalistic religion-based identity that separates, and at the same time fully recognise the divine mystery and enter into a relationship with it?' He pauses before answering his own question. 'Each religion has its story, but we don't yet have a sacred story that can somehow reconcile all of those views. We don't, of course, want to reduce that to such a simplistic and bland common denominator that all of the profundity is lost. So what we are seeking is a certain coherence which respects the distinctiveness of each religion.'

'So what I wish to propose to you is a vision of "planetary prophetology",' he continues. *Now we're getting wacky*, remarks a voice in my head. Pir Zia embarks on a careful explanation of how the great world religions had begun with a moment of revelation, a heightening of awareness which indicated that the boundaries of the founding prophet's ego had been transcended. 'Christ in the desert. Mohammed in the cave of Mount Hira. The Buddha under the Bodhi tree. They are human beings like ourselves. And yet they have become so suffused with awareness of the unity of being that their whole orientation has changed: they're no longer acting, as we do for the most part, on the basis of personal interests, expectations and agendas. So the prophets are exemplars of the highest order. And now, in an age of openness, it is possible for the chain of transmission to pass between prophets of different faiths, so that a Muslim, for example, can come under the spiritual influence of the Buddha without rejecting his faith or community. There's a certain point on the mystical path where one really can proceed no further until one has taken the turn to pluralism, until one has become universal. When we grasp one articulation, one act of divine speech and deny all others, we're not listening any more to universal history. It has become more about ourselves, the boundaries of our condition, than our access to what is seeking our attention.'

While he has been speaking, a sense of all-rightness has stolen over me; I have the impression of a much older person speaking. I look around to check others' reactions. The audience is as fully focused on Pir Zia as he is on them. Somewhere, at least, the grown ups are in charge.

He moves onto the question of how ordinary people can access Sufi wisdom. 'There is an interzone, which the prophets have entered, been absolutely transformed and come back with a message. This intermediate zone is the world of dreams, myths, and archetypes, and all of us can partake of the legacy of prophecy through dreams and meditation.' He lowers his voice confidentially. 'In the morning, if you're rushing off, an opportunity has been missed. There are times of the day which are more conducive to awareness, which means that one becomes more conscious of the message of the prophets.'

Then, thanking us for our 'quality of attention', he folds down his eyelids, crosses his arms over his heart and, without leaving his chair, seems to go elsewhere. I consult my mobile. He has been speaking for an hour and twenty minutes, without notes.

The line queuing to speak with him consists almost entirely of women. At its head, Pir Zia engages in an intimate consultation with each person, sometimes listening, sometimes lowering his lids and opening his arms to encircle a petitioner with silence. I don't want to consult him, but I do have a question about the chain of transmission that lay at the heart of the Sufi way. Wasn't it rather elitist, exclusivist: part of exactly what he had just been speaking so eloquently against? My turn has come. Close up, this spiritual leader seems unfeasibly young; his skin has the peachy plumpness of a twenty-something. Could this really be the same person that, minutes before, had carried the whole audience with his particular brand of elder-wisdom?

I explain my question, and the dark eyes flicker with recognition.

'Yes,' he nods, 'You could say that. But the line of transmission isn't always inherited – I'm not obliged to take it on. It goes in and out of families: sometimes it stays in a family; sometimes not. The line has been unbroken in my family for many generations, but it's not an absolute thing.'

I wonder whether being born into a family with a certain background is a factor, in the way that being born into a musical family would be more likely to foster a musician?

'Yes, certainly that helps,' he replies. 'In my family, we value this work, so we want to continue it. But I haven't chosen my successor yet.'

Later that week, sleeping later than usual, I had a dream. I was in the field on the other side of the river from my childhood home on the banks of the Severn. It was, as ever, bleak and empty, a flat plain you got to via a patch of dusty ground on the other side of the bridge. There, between ditches shrouded in willow trees, you had the choice of two tracks: one that led, through pyloned fields, to nowhere in particular; the other running along the edge of the field to the treacherous weir and a lone dwelling inhabited by a family who, rumour had it, were Strange. Every so often, R and I ended up there when we had exhausted all the other options. We would trail along one or other of the tracks in desultory fashion, sometimes retrieving a discarded porn mag out of a ditch with a stick. But despite the subtle hostility it exuded, the barren field never yielded anything of interest.

In my dream, a second image of a desert hovered over the field. There was a range of high, golden dunes; people were sliding down them and laughing as they played with the soft, fine-grained sand. To the right of the dunes appeared a vast expanse of rocky desert, jagged and shimmering with inhuman beauty: the kind of mesmerising rockscape I had seen from Mount Nebo and Mount Sinai. Laid out alongside the dream desert – or was it underneath? – the green-brown river and field remained, as if projected onto a giant internal screen. But it was nothing compared to the light and life dancing in sand and rock.

In my waking life I had been to several deserts including the Western Desert in Egypt and Jordan's Wadi Rum. But the king of deserts, as far as I was concerned, was the Sahara, where I spent a week or more each time I worked on the desert race. The vast horizons, the great expanses of space immediately opened up space in mind and body; it was possible to empty your mind, to simply be. The absence of things brought the little that was there clearly into focus: the desiccated desert flowers that you could pluck from the sand; the twirly precision of a single, distant tree; the black beetle scurrying excitedly towards the trickle of fluid when you went for a pee behind a rock. It was a nature minimalist's Eden: you could have a clear perception of almost everything you encountered. One year, it rained for the first time in seven years in that particular part of the Sahara, causing strange fissures to appear in the desert floor. Walking across the emptiness, I was brought up short: out of a large crack in the ground came a large, round gourd of brilliant yellow.

Every day, as the race progressed, the entire camp moved to another part of the desert. Each place was different: there was the stony desert, where the ground was littered with sharp black rocks; the mountain desert with its valleys and blocks of shade; and the growing desert punctuated with trees and scrubby bushes. It was rarely completely flat; something was almost always breaking the horizon: a table-top mountain, a craggy range of orange-and-black rock and – my favourite sight – the skinny black limbs of a lone tree. The golden dunes of desert-cliché were comparatively rare, which was just as well, given how hard they were to walk on, with the sand clawing your feet and dragging you back.

It was not easy to find solitude in the desert. You could see a lone figure approaching from a long way off, which could mean fifteen minutes of assessing whether they posed a danger. Was it a colleague from the camp, a Moroccan going about his business or a Bedouin hoping to profit from the loose morals of a lone western woman? But wherever we were, I always kept the Golden Hour, walking out into the desert just before sunset, getting far enough away to feel alone but still know the way back. Then I would settle down and watch the amber light flood the surface of the earth. The sun dropped quickly in this part of the world, seemingly speeding up as it approached the horizon; you had to be alert if you wanted to see the exact moment when it dropped out of sight. Then there came the strange effects of the fading light, often suffused with red, sometimes a greyness that was almost tangible. I would stay until the last possible moment before rapidly striding back to the twinkling lights of the camp. From experience I knew I had half an hour between sunset and the point where it was too dark to be wandering around the desert alone.

After I stopped working on the race, it was several years before I set foot in the desert again. I had decided to take a proper holiday, one that avoided the usual nosing about the Middle East. Instead, I would be an ordinary tourist on a winter yoga holiday. Egypt was the only other affordable option: there would be yoga morning and night, and an optional trip to the desert. I'd never been to Sinai; it would be rude not to sign up.

The Land Rovers carried us off-road into the desert: a group of holiday-makers, a yoga teacher and Egyptian guides. Sinai was very different from the Sahara: the sand had a pinky hue, the rock a greenish one, making for a real geological prettiness. The desert floor was stamped with little table-top mountains as neatly as if someone had printed a fabric. I was intoxicated with the beauty of the place. After about twenty minutes, the Land Rovers came to a halt and we tumbled out. There was to be a yoga session among the dunes, but I couldn't concentrate on postures; it was the Golden Hour. I excused myself to the teacher, indicating the direction in which I intended to walk. She nodded understandingly.

Ten minutes later, a band of dunes separated me from the group and I was in a flatter, bleaker landscape dominated by rocky outcrops. The sound of the wind coursing over space was familiar but, above all, there was a feeling of overwhelming relief, as if a pressing weight had been lifted from my chest. How had I managed all this time without coming here? Only, it seemed now, by an act of supreme forgetting. The sun was sinking, but this spot wouldn't do: I couldn't see it properly from this angle. Adjusting my direction, I walked on some more, finally choosing a place where a particularly impressive table-top mountain was directly in my line of vision, to the left of the lowering sun.

I wanted to absorb as much of this vastness, this concentrated silence, as I could in the limited time that I had. I sat down on the desert floor. Trying to still my anxiety about the time, I looked at the mini-mountain in front of me, a haze of red-grey dust gathering around it. Then, suddenly, a phrase sailed sideways into my head.

I AM WHAT I AM, it announced confidently.

What? I was tempted to laugh at this Old Testament-style invasion of my consciousness. I had forgotten I was in Sinai, almost believing myself back in the Sahara. As I stared at the rock ahead, the phrase recurred, less insistently. I began to relax; the tone fitted quite naturally with the grandeur of the place.

'I have been here all the time. Remember me,' added the voice.

It was growing dark; I had lingered too long. Confused, amused and grateful for my strange experience, I set off in the direction of the others, walking rapidly. It was further than I thought back to the dunes – desert distances are deceptive – and I was relieved to be finally struggling up the crest that separated me from the group, the sand dragging against my feet. Yet at the top, there was nothing beyond except another dune. I glanced at my water bottle. Just an inch left. I had brought neither torch nor compass. I struggled up the second dune. Still nothing. I was started to panic and making calculations about what the group will do if I don't reappear: surely they won't leave without me?

I'd now crested a third dune, and there was still no sign of human life. The remaining light was fading fast. Well, even if they didn't find me tonight, they would look in the morning. Without the burn of the sun, a solitary overnight stay in the desert would be unpleasant, but not fatal.

Over the fourth dune, I saw a Land Rover perched some distance away, in a direction different from the one I expected. People were trudging towards it, yoga mats slung over their shoulders. Someone waved. Minutes later, I was back among people, gossip and laughter: the yoga session had ended abruptly as several participants, feeling the sudden chill of the evening, had rolled themselves up in their mats and refused to move.

The next morning, as the sun rose over the craggy horizon, the desert wore its sweetest face. In the early light, the sand was the most delicate shade of eau-de-nil, and a gentle breeze fluttered over my skin. Pure, pure joy. I took my toiletry bag a few rocks away so I could carry out my morning routine in privacy. Back at the camp, the Egyptians were exchanging the customary greetings: Saber al Nour, Saber al Asal, Saber al Wurd, Morning of Light, Morning of Honey, Morning of Roses. They were baking bread for breakfast in the embers of the fire. While the others went to do yoga, I cut class to sit idly around the fire with them. They told me that some tourists, usually Germans, booked desert trips lasting forty days. I felt a stab of envy.

The day passed quickly. Our guides were good at their jobs, and knew the go-to places in this part of Sinai: we trekked through a canyon of chalk-white stone and rolled down some particularly steep dunes. Then we lunched at an oasis and bought beaded souvenirs from itinerant girl-sellers. I was in denial about the fact that, having just got back to this place of places, it would soon be time to go. And, all too soon, the four-by-fours were speeding over the desert, the drivers doing their usual tricks-for-tourists: racing each other, waggling the wheel until we're almost flying over the sand. We women screamed appropriately.

This final stretch of the desert was full of small, perfectly proportioned trees, their twiggy arms dancing in the breeze. I looked back out of the rear window, watching the desert slip away ... *Always remember me. Always remember me*, it seemed to say. We were nearly at the road now, and the other passengers were chatting hard about the evening's activities. I put my sunglasses on. I didn't want them to see that, like a child dragged away from a good time too soon, I was crying.

Had my dream of desert and field taken me into the interzone that Pir Zia had been talking about? It was an apt illustration of the polarities that characterised my personal history: town/country; English/foreign; adventure/security; one ancestral line full of facts and voices, the other of silence and absence. I am pleased to have this internal image of the co-existence of two such different places, possibly the resolution of the conflict they embodied, and store it carefully away.

Whatever its personal significance, it was time for me to find out more about the practice of Sufism, to see what other twenty-first-century Britons make of this ancient tradition. I know that The UK Sufi Order meet on Monday evenings at The Centre for Counselling and Psychotherapy Education in Little Venice and so one day after work I make my way towards a mansion of stucco cream that stands on a promontory on Regent's Canal. Willow trees bend over gaily painted canal boats and troupes of ducks paddle tranquilly across the water. The traffic of the Westway roars overhead.

I walk through the pillared entrance and pause: which of the closed doors are the Sufis behind? The building has several floors and many rooms, many containing psychotherapists; the waiting room is packed with people anxiously eating sandwiches ahead of their sessions. Finally, I come to a door with a pile of shoes heaped up outside; from behind it I can hear chants of 'Assalamu aleikum'. I know that the hour before the class is given over to an informal preparatory session but have no idea of what it consists. Cautiously, I turn the handle. The room is large and elegant, designed to accommodate a large number of guests with bay windows that take up most of the west-facing wall. In the pool of light that floods one end, a dozen people are slowly weaving a circle, chanting as they move. They seem utterly absorbed in the intricate choreography they are creating: intimate, self-contained, and entirely removed from the concerns of the day. I can't see how I can possibly be a part of it. I feel a strong urge to bolt.

Resisting the urge to run, I make for one of the chairs that line the wall and sit down to examine the circle. Each person's hands are crossed across the chest and, as they turn, they bow and raise their upper bodies, looking deep into the eyes of the next person. The upturned faces are beatific. I recall with surprise that it is early on a weekday evening in central London; the members of the circle are mostly in their thirties and forties, all white and smartly dressed and I wonder how they have managed to shake off the dust of the working day so fast. 'Look into your heart' instructs a soft, male voice periodically. Meanwhile, other people are drifting quietly in to the room and taking up meditation postures on the carpet.

Suddenly, the circle is breaking up. Wordlessly, everyone takes a chair and places it in a large semi-circle, and I follow suit. We sit, bathed in the light of the westerly sun, as the teacher begins to speak. According to the teachings of the *murshid*, he tells us, our subtle centres do not get enough sustenance in ordinary life and tend to atrophy. The Sufis call them *latifas*, the Hindus *chakras*. 'Everyone has read a book about them, and where they are: two inches below your navel, and so on,' he continues softly. 'Please forget all that: they are not in the body, but in a parallel universe.' But there are, nonetheless, two channels to the *nour*, the light: the subtle breath and vibration.

I glance at the other side of the semi-circle. Legs are firmly planted on the floor, hands resting in laps, and eyes are closed on upturned faces. Participants are not so much listening as luxuriating in the mood created by their teacher's gentle presence. He pauses and looks round at us acutely, with the kindness of a teacher for very small children. 'I'm talking too much. I'm going intellectual.' The semi-circle makes no response. 'No? Well, I'll go on, and tell you anyway.' I suspect he is right, but that the group are content to bathe in the light, both literal and metaphorical, on any terms. Their eyes are closed, their mouths curled up.

The early seekers of the light, he goes on, troubled the religious establishment, who saw their unorthodox approach as a return to polytheism. 'The fear of the early church was that they would fall back into the polytheism of the pagans. But polytheism was not worshipping idols: it was the belief that God was in everything, and everything was in God. There is a God that is knowable, and there is a God that is unknowable, beyond everything. If you believe that, then polytheism and monotheism are unified.'

He stops speaking. I am impressed. Without any fuss or fanfare, he has arrived at a solution to one of the greatest theological disputes going. But there is no reaction from the rest of the group.

'Now, shall we do something else?' A perceptible shudder of agreement runs through the semi-circle. *Yes. This is what we want. More of The Bliss.* Settling itself more deeply into its meditation posture, the group begins to chant 'Ya Nour'. The sound builds quickly, developing in strength and depth, and acquiring a metallic quality suggestive of pipes; it is hard to believe that such a metallic sound is made of human voice alone. Now it is circular, as if a wall of sound is enclosing us. The light of the near-horizontal sun blazes into our faces, adding to the sense of unreality.

All too soon, it ends. The teacher brings the session to a close with a story from his life. Once, chanting in a cave in Turkey in 1985, he had been overwhelmed by the powerful sound created by the echoes. 'I was so gone, so incredibly high. I felt I was so near to annihilating every atom in my body, becoming one with the vibration.' He laughed self-deprecatingly. 'I wanted it so much. I could taste it. But you know, some things get harder the more you try. I couldn't let go. I was trying so hard, and I was sweating.' The row brought the guard who told him, in several languages, that the caves were closed. 'Perhaps he was my guardian angel, and it wasn't time to get annihilated yet.'

The semi-circle has scattered and is now putting away chairs. Acquaintances greet each other with enthusiasm. I hover for few moments – it seemed strange to leave without speaking to anyone – but everyone seems otherwise engaged. Slowly, I make my down the stairs and back out to the street.

In the tube, a white board has been placed by the ticket barrier. My heart sinks. Station staff only bother to create an impromptu sign when there are severe delays to announce, or maybe a line closure. I stop to read the squiggly black capital letters.

GOOD EVENING FOLKS
YOU THINK YOU LOOK LIKE YOU HAD A BAD DAY.
HAVE   YOU SEEN THE GUY BEHIND YOU?
HAVE A PLEASANT EVENING.

I feel strangely comforted by this down-to-earth piece of British drollery. I am feeling a little disembodied; while interesting, the zikr had been a curiously bloodless experience. In future sessions, I must make more effort to integrate, I tell myself: it is surely part of Sufi tradition that you have to demonstrate your readiness to participate before things start to open up.

But as the weeks stretch into months, I find repeated excuses to justify the missing of each coming session: I was tired; it was Monday; next week would be better. Nor can I discern anything about my resistance that suggests overcoming it would be beneficial. Finally, I admit it to myself: I simply do not want to go back into this particular world. Instead, I do some more research and resolve to explore a branch of Sufism more typical of British Islam.

The Naqshabandis-Haqqanis are an order who combine Sufism with the strict observance of Shariah. Devout Muslims, they claim a spiritual lineage that goes back to the Prophet: it is said that the head of the order Sheikh Nazim, a Turkish Cypriot living in Cyprus, is descended from Abu Bakr, the first caliph and Mohammed's main companion. The emphasis on spiritual transmission was useful in a culture where the interweaving of politics and religion made society vulnerable to pretenders seeking to build rival power-bases: insisting that a Sufi master had a track record and was recognised by other spiritual leaders provided a system of checks and balances. Accordingly, the Naqshabandis tend to be suspicious of claims to enlightenment based only on the experiences of individuals; they prefer to recognise signs of spiritual development that could be corroborated by other sources, such as written texts or witnesses. This was a communal spirituality which stressed the need for a teacher to guide the seeker on their journey towards God.

The Naqshabandis had come to the country as part of the wave of immigrants that had come to Britain from the Indian subcontinent in the 1950s and 1960s, and were now the most prominent Sufi Order in Britain. It was impossible to know how many considered themselves to be Sufis, but in 2006 a new organisation called the Sufi Muslim Council claimed to represent the 'silent majority' of British Muslims. According to its leaders, up to eighty per cent of Britain's two million Muslims came from the Sufi tradition, a peace-loving form of Islam that was a long way from the hardline, politically engaged image the religion had acquired in the wake of the London Bombings.[81] The politicians grabbed the claim eagerly.

Despite my travels in the Arab world, I had almost no first-hand experience of the world of British Asians. The one exception was of a segregated wedding in which the bedecked bride sat in glittering isolation on a dais before an audience of women and children. Her husband, behind a screen with the other men, remained out of sight until his new wife instructed him, over her mobile phone, to 'get out here'. The preacher talked about westerners being the 'enemies of humanity' while we, a little group of western guests, got crosser and hungrier as we waited for our curry. Afterwards, we learnt that MI5 had also attended the wedding. I needed to get a fuller picture of British Islam.

DIVINE MUSIC

'Why is it you can never find a hijab when you need one?' I mutter into the blanket box, throwing towels and pillowcases around a bedroom already littered with the week's clothes.

It is a Friday evening on the first cold night of winter, and the end of a tiring week. The voice on the other end of the phone when I rang to check the details of the zikr was young and eager-sounding, typical of many of the British Muslims I had interviewed over the years. I should enter the mosque through the sisters' entrance, he advised, and while it didn't matter that I wasn't a Muslim, I should still wear a headscarf. I'm not entirely comfortable with being told to wear the hijab in my native London, having only rarely been expected to do so even when travelling in the Middle East. But covering my head will, I reason, help me get under the skin of this more conservative Sufi community. This time, I'm not going to tell the people I meet that I am writing a book: it will only make them wary, and skew their attitude to the newcomer. Instead, I will begin my explorations as a white woman seeking spiritual enlightenment in Islam – a common enough profile in modern-day Britain – under the cover, both metaphorically and literally, of the hijab.

In the end I settle for one of the big scarves I have long worn as protection against the British winter, and take the bus to Tooting. It is only three miles from where I live, but Tooting High Street, with its halal shops and brightly lit cafes full of extended families, could be in the heart of some Middle Eastern city. I walk on, past an Islamic bookshop, until I reach the mosque on Gatton Road, a red-brick building that blends well with the surrounding Victoriana. The sisters' entrance is clearly marked. I peel off my boots inside the darkened corridor and pad into the women's section. It is, in fact, only one end of a bigger room that is divided down the middle by a faded green curtain, and it is entirely empty. From the little I glimpse as I go past, the other side of the curtain is packed with men and boys. A young, emphatic voice is giving some sort of address. I sit down on one of the sofas and try to follow the thread: it is something to do with the companions of Mohammed, but more than that, I can't tell.

It is relief when a female figure steps out of the darkness of the corridor. She wears a kind of headdress I have never seen before: a baklava of black-and-white cotton jersey with an optional yashmak that can be drawn across the lower part of the face at will. She, too, seems relieved at the presence of another woman, drawing me into the adjoining bathroom, where we whisper conspiratorially while she performs her ritual washing. I have the comfortable sense of being taken under a sisterly wing; my new friend has ready answers to my questions. The sheikh is in Ilford, she tells me; the people of the zikr follow him wherever he goes, so it is possible they won't come tonight; we will have to wait and see. These occasions are often segregated; even her wedding had been so. She touches the fabric of my scarf lightly. Yes, I do need it, otherwise I would feel like I didn't fit in.

We continue our whispered conversation on the sofa. She is, Sana tells me, a divorced mother of two, and comes to the zikr only sporadically. 'I'm not very committed.' She looks into her lap sadly. 'I come for a while, and then I don't … I like to talk to the sheikh.'

Her face is suddenly lit with enthusiasm. 'I believe in God, though.' She pauses. 'Do you know the prayers?'

I shake my head. 'I know some of the philosophy. I've read a bit of Rumi.'

Sparks of pleasure dance across her face. 'Rumi says if you see a fault in others, it's because you have it yourself. Then, he says, don't worry if you don't have that fault, because you'll have it later.' There is a pause while she lets the joke sink in. Then we both laugh, swaying slightly on the sofa.

On the other side of the curtain, the talk is coming to an end and the youngest of the boys, visible through the gap in the curtain, are stretching restlessly. Soon, the group is trailing out and older men are hurrying in, plastic bags clutched against their salwar kameez, casting murmured assalamu aleikums in our direction.

As the preparatory prayers begin on the other side of the curtain, Sana takes to the floor, bowing and kneeling as she goes through the various recitations. When chanting indicates the beginning of the zikr proper, I join her. We sit, cross-legged, as next door the fluorescent strips are turned out, leaving only a narrow line of light below the bottom of the curtain. A strong draught whips across the ground, and we wrap our winter shawls tightly around us. I can't help but notice that the women have got the reverse side of the hanging, which is made of two pieces of material roughly sewn together. There are gaps where the seam is coming apart, and stray threads dangle from the hem.

'Do they always have the curtain?' I whisper.

'Yes.' Sana rolls her eyes regretfully towards the barrier that separates us from the sheikh, the heart of the zikr. 'I wish they didn't. But they do.'

It is strange sitting here, in the draughty darkness, on the other side of something significant. But I draw comfort from the female figure beside me, and try to concentrate on the sounds. The chants begin quietly, the men's voices gathering in strength and volume just behind the leading voice, rising in unity until, at the peak, the lead voice suddenly cuts them off, instituting a moment of silence. Then a new movement begins, and a different mantra and melody gather and rise to a culmination. The Arabic words are familiar to me, but recited so fast that I can't possibly participate.

Finally, the zikr is coming to an end. As the last chants die away and are replaced by murmurs and scuffling, Sana rises and I follow suit. With a mixture of sweetness and embarrassment, she kisses me three times; then, clumsily, we try to form the circle that brings things to a close. But something else is happening on the other side of the curtain. 'Let's see what's going on,' whispers Sana, and stands on her tiptoes, trying to look through a gap at the top where the seam has come apart. I duck down to the floor in an attempt to see something underneath. An expanse of carpet stretches out emptily. Then, realising how embarrassing it will be if the men on the other side see my disembodied face staring at them, I hastily stand up.

'I think we can go now,' says Sana. After the zikr, the women usually sit down and share cake and chat, she adds, her face splitting with pleasure at the thought. Passing the end of the curtain on our way out, we finally catch a glimpse of a close, intimate circle of men clustered together in the far corner of the room, as if gathered around something very special.

'There are some zikrs that are not segregated,' she tells me as we put our shoes back on in the corridor. 'There are others which are more open-minded.' She is, I realise, apologising.

'Hamdillah you were here,' I tell her.

'I was glad you were here, too,' she replies.

'Maybe your ancestors were Muslims,' she adds hopefully. 'Maybe,' I agree, inwardly doubtful about the possibility, but recognising the comment as a kind of welcome to her world.

Sana had suggested that we go to a Friday zikr together, and invited me to have tea at her house beforehand. So one bitterly cold night, I take her up on her offer and set off for Tooting on the bus, a Victoria sponge perched on my lap.

On her home ground in a tiny terraced house, her head uncovered, Sana seems different: her hair and personality more expansive. A British Pakistani, she had married a British man who had soon proved abusive, leaving her to bring up her two boys alone. Her account helped to explain the sense of loneliness that clung about her: a single mother whose nest was beginning to empty. But as we talk on, it becomes clear it was also to do with her relationship with the Muslim community: while she is clearly Muslim to the core, she feels as if she is an outsider. 'I'm always on the outskirts, on the edges.' She laughs ruefully. 'I've really never felt I belonged anywhere.'

Now I am laughing. 'How come I'm always finding people like you?'

I confess my writing project, swearing her to secrecy and making it clear that, rather than signing up to a particular group, I want to get a fuller picture of British Sufism. Sana is supportive of the idea, and promises to think of ways that I might do this.

The zikr, this time, is different. Women of all ages flow in, with tots and teenagers in tow. They quickly fill the space on their side of the curtain with chatter and laughter, settling themselves comfortably on the carpet. When the chanting starts on the other side, Sana comes and sits next to me. As the mantra 'Ya nouri' is chanted, she hands me some prayer beads to tell. 'By repeating this, you are getting in touch with God, you are calling your God,' she instructs, her manner grave and parental.

But it is hard to concentrate when surrounded by so much activity. The children whir like tops, and a few go to explore life on the other side of the curtain, where they are welcomed affectionately before being sent back to their mothers. I have difficulty staying cross-legged for long, and envy the ease with which my elderly neighbour has planted herself into the floor, her skirts and shawl spread leafily around her. But at least the sequence of chanted prayers – shouted by one small girl clearly delighted to have them by heart – is becoming familiar. I am beginning to hear that, like western symphonies, the chants enact a musical journey: the initial cajoling of the listener builds gradually to a climax, which is followed by a harmonious resolution.

With the heating on and the company of women, this time life behind the curtain is warmer, both literally and metaphorically. When the final circle breaks up, a few of the women approach me, ask a single, tactful question about where I am from, and then withdrew, swathed in gentle smiles. Only the western convert poses the question directly: 'So what brings you here?' As I consider how to respond, Sana steps in swiftly, answering protectively: 'Alex is very interested in Sufism.' Then, as packets of fairy cakes and digestives circulate, we all sit on the floor, lamenting the winter exhaustion that everyone, to a woman, is feeling. It is nearly eleven, a couple of children have gone to sleep, and one mother makes as if to join them, rolling semi-comically on the carpet.

Yet as we make our way out, I sense that Sana is disappointed in the proceedings. Her demeanour with her fellow Muslims is reserved, less spontaneous than earlier in the evening; it is obvious she is less than comfortable with them. As we put our shoes on in the dark corridor, she expresses her frustration at her lack of belonging, at her difference from her more conservative counterparts. 'I even have to bring my own friends,' she says with exasperation. She is quietly experimenting with various Sufi groups, searching for one that might suit her better, as I plan to do in my exploration of British Sufism.

'Don't tell them you have another sheikh,' she advises. 'You're only supposed to follow one, to have loyalty to one.'

'What would happen – would they exclude you?' I ask, intrigued.

'They'll just go cold on you,' she replies.

Despite being on the wrong side of the curtain, I do get to talk to the sheikh. A kind of public zikr is to take place on a Saturday in the shopping centre at Sutton, part of a small exhibition of Sufi art and calligraphy. The sheikh will be there, in a mixed, more relaxed setting, and there will be a whirling dervish. Sana picks me up at Tooting and we drive deeper into the suburbs, getting thoroughly lost in the rows of terraced streets. But eventually, we arrive in the town centre, park in the multi-storey and head for the shopping centre, to find the unit that has been given over to community use.

The shopping centre is large and sprawling; the unit, tucked away in an uncommercial, hard-to-rent corner, is difficult to find. But the security guards are unusually helpful when Sana asks for directions. 'Are you from Pakistan?' asks one, his face lit with interest. 'I am, too.' A second, uniformed young Asian leads us most of the way.

Sitting in the small, brightly lit unit, amid an array of coloured canvases and tables laden with soft drinks and cakes, is the sheikh and his family: a daughter, his ex-wife and a variety of sisters and children.

We admire the screens, with their vivid swirls of colour and circles punctuated with gold Arabic calligraphy. The artist behind them is large, serene and earth-mothery, with something of the Stoke Newington bohemian about her. As her toddler spoons up the foamy dregs of a takeaway coffee, she enthuses about the benefits of the weekly zikr. 'I feel lighter, freer, after' – her crossed hands fly away from her chest – 'like everything from the week has been lifted.' I ask if it is always like that. She considers a moment. 'It used to be really long. Now it goes fast, and it seems really short.' Her smile broadens. 'Because, you see, it's the ego which says, "Oh I want to watch that TV show, go and have something to eat".'

The dervish is taking his time. We admire the artwork, with its curls of gold and Arabic inscriptions, some more, gradually edging towards the sheikh, who is standing within touching distance of a table. As the introductions are made, I realise he needs the security: a shuffle and slight slur of speech suggest a stroke. The aquiline face above the long white beard is not Asian; the sheikh is Palestinian, born of a Lebanese mother, and often goes to Beirut. I am on familiar territory, the places he speaks of unfurling in my mind under a blazing Middle Eastern sun. He has been leading the Tooting zikr for fifteen years, he explains in halting English, taking over when the previous sheikh died. His own Sufi master is Sheikh

Nazim, who lives in Cyprus. Every now and then, he will visit him for a spiritual top-up.

What, I wonder out loud, is the function of the various elements that make up the zikr?

For a while, it seems as if the sheikh isn't going to answer.

'It's like medicine.' The words come slowly. 'You have one thing for each condition.'

The zikr follows a certain formula, he goes on, that was designed to bring the angels down into the human gathering. 'But the devil comes too,' he adds ominously. 'He knows there's something going on, so I call upon spirits to protect me.'

Silence. Mindful of the sheikh's frailty, I am wary of bombarding him with questions.

'Shall we go to Cyprus?' he asks suddenly, with a roguish twinkle.

I laugh. I could easily sail across to the island when visiting Beirut; the Lebanese pop over all the time. The ice broken, it is easier to say what is on my mind. 'So what's the point of the whirling?'

Whirling is another way of invoking the divine, like the chanting of the zikr, the sheikh responds. But it has to be treated carefully, as it is dangerous for some people. 'You can go mad.' He whirls a warning finger upwards. Generally, it should only be done by the dervishes themselves, with those present looking on.

'I'm not allowed to do it,' he adds. 'You need to have the permission of your sheikh. Once I did it, and I fell down. That was because I didn't have permission.'

'So how does it have an effect on the other people?" I ask, puzzled.

Another pause. 'They are bringing things down, and putting them into a basket. Then they give things out. If you seem interested, they will give you one.'

There is a flurry at the door. The dervish has arrived. He is two hours late, having had difficulty parking and then getting lost in the shopping centre. But his appearance, with his blue turban, baggy Turkish trousers and long waistcoat, is rewardingly dervish-like. A couple of small boys with huge dark eyes canter at his sides. Below his turban, I notice, the dervish himself is pale-skinned and blue-eyed.

He kisses the sheikh's hands, and prepares to whirl.

'He says anyone can join in,' announces the artist. The three of us, mindful of the sheikh's words about the dangers of neophyte whirling, exchange glances. There is a general shrug. The rules are strict, yet flexible.

Someone presses a button on a portable CD player, and the dervish begins to revolve, his soft shoes allowing him to turn easily on the laminate floor. His eyes are closed, his head bowed; one hand points up, the other down. As he gathers pace, a boy of about eleven joins him. He is a stout child, and he holds his arms stiffly, his expression self-conscious as he turns himself ponderously. The onlooking adults encourage and caution him by turns. The dervish is now in full spin, apparently oblivious to his surroundings, the stolid figure of the boy moving faster at his side. Then the music and the dervish stop, and the boy stumbles to a halt, visibly disoriented. 'Look at Mama!' cries someone.

As the dervish embarks on another whirl, a couple more children join in. The first boy is having another go. This time, he moves smoothly, his arms flowing into the movement as he spins faster and faster. As this second whirl comes to an end, the sheikh focuses his gaze firmly on the boy, willing him to steady himself as he gradually stops spinning and folds into a kneeling position on the floor. An air of congratulation fills the shop unit. 'That was his first time!' explains one of the women triumphantly.

Sana and I go to say our goodbyes to the sheikh. 'See you in Beirut.' He nods at me.

'We could go clubbing,' I rejoin, and get an answering gleam of amusement.

'I'm *trying* to teach her to become a good Muslim,' says Sana apologetically.

Clearly, I am never going to be a good Muslim in the sense of following rules set by a culture very different from my own, and it is clear that if I am to get further into the Sufi world I need to find a more open zikr. Surfing the web soon turns up a website featuring a more promising gathering: 'Everyone is welcome to experience Sufi Zikr Meditation based on traditional Sufi practices established over 1500 years ago', declares a sidebar.[82] This group of Naqshabandis meet on Thursdays in Maida Vale; there is a map, and a picture of the church hall where the zikr takes place. The Sufi webmasters have even posted a video so that all might share in the proceedings. I click 'play', but all I can see is a few men sitting on the floor in a darkened room; the chants are only semi-audible ... maybe you have to be there.

It is a long walk from the station to St Peter's Church Hall, between the moneyed terraces of Maida Vale. The modern entrance is unassuming, but a billboard on the pavement makes it clear I am in the right place: SUFI MEDITATION: ALL

WELCOME. I convert my scarf into a loosely worn hijab and step over the threshold.

Plastic, cleaning fluids, tea: the familiar smells of an English church hall. The room is small, with chairs stacked around its sides and a kitchen with serving hatch at one end. But as I hover in the doorway, the place is undergoing a transformation: several Asian men are laying out carpets; another is setting a video camera on a tripod; a couple of others are carrying big metal pots into the kitchen. The men are mostly in their late twenties and thirties, and wear stylised turbans of stiff satin in greens, blues and golds. They nod smilingly in my direction. An older man, with deep-set eyes under bushy white brows, is sitting cross-legged on the floor, apparently oblivious to the activity around him, murmuring prayers. Then, when everything is ready, one of the young men goes to the doorway and sends a wailing call-to-prayer deep into the night.

The men arrange themselves in rows, but only one woman places herself behind them, a willowy East African. I sit on one of the plastic chairs with another western woman and watch the prostrations that accompany the opening prayers. The single female figure is in continual movement, bowing, kneeling, standing. To my surprise, I find I am longing for the moment when the zikr proper will begin: I want to be floor-level, among others, safely enclosed in darkness and sound. Despite its chilly segregation, the Tooting zikr must have had an effect on me, after all.

Lights out. The three of us form a cross-legged circle behind the men, and the sheikh begins to speak. The talk is of gardening and of the necessity of regular tending; if the garden is the soul, and the walls the ego, one's plot is under continual threat from weeds. The analogy is familiar; this is the religious imagery of the East, with its cooling green oases amid dusty cities and arid deserts. It is no coincidence, adds the sheikh, that the Naqshabandis' spiritual leader's favourite activity is gardening. He makes frequent references to Sheikh Nazim, and each mention of the leader's name generates murmured thanks and praise among the men. The sheikh's measured tones are familiar, too: his voice is unmistakeably English, and his turns of phrase suggest a sermon in an Anglican church.

The chanting gets underway. 'Seven times, this one,' instructs the sheikh quietly, and the male voices quickly build the sound. Meanwhile, more women have slipped in and joined our smaller circle – one squat figure plonked comfortably beside me is rocking slightly, apparently in a state of complete absorption. I register a twinge of envy: how did she manage to slip in from the street and enter this altered state so quickly? Yet as the zikr goes on, I find it impossible to remain unaffected. Somehow, the sound is growing denser, growing closer as it encircles me; it is getting very hot in my thick jumper and headscarf. I am enclosed within a sonic space that did not exist before. The chanting is now unified, issuing as if with one breath from a single creature, part of myself notes in amazement. Then I'm caught up with what is going on in my own body, a physical tide rising from the base of my abdomen. It is accompanied by a strong feeling of nausea.

'We will have a meal together now.' The East African woman is beside me. The lights are back on, and plastic plates with curry, rice and noodles are being handed out; everyone is sitting in a neat rectangle around the carpets, which serve as a table. As we eat, my companion talks freely about how her family fled their native Somalia. As Sufis including a Sufi master, they had fallen foul of the religious extremists who were terrorising the country; in the eyes of the Wahhabis, Sufism was an 'innovation' that was '*haram*', forbidden by God.

In the liberating indifference of Britain, she put aside all religious questions, and forgot about Sufism for some time. But then a Spanish woman had told her about the Maida Vale zikr and, eight years on, she no longer felt there was a conflict between the two forms of Islam. 'You could say Sufism is too soft, too much about love, while the other, extreme form of Islam is about fear,' she tells me smilingly. 'The thing is to avoid both extremes, to do as Islam teaches, and tread a line in the middle.' Her slim brown hand cuts a line in the air. 'Like with a parent: you feel the love, but also the fear if they are angry.'

Like a lot of Sufis, she had, meanwhile, trained as a psychotherapist and found that the ancient spirituality and modern discipline had much in common. Her own therapist was an atheist, causing her to question whether she should have found a believer. But in the end she was glad because the experience obliged her to explain her faith, such as the fasting of Ramadan, to her therapist. She smiled broadly. 'And, of course, in explaining it to her, I'm also explaining it to myself.' Being a Muslim starts with the *Shahada*, the profession of faith that states there is no God but Allah and Mohammed is his prophet, she goes on. Then there is the obligation to pray five times a day which, like psychotherapy, works on mind, body and spirit; it is important to remember that prayer is about the body as well as the soul.

'Do you take part in other Muslim worship?'

'Oh yes, I'll go anywhere. I've tried everything,' she replies cheerfully. At one point in her spiritual explorations, she had become anxious about the legitimacy of her syncretic approach and consulted a Sufi master about whether she should, after all, stick to one sect. No, he had told her, being a Muslim is not part of a club. Go where you feel comfortable. If you find a group where your heart is at peace, stay with it – that's your way to God.

After the meal, the people around me become concerned about my long trek across London, and a lift materialises. Rahil, a young family man who lives in south London, is to drive me home. He and his mother, the provider of the food, carry the huge pots out to the car, and I get into the back seat. Late on a week night, the streets of London are almost empty, and Rahil is a proficient navigator; in no time we are coursing down the brightly lit Edgware Road and heading towards the river. His eyes flicker in the driving mirror as we talk; I can tell he is curious about who I am and why I am interested in Sufism, but is too tactful to probe. He himself, he volunteers, is a former follower of Wahhabism who has since discovered that God works through love rather than force.

Here is my opportunity to ask about this Sheikh Nazim that everyone keeps mentioning. He is, says Rahil, thought to be a descendant of Rumi and Abu Bakr, part of a line that goes back to the Prophet. For the Naqshabandis, there is no other leading sheikh in the UK, so most followers periodically go to see Sheikh Nazim in Cyprus, where he received a constant stream of visitors. I should go, said Rahil: he would always make time for me. And although he is now very old, he still has not chosen a successor.

'So what happens after he dies?'

The eyes in the mirror flicker.

'No one knows.'

I sleep well that night, my body somehow lighter on the mattress, suffused with an unusual level of physical well-being that lasts well into the next day. That weekend I check out Sheikh Nazim's online presence. His website is clearly a collective effort by followers, and displays neither communication savvy nor technical skill. But it is packed with information and resources for the faithful: there are videos, broadcast prayers and, everywhere, pictures of the Sheikh himself, a bushy-browed man who wears a turban and varying expressions of geniality and sagacity.

Over the following months, I go back to the Maida Vale zikr intermittently. The female attendance varies hugely; the women, perhaps more constrained by childcare and domestic duties, dip in and out more, but there is always the same core group of men. But the welcome is consistently warm; the men nod and smile, while the women press food on me. After a few sessions, it becomes easier to slip into the peculiar state induced by the chanting; by the mid-point of the zikr, the sound penetrates my body, as if operating at a cellular level, and I can no longer determine the boundary between the vibrations out there and those resonating within. The zikr seems shorter, and I am sorry when it ends.

One evening, the usual sheikh absent, one of the younger men leads the proceedings. His voice is stronger, his approach more energetic and at the culmination of the chanting, I have the feeling of being entirely taken over by the sound. Warmth spreads through my limbs. HAH HAH HAH says the circle; there is no way of staying outside the vigorous rhythm: you can only surrender. Then the chant becomes breathier, like the breath from a single creature. My eyes are watering involuntarily, and I become aware of the beginnings of a familiar, rather more worldly feeling rising inside me. Quickly, I put a stop to it.

Afterwards I feel agreeably drained, as if having done some vigorous exercise followed by a hot bath. I go home and sleep soundly. The next day at the office, the paper falls open at the advice column of a sex therapist. Briefly, I toy with the idea of writing in: *Dear Auntie X, Thanks to a group of devout Muslims, I am experiencing sensations of a climactic nature. There is no physical contact or inappropriate behaviour of any kind. Is this normal?* I fold the supplement shut and go to lunch.

The opportunity to consult someone more informed comes at the next zikr, when I find myself sitting next to a young woman I haven't seen before. Marina is a health professional who has discovered Sufism in adulthood; although her own order is in Germany, she appreciates the Maida Vale zikr for its openness. 'Are you comfortable here?' she asks, as the bowls of nuts and dried fruit are handed round the carpet-table. I am, to an extent which surprises me, I tell her.

Marina laughs. 'Yes, it's really connected here.' She thumps the cupboard behind us. 'Really plugged in. When I first came, I vomited afterwards.'

Now is my chance. 'So is it usual to experience quite, er, strong physical feelings during a zikr?'

'It isn't, but it can happen. It's the cleansing.'

The power of the zikr, she says, lies in the language that is used; the words work like a code, carrying energy. Her explanation echoes the traditional Islamic view that the language of the Koran is sacred; its power deriving more from the effect of the recitation rather than the content of its claims.

But, Marina goes on, even if you choose to disregard the religious significance, the zikr will still have a beneficial effect. 'You can go and get the energy boost – it lasts about a week – or you can try and live the spiritual side in your life.' She goes to Germany every month, to see her spiritual adviser and get the guidance that can only be provided by your own *tariqa*.

I wonder why finding the right *tariqa* is so important.

'It's like a carriage, with Sheikh Nazim as the locomotive,' she replies. 'People can get into any of the carriages that they want – they may be more comfortable with one group of people, just fit.' She pauses. 'Of course, some of the carriages are nearer to the front than others. The Naqshabandis are the most powerful order I've come across. They say it's because Sheikh Nazim is descended directly from the Prophet.'

The psycho-spiritual effects of sound have long been recognised by non-western traditions. Shamans use the effect of drumming on the brain to induce a state of altered consciousness; eastern faiths exploit the capacity of the chant to send vibrations through the body and create an audio whole that transcends the individual. That the human body is essentially rhythmic, governed by the continual beat of heart, pulse and breath goes a long way to explain the profound effect of music on mind and mood. I had experienced first-hand the musicality of Arab culture, from the ubiquitous pop songs of the street, to the euphonious recitations of the Koran that poured out of televisions every Friday. The musicality was in the language itself, as I had become aware during my attempts to learn the language. 'Hear the rhythm,' my Arabic teacher had urged. I was getting nowhere trying to grasp the logic that underlay the three regular verb patterns in conceptual terms; this was about listening. He sounded out the shapes on the page. Suddenly, hearing an aural pattern reminiscent of Do Re Mi, I had it.

It seemed ironic that conservative branches of Islam sought to eradicate all traces of music from the lives of the devout. And the ban on music didn't just affect Muslims in Afghanistan: the Muslim Council of Britain estimated that around ten per cent of the country's Muslims considered music lessons inappropriate for their children.[83] Perhaps the strength of this anti-reaction was testimony to the power of music over body and spirit.

Personally, I preferred a spirituality that worked with the body rather than trying to suppress it. But I noticed that, after a few sessions at the Maida Vale zikr, it was the very intensity of the sound that I found off-putting, part of the reason I didn't often make the trip across London to attend. With Britain plunging deeper into recession, my working life was becoming increasingly fraught. Stress was taking its toll on my nervous system, and my senses couldn't cope with any extra stimulation. But peace had broken out on the domestic front. A suspended ceiling had solved the problem of the stomping coming from above, while my downstairs neighbour and I enjoyed a relationship of mutual acoustic tolerance. Once his girlfriend had moved out, a guitar moved in, and for months the baby steps of learning to play the instrument would drift up through the floor, usually in the form of the opening chords of 'Hotel California', repeated again and again. But over time, his playing came on so well that one day, hearing the sounds of Pink Floyd from the bottom of the garden, I believed it to be a studio recording rather than a live imitation. My neighbour seemed undisturbed by my eclecticism which spanned folk, musicals and large quantities of Arab pop, telling me over the garden fence: 'You have impeccable taste'.

Ramadan. The Holy Month, and the highpoint of the Muslim year. I had to admit that my experiences of The Beautiful Month in the Middle East had been pretty negative. Entering a shared taxi meant taking your life in your hands: the drivers, after a long, hot day without food, water or cigarettes, were desperate to get home for the meal which broke the fast. They drove like maniacs, cursing each other roundly as they went; it wasn't unusual for fights to break out on the dusty roads. Although there were exemptions to the obligation to fast – if you were ill, or on a journey, for example – in the most conservative areas there was pressure for all to participate. At clinics, the diabetic and elderly refused to take their medication, jeopardising their already-fragile health. Having low blood sugar, I found myself in a hypoglycaemic heap on more than one occasion after those around me had made it difficult for me to eat.

This year, my British Ramadan didn't begin well either. On the first day of fasting, my Arabic teacher sent me a text, cancelling the lesson. It was the latest in a string of cancellations from him, and I was already on my way to our meeting place. His behaviour encapsulated my problem: while I believed people when they said Ramadan was an opportunity for the cultivation of virtue because so many of them said it, so sincerely, the conduct often suggested otherwise. But I was curious to see how the Sufis would celebrate the festival. So, as the Muslim world declared Eid had begun, I set off across town for another zikr.

The hall is empty apart from a kind-faced man in his sixties who is putting out the carpets. Eid had been declared a day earlier than expected, so the others are eating and will be along later, he tells me. Although not part of the group of younger Asians, I have seen him at the zikr many times before, and he is always friendly. We chat while we wait; he's only been coming to the zikr a couple of years, having had 'many problems'. A visit to Sheikh Nazim in Cyprus had resolved them all. I am puzzled. How could a brief encounter with one other human being be so life-changing? Was it his words, his presence? My interlocutor, smiling sweetly, struggles to find the answer. Yes, it was his words and his presence, but he can't really describe ...

'Eid Mubarak!' The group fill the hall amid hugs and cries of joy. The long month of fasting is over; the time of celebration is here. There are grumbles about the confusion of when Eid, determined by the sighting of the new moon, would begin; increasingly it is being called by spiritual leaders in various parts of the world at different times. 'We follow Turkey,' says one turbaned young man. 'We should just call Saudi Arabia,' says the woman next to me. The sheikh has brought a large tambourine 'for Eid', and this time the zikr is a noisy affair, the energies it produces rather scattered.

At the meal, the conversation is animated. A pastor in America has been burning Korans, and he wants to make it an annual event. 'They want to erase the Koran. But you can't: it's written in people's hearts.' The young man is passionate, his hand pressed against the left side of his chest. The young woman next to me, a Pakistani with an English-American accent, wants to know if I've been to the zikr before. Recently, I haven't felt up to the intensity of the experience, I tell her.

She considers my response seriously. 'It's intense because we invoke the divine. It is dangerous to do so without a *murshid*. People have even died.'

'In zikrs?' I am astonished.

'Yes,' she replies gravely. 'It has happened.'

The intensity, she goes on, diminishes as the *murid* ascends through the various stages of spiritual development. One sign of progress is feeling your heart beating in tune with the rhythm of the zikr, as group and individual merge. You also feel it in the psycho-spiritual organs known as the *lataif* that run along the front of the torso. 'The first place is here' – she indicates a place to the left of her breast. 'It affects people different ways. I always cry in a zikr.'

It is later than usual: time for *isha*, the night prayer. The men re-form their circle; we women sit in a long row, our backs propped comfortably against the cupboard. Tonight is a family event, with several children present, and their higher voices leaven the sound of the prayers. A little boy asks his mother's permission to join his father, and the smaller, prayer-capped figure becomes an almost exact replica of the man whose knee he clutches. Beside me, the woman I had been talking to earlier is sniffing loudly. Another woman fetches her a box of tissues. Afterwards, the hugs are especially warm.

Sufism, I was concluding, was an authentic spiritual tradition that was very much alive in contemporary Britain. But was it mine? As far as I could see, being a Sufi in Britain always seemed to involve being elsewhere: attending a *tariqa* in Germany or India, checking for the rise of the moon over Saudi Arabia or Turkey, popping over to Cyprus to consult the top sheikh. I could see that I was benefiting from the energy boost Marina had spoken of every time I went to a zikr. I was comfortable with the people, grateful for their warmth and easy generosity, and the practical materialism of Sufi spirituality, its attention to the needs and workings of the body, sat well with me. But in Sufi terms, my limited involvement meant that I was only 'warming the heart'. There was no pressure from anyone, but I knew that to go further in this tradition I would have to become an initiate, to follow the guidance of a teacher and become a 'committed one'.

Time to bite the spiritual bullet. I did not belong here.

I walked away from the hall, between the darkened terraces of Maida Vale, powered by a strong sense of physical wellbeing.

BACK TO NATURE

The British have a long tradition of quietly recognising nature as something of intrinsic value and of finding practical, understated ways of expressing our love for the natural world. We're a nation of gardeners, of walkers, of animal-lovers. If an Englishman's home is his castle, then perhaps his God could be found in his garden. Perhaps I would find a clue to the twenty-first-century spirituality I was seeking quite literally on my own soil.

But why does relating to nature have to be so uncomfortable? I look on with incredulity as my contemporaries valiantly demonstrate what it takes to be a lover of nature: Ray Mears building a shelter under the dripping trees and feeding on insects cooked over a fire kindled – if he's lucky – by rubbing together two expertly selected stones. Even a literary type such as Robert Macfarlane, in his quest for wild places, beds down on cliff-edge and icy mountain-top.[84] Exploring some eastern land, the travel writer Dervla Murphy simply parks her bicycle and sleeps in a ditch. The message is clear: closeness to nature involves hardship; if you want the chance of communion or epiphany, you are required to show a certain robustness, something akin to asceticism.

Not me. You're more likely to find me under a duvet, watching the clouds as they process slowly past the window or, on those rare English days when there's an ambient warmth of at least twenty-five degrees, lolling under a tree, gazing at the exact point where the sun catches the edges of the leaves. Occasionally, I feel sorry about this, but not for long. There must be a place in nature's kingdom for us, the non-toughies, the ordinary souls who love from a position of relative frailty. My body expresses its relationship to nature through a heightened sensitivity to the seasons and diurnal changes: with winter comes an overwhelming urge to hibernate; with spring heightened energy and exhilaration. Damp days can bring on flu-like symptoms: a fuzziness of head and aching of limb, while my rhinitis means that sudden changes in temperature or humidity can trigger a sneezing fit. Most people think I have a cold, but I know the truth of the more poetic interpretation offered by a friend: 'You're like a pine cone,' she said kindly. 'You open and close, depending on the day.'

Perhaps this goes some way to explain why I've always been obsessed with the weather, even by English standards. ('You should live in a lighthouse,' said my mother tartly, as I leapt from my chair for the fifth time during lunch to check what was happening, that particular moment, in the skies. 'Then you wouldn't have to keep jumping up to look out of the window.') 'Why do you begin every piece with a weather report?' asked a fellow journalist who regularly subbed my copy. I noted the need to vary my intros, while privately attributing my meteorological obsession to living on an island where the ever-changing weather is woven into the very weft of experience.

The flat had taken a year to find, the difficulty of the search enhanced by the fact that Madam wanted a flat that was light – so no basements – but which nonetheless had direct access to a garden. After months of searching, estate agents would greet me in the street by name, a glint of amusement showing beneath a veneer of commercial politeness. Finally, with prices rising and time running out, a promising set of pictures appeared on the website of a small agency I wasn't registered with, showing spacious Victorian rooms and a back door opening out onto a vista of seductive green. 'And *this* is the best bit,' said the estate agent, leading me down the dozen back steps and trying to make his way manfully through the forest of brambles that towered over our heads. It was, as far as I could tell, a good-sized garden for London, but one that hadn't been cultivated for years.

The price of this patch of relative wildness was settling south of the river, in an area with which I, a born north Londoner, had no connection. The Fresh Air Suburb, as it was dubbed in the 1900s, perched on the hills above London, offering a Janus-faced view of the world: turn one way, and you saw the city skyline, jagged with shiny high-rises; turn the other, and the green vistas of Surrey and Kent fell away into a blue haze that could be mistaken for the sea. Only two hundred years before the area had been rural, with just a few farmhouses and cottages dotting the wooded hills. It was still sparsely populated as late as 1849 when one Mr Leach, on one of his local foraging expeditions to gather flowers and berries, disappeared into the wild around Anerley and was never seen again.[85]

Even in the twenty-first century, the area's many parks and pockets of woodland made it hard to see it as fully urban. The move brought an instant cure to a compulsion that had regularly beset me when living in the heart of London, propelling me spontaneously outside and causing me to walk several miles to the nearest big park, as if my feet were being controlled by some external force. My new home was already in a green space: the back looking onto gardens, allotments and, beyond that, a wooded hill. The transmitter on its crest was a visual barometer of the mood of the day, its top half disappearing into a grey mist when the clouds were low, its red lights an early signal of the deepening gloom on a winter's day. The sounds of traffic and passers-by were replaced by birdsong by day and the screams of foxes by night, and on stormy days the prevailing south-westerly wind ploughed through the trees, and rain beat against the glass.

I'd been there a year before I realised that the area reminded me of somewhere I had always known. It was, in fact, a benign version of my place of origin on London's northern hills, with its long-limbed old trees and lofty views of the city. My new habitat even had a mirror image of the Ally Pally, the collective memory of a local landmark, the ghost of a people's palace, made almost entirely of crystal.

The eye craves green. Outside the kitchen lies my green room, a verdancy that encloses and soothes. Even in the depths of winter, when the back door can remain firmly shut for days at a time, I know that there is this other place, a place of repose and escape that I can slip into, visually or physically.

But on a practical level, it is a difficult garden to bring back to life. Beneath the dense brambles and weeds that cover every inch is a heavy clay soil, dense and unyielding. The overhanging trees and position of the fence mean that, while half the plot sits in sunshine of almost Mediterranean brightness, the other languishes in shaded woodland. My green-fingered neighbour Jane sucks in her cheeks when she visits for the first time. 'Oh, dry shade. Very tricky. Have you thought of pots?'

I have not. Nor will I countenance the fashionable decking that the estate agent so blithely suggested. Nothing will do but grass, green green grass. So I start digging. The plan is straightforward enough: turn over the soil, and remove as many of the weed-roots as possible before sowing grass seed. But the ground throws up constant resistance in the form of rubble, the legacy of the house's conversion into flats. There are chunks of stone, coils of rusting metal, bits of plastic, an infinite variety of unidentifiable objects and endless shards of glass. In one week alone I fill twenty-five plastic bags. Each time I return to the garden, the unseen forces that really govern the land – the wind, the rain and the wildlife – have turned over the earth to reveal yet more fragments, glittering up at me, threatening to scar a visiting toddler.

One day, the earth yields up something more interesting: a fragment of china bearing the letters 'EAM'. Instantly, my brain completes the word 'Eames', the name of the family into which my grandmother married, that of the never-known grandfather who jumped into the Thames. I turn the fragment in my hand and examine it closely. It's a chunky piece of crockery emblazoned with letters that exude a cosy domesticity, obviously part of a word such as 'cream'. I find this intimation of a connection, however tenuous, between my new area and people from my past comforting and put the shard on a post for safe-keeping.

As a new gardener, I'm starting from scratch in terms of knowledge. But as I glean scraps of information from relatives and gardening programmes, I quickly come to understand one thing: nature has its deadlines, and they're even less negotiable than those of journalism. Desperate to sow the grass seed before the soil turns cold so that roots can establish before spring, I dash in and out, digging and raking in between phone calls for an article and preparations for a trip to Lebanon.

A week later I am having lunch in Beirut and telling my host about my new passion. 'What will you plant?' he asks.

'Roses!' He laughs as I lift a forkful of tabbouleh to my mouth. 'Why do the English always have roses? It's as if there were no other flowers.'

Curiously, the garden brings me closer to wildlife than I ever was when living in the country. Set a good distance away from the houses, and connected to gardens and allotments with hedges and ground-cover, my uncultivated patch is clearly regarded by the local animals as unclaimed territory. Every time I go out, there is fresh evidence of digging, eating or defecating. At first, disarmed by the unexpected presence of bright eyes and fur, I behave like a sucker, scattering hazelnuts for the squirrels and speaking sweetly to the cats. Then, seeing the daily destruction of my efforts to bring the soil back to life, I wise up, boarding up the holes in the fence and generally establishing my territory. Standing at the top of the kitchen steps one lunchtime I see a fox in the middle of the lawn, a large, dead hedgehog in his mouth. 'Leave, please,' I instruct in my strictest voice. The fox immediately drops the hedgehog, and looks nervously towards the hole in the fence. 'And you can take that with you,' I add schoolmarmishly. The fox picks up the prickly corpse in his long jaw and makes for the exit. Apart from the odd bone deposited overnight, I don't see foxes in the garden again for some time.

But the quiet moments in the garden, when they come, make all the effort worthwhile. Standing in the weakening light of the westering sun, the smell of the newly turned earth in my nostrils, I am returned to ground level, to something approaching that absorption in nature I knew as a child. As a grown-up gardener, there's something about working the earth that is both penitential and uplifting. It's easy to see how the tending of gardens is so easily recruited to serve as a religious allegory, a metaphor for humans trying to engage with a reality they only half-understand, one which involves both struggle and reward.

As the year moves deeper into its darker half, my eye craves orange and yellow. I buy a patio rose with blooms of fluorescent orange and put it within sight of the back door. Down in the garden, I plant some crocosmia for its tips of flame, and fall for *coronilla glauca*, an ebullient little climber with bright yellow flowers and frilly leaves. It blooms all winter, trooping the colour even in the iciest conditions. I scatter honesty seeds, harvested from my godmother's garden, in memory of my grandmother. In January, after the turn of the year, I plant my roses.

Spring, after a long winter, is late. Nothing is coming up; the heavy clay soil remains dark and unresponsive. I look in vain for the puschkinia and scilla that flowered so resplendently the year before, illuminating the shady side of the garden with their strangely sculpted white heads. Maybe the squirrels, digging more deeply and desperately for food as the dead time drags on, got the bulbs. Much of my previously successful lawn has gone bald, leaving patches of bare earth. I think crossly about the fruitless effort, time that could have been spent earning money, walking or seeing friends.

O me of little faith. Days later, the buds are there, as intricate as asparagus tips, poking out of the earth. The grass seed sown to cover the bare patches sprouts almost overnight: scattered on Sunday, by Tuesday morning there are delicate strands of lime-green almost an inch high. A poppy opens suddenly, waving skirts of yellow silk. The contorted branches of the tree I planted in the corner, a deciduous larch, sprout the makings of its cones: pink buds against fresh green needles. In a flash I see the natural genesis of a colour-combination I've always loved in fabrics.

By April, everything is bright and beautiful; we're having one of those early heatwaves that are becoming a regular feature of the English year. On Easter Saturday, I'm out in the garden, doing the chores of early spring. Working tranquilly away, I notice that a pointed brown face has emerged through a gap in the fence, followed by a good-sized body. It sits motionless in the corner, sunning itself. Normally, of course, I'm terrified of rats: they invade the compost heap, chomping away on vegetable peelings, their fat, furry bodies burrowing away fast at the sound of my scream. But this one has a different demeanour, gratefully soaking up the mid-morning warmth, his nose a-quiver, a large bead of blood on its tip. I don't scream and he doesn't run, so for a sunny quarter of an hour we co-exist peaceably, me working my patch and him resting in the corner, his body gently palpitating until he turns and slowly shuffles back through the gap in the fence.

With hindsight, my encounter with the dying rat seems prescient because, three days later, my father is dead. My mother takes to her bed, pleading a fatal stomach condition despite five medical opinions to the contrary. I lie on the sitting room floor, discussing the funeral arrangements with my brother. I can't sit up because my own stomach, flooded with stress-induced acids, hurts so much.

The next morning, the phone goes. The voice on the other end is hesitant, and has a soft local burr that I have known almost forever. It is S, my friend-from-down-the-lane from the Big House. We are rarely in touch these days: I'd last seen her outside the supermarket six months before, having just learnt of my father's diagnosis. She doesn't know if she's got the right number. But she needs to speak to me urgently because she's been troubled by a dream in which she saw me stricken with something like appendicitis.

Awake, she told the man beside her: 'Alex is in pain. I think her dad's died.'

'Rubbish,' said her husband.

The 'principle text' of the English passion for the countryside, according to Richard Mabey, is a modest little book about the natural life of a parish in southern England which has never been out of print since it first appeared in 1789.[86] *The Natural History of Selborne* by Gilbert White was the published correspondence between a country curate and two eighteenth-century naturalists, Thomas Pennant and Daines Barrington. With his detailed observations of the local flora and fauna, White was unwittingly pioneering a new way of engaging with nature that endures to this day, one that recognises both the otherness of the natural world and its relationship with the human.

Born in the Wakes, the family home in Selborne, the young White went to Oxford and then, like many educated men of his time, entered the Church. But the living of his local parish was unavailable, and half-hearted attempts to get a position elsewhere foundered on his reluctance to leave home. So he settled for a series of temporary curacies in Selborne and the surrounding parishes. As a young adult, he travelled extensively around the southern part of England but never went further north than Derbyshire, considering, as Richard Mabey records in his biography, the Sussex Downs to be 'a vast range of mountains'.[87] Although a sociable man who had visitors for weeks on end, in later life White disliked travelling long distances, sometimes upsetting friends and relations with his refusal to visit them. Despite his obvious need for stimulation – he often complains in his journal of the lack of like minds with whom he can discuss natural history – his sensibility was a local one, and the parish of his birth exerted a pull more powerful than all other places.

It is tempting to attribute White's extreme rootedness to the peculiar geography of Selborne, a place enclosed in a valley so narrow that when in it, you see nothing of the world beyond, and when above it disappears from view. Within the valley was a micro-landscape of sloping pastures bounded at one end by a huge tree-covered hill known as The Hanger that was unusually rich in plant and animal life. 'The parish I live in is a very abrupt uneven country, full of hills and woods, and therefore full of birds', writes White. Located on a geological faultline where the chalk of the South Downs met with sandstone, it had a variety of soils including 'a black malm' and 'rubble stone' which 'moulders to pieces, and becomes manure to itself'.[88]

Selborne was linked to the outside world by hollow lanes, sunken roads so overhung by the trees growing up their sides that stepping into one was like entering a tunnel. White is at pains to describe their influence on the psycho-geography of the village:

> These roads, running through the malm lands, are, by the traffic of ages, and the fretting of water, worn down through the first stratum of our freestone, and partly through the second; so that they look more like water courses than roads; and are bedded with naked rag for furlongs together. In many places they are reduced sixteen or eighteen feet beneath the level of the fields; and after

floods, and in frosts, exhibit very grotesque and wild appearances, from the tangled roots that are twisted among the strata, and from the torrents rushing down their broken sides; and especially where those cascades are frozen into icicles, hanging in all the fanciful shapes of frostwork. These rugged gloomy scenes affright the ladies when they peep down into them from the path above, and make timid horsemen shudder while they ride along them; but delight the naturalist with their various botany, and particularly with their various *felices* with which they abound.[89]

While his naturalist peers were scouring the remotest corners of the British Isles for new discoveries, White was examining what was under his nose in minute detail. Much space is devoted to the habits and instincts of birds, including the migratory movements of swifts, swallows and martins, with an attentiveness to detail that accords them their own ways of being. Yet surprisingly, given his role as a clergyman, he never uses his observations as a springboard for theology. He makes the odd reference to the Creator in the vein of John Ray, the seventeenth-century naturalist and theologian who believed that God could be best understood through his creation, but generally, God is absent or, at most, implicit and in the detail. *The Natural History* reads more as an early expression of an ecological spirit which attempts to see nature in its own terms, blending a spirit of reverence with a scientific approach. In this respect, White's legacy struck me as quintessentially modern, and I wondered whether it might throw some light on our relationship with nature in the twenty-first century.

My entry into the latter-day world of Gilbert White came via a leaflet picked up by chance at a plant sale. The South London Botanical Institute was organising a day trip to Selborne for botanists. Listed amid details of Lichen Workshops and Field Meetings, the excursion promised an opportunity to observe those obsessed with the detail of natural objects. I signed up straight away.

The train to the nearby town of Alton is full of parties of Asians on their way to the Jalsa Salana, the annual convention of heterodox Ahmadi Muslims. Women and men cluster together in their respective groups, and relatives pass each other titbits of food. Outside the carriage, it's a moist, mizzling kind of day and although it's July, a thick blanket of fog covers southern England. Yet, peering anxiously out of the window, I can see streaks of duck-egg blue on the horizon.

At the station, we are met by our guide for the day, June Chatfield, a locally based biologist who teaches for the Institute. She emanates energy and knowledgeable enthusiasm, her dark eyes alert beneath white hair loosely pinned into a French pleat. A former curator of his house and garden, she knows a lot about Gilbert White. She shepherds us towards an ancient Peugeot, and I climb into the back. Moss grows out of the window frames, and the seat is strewn with straw for transporting tortoises. Soon, we are rattling away from the flatlands around Alton and descending into the hills that enclose Selborne. 'They've forgotten us out here,' says June cheerfully. 'We still have five-digit phone numbers.'

As we wait in the village car park for a party of botanists from Kew, she regales us with tales of the travails of preserving White's legacy. As curator, she had been involved in the purchase of the manuscript of *The Natural History* some thirty years before. The museum was up against a rival bid from a pension fund whose managers cannily recognised this interesting piece of the national heritage as a good investment. With a little over a month to find the money, fundraising was a challenge: BT pricing bands meant that using the office phone in the mornings was forbidden, so all calls had to be fitted into the afternoons. The money raised didn't stretch to the introduction of *The Natural History*, but when the wealthy American who bought it discovered whom he had outbid, he was so mortified that he gave it to the museum. Now, with the museum a charity, and the house supported by a tea parlour and gift shop, things are less precarious.

But the spirit of the naturalist who had brought our party to Selborne seemed all-but-lost amid the tourist bustle. 'Where's Gilbert White?' asked one of the botanists mournfully, surveying the well-maintained car park and spanking new toilet block. 'Where's Gilbert White?'

When the party is complete, we set off for the village centre. The 'single, straggling street' of White's first letters is unchanged: low-roofed cottages line the narrow thoroughfare, while behind, the wooded mass of The Hanger fills the horizon. We make our way to the church of St Mary's, pausing to admire the fourteen-hundred-year-old yew. Inside, a stained glass window in the south aisle, depicting St Francis surrounded by birds, marks the centenary of White's birth. A second, triptych window marking his death pays homage to his various roles: 'For a faithful priest ... A humble student of nature ... A writer of genius'. The needlepoint hassocks of parish blue, instead of the usual crosses and flowers, abound with creatures: foxes, hares, herons and owls.

But it's outside the church that the action really begins. 'There's an owl dropping!' exclaims June, bounding towards a tombstone.

Set apart from the others near the boundary with the neighbouring fields, the grave is clearly a favourite perch, the stone splattered with excrement. June peers carefully at the dropping – a large patch of light brown fluid containing lumps of undigested matter – and decides it is more likely to be the product of a crow. We file out through the little wooden gate at the rear of the churchyard and into Church Meadow. A steamy heat rises from a stretch of uncut grass to the right, and the air is filled with the grasshoppers' song; it is beginning to feel like a proper English summer's day. Yet there is something odd about this landscape, with its exaggerated proportions and sharp angles: within a few yards, the ground falls sharply away into a wooded valley where outsize tree trunks stretch from floor to sky. The meadows tilt at steep inclines, and things are growing everywhere, banks of nettles jostling with tussocks of grass. The fecundity of the place, says June, is due to the above-average levels of precipitation caused by the surrounding hills.

'Ah!'

She's spotted something, a large piece of sponge growing out of the base of the large oak sited halfway down the slope. It's golden, the size of two large hands, oozing out of the trunk as appetisingly as an over-ripe camembert. The group gathers round, commenting on its function and chemical composition. The organism is identified as *inotus dryadeus*, a fungus specific to oak. 'I've known a lot in Somerset, but not here,' says June. 'Maybe it's because of climate change.' She adds with satisfaction: 'You come to a place you've known for donkey's years and you never know what you're going to find.' A tall man does what I'm secretly longing to do, putting his finger on the golden crust and licking it. 'How does it taste?' I ask curiously. He hmms and considers, eventually pronouncing it 'sort of nectary'.

We continue to the bottom of the field-valley, pausing to examine the tangled crown of a wind-felled oak. Its upper branches are covered with yellow-grey growths that mingle with the limier greens of its leaves. 'It's a wonderful way of getting into the lichens, which you can't normally,' June enthuses. 'This gets you right into the top canopy.'

Moments later, she's almost in the stream that separates the field from the woods, standing on the muddy foreshore to study the plants that grow in the water. 'This is "fool's watercress", or water mint.' She proffers a green frond with little white flowers. 'It's a member of the carrot family: when you crush them, they smell of parsnips.' I nibble a few of the dark green leaves. They have a distinctive spearmint taste, and an undertow that is almost metallic. Wordlessly, a young woman approaches me with another waterside plant: a forget-me-not with petals of the palest blue as if the flowers have been diluted. Other botanists are comparing grasses at the stream's edge, peering through eye glasses, getting reference books out of rucksacks to check features that puzzle. Fragments of discussion drift through the air. 'I'm puzzled by the difference between these two kinds of grass,' confesses someone. 'Oh, and this one has hairy nodes as well,' says someone else.

I observe the naturalists as they crouch, lean, pick, and show. No one, not even the oldest member of the group, seems to have the slightest concern about muddying clothes or overstretching limbs, getting into the oddest positions in the pursuit of botanical truth. Like adult children, they are entirely absorbed in their study of the detail of the world. This lingering over nature is very different from the approach of the walking groups I'm used to, with their relentless drive to notch up the miles, attain the destination. Eventually, we make it across the stream and enter the beechwood a few yards away. Under the dark canopy of the Short Lythe lies another strangely exaggerated world. The trunks of the trees reach up through different layers of matter, the steepness of the slope exposing roots that form a network of holes and burrows.

While the botanists collect in groups along the path, examining pieces of vegetable matter, I decide to reap the benefits of this leisurely pace, and sit down by the brook. I miss the childhood activity of messing about in the streams of north Gloucestershire; it's been difficult since to take such pauses in company, with the perennial obligation to keep walking and talking. The water that bubbles over the pebbles is clear, refracting the play of sun and cloud and accenting the tones of stone, twig, earth. I draw its smell deep into my body, feeling it course through my airways, willing it into the upper reaches of my skull. Unlike the streams I used to play in, scented with sewage or decaying willow, the smell of this water is clean and metallic, a cousin of the mint I ate earlier.

Slow-slow, slow. After a picnic lunch in Church Meadow, we meander through the village towards one of the hollow lanes made famous by White. We make poor progress down the High Street, pausing frequently to examine plants growing out of garden walls. 'Mmm, botany pace,' murmurs a woman from Dulwich as we stop for the nth time. On a previous outing, she tells me, the group spent half an hour examining a wall in the centre of town because of its spleenwort. But finally we arrive in what used to be the main road to Alton.

And it is 'in'. With branches overhead and the vegetation curling around the sides, it's like being in a tunnel; the surrounding fields tower above my head. The tree roots rise like church pillars, and the earth-walls are flecked with chunks of butter-coloured stone. Two hundred years ago, the lane was a major transport route for moving livestock and crops, and continued to provide an alternative network even once surface routes had been built. Even now that the lane is tarmacked, explains June, its sunken location means that the water courses down its sides, forging deep runnels into which wheels get stuck.

She and I fall into step as we progress up the hollow lane, towards the light coming from the open field that lies beyond the circle of bank and trees. She tells me she's writing a contemporary natural history of Selborne, something that will record the details of its flora and fauna of the early twenty-first century. What better name for a communicative botanist than Chatfield? I've stumbled across a latter-day Gilbert White. I find this evidence of the continuity of purpose, of the love of a place in all its specificity, supremely reassuring.

Gradually, south London is yielding up its wild places. One weekend, walking home after a gardening workshop on the allotments a couple of hills west, I discover it's possible to play a kind of green space touch-off-ground across a good portion of my neighbourhood. I keep almost entirely to woods and parkland as I make my way a mile across country to the park at the end of my road. I am treading the remnants of wild Surrey, the great North Wood that covered the hills of the north of the county, stretching as far as Camberwell. Their scattered communities gradually evolved into villages and suburbs, ending some ways of life and introducing others: by the eighteenth century the Croydon-based charcoal burners that supplied the city with fuel had disappeared, as by the nineteenth had the inland smugglers who used the woods and green lanes for cover. The idyllic spot – within easy access of London, but situated pleasantly above it – was a prime target for gentrification, and the gypsy encampments which had populated the forest for centuries were replaced by wide leafy streets and

Victorian villas. The views and meadows made the Norwood hills a prime site for the new age of recreation: the discovery of a mineral spring on Beulah Hill – 'one of the purest and strongest of the saline spas in the country', according to one Professor Faraday – brought city-dwellers until it was superseded by the greater attractions of the Crystal Palace.[90] But the past lives of the area lived on in the names of its streets: Sylvan Hill, Gipsy Hill, Fox Hill.

The more green spaces I discovered within walking distance of my new home, the greater my appetite for open land. I had disregarded the green splodge that lay a bit further south on the map, believing 'country park' to be an oxymoron. But a chance conversation with Jane suggested that the place was worth investigation so, early one summer's evening, I set out on foot. Increasingly troubled by my shrinking world of work, I needed a reminder of what was real. The economic world I knew was dissolving and fracturing with terrifying speed, and it was clear that no one knew what to do. Having had work whenever I needed it since the age of fifteen, I was now in uncharted territory. Magazines folded or reduced pages; the last of my regular clients announced overnight that, due to cuts, it no longer had any freelance work. New opportunities were rare and even responses to advertised assignments often got no reply. More frustrating still were the solicitations that led to a series of time-consuming communications that usually ended with the revelation that the budget wasn't there/the key decision-maker couldn't decide. I seemed to be caught in an endless, speculative discussion about things that didn't really exist.

The streets of south London were lined with chicken and kebab shops and coursed anarchically with cars and people. I paused to examine my map and a youth with a French-African accent stepped out from a doorway to offer his assistance. Finally, after roads of terraced houses, a mass of green filled one side of the street. A narrow path curled off between the trees. Moments later, I was under a vast white horizon, dusty tracks crunching underfoot. Paths snaked off between drifts of head-high cow's parsley, and the air was suffused with a distinctive willowy smell reminiscent of the streams and rivers of Gloucestershire. I felt my breathing slow. Some pine cones littered the verge. I picked one up; it fitted snugly into the palm of my hand, woody, substantial, yet delicate: the best executive stress toy not on the market.

Later, Jane takes me next door to her allotment, where the sun-drenched trees and bushes are fructifying madly. We pick plums. I feel better.

In the autumn, I get headhunted to edit a new political magazine. It will be interesting work, in a field I know well, and on the part-time terms I ask; it's almost too good to be true. There is a smart launch in Westminster, with carefully worded speeches and a large government minister. Within weeks, it *is* too good to be true. The boss of the company, a diagnosed manic depressive, has built his company on delusional figures, and the projected income is not materialising. He clears the scene and, amid a sweep of redundancies, the magazine is purchased by a philanthropically minded entrepreneur. I am summoned back to the office to restart work on the forthcoming issue. A week later, the new owner takes a closer look at the figures and hurriedly pays off the few remaining staff. I'm reminded of a Spanish saying, expressive of a bleak Catholicism: 'Dios aprieta pero no ahoga': God gets you by the throat, but He doesn't actually strangle you.

I decide to eschew office life, with its desk-level politics and corporate guillotines, once and for all. Instead, I will supplement my freelance work with a locally based micro-business. My model is the skilled tradespeople who have done work on my flat: the plumber, the electrician, the carpenter; my aspiration for a straightforward exchange of skill and labour for payment, in which the worker retains her dignity and independence.

Gradually, as the days take on a new pattern, I realise that another exemplar has unconsciously established itself in my mind, something akin to the deliberately varied routine of monastic life. My daily pattern, solitary writing followed by two or three hours of practical tasks and then people-based work for the rest of the day, is far from the disciplined timetable of prayer and work of the monastic day. But nevertheless it owes something to the insight that human life is best lived when body and soul are allowed to follow their natural rhythms. Tide in, tide out.

It is late March, and I am heading west for a weekend of walking with B. After the long drag of winter, we mean to stretch our legs and clear our heads, while satisfying a yen to explore Somerset, the county next to the one we grew up in, but largely unknown to us. We book into a rural B&B, a cottage folded into the land near Solsbury Hill, and anticipate the combined pleasures of familiarity and discovery.

The houses in this part of North Somerset are solid, well-proportioned constructions of the local limestone, which are perfectly attuned to the landscape. Affluent, serene Bath seems to have achieved a harmony with its surroundings rarely found in British cities. When you walk its honeyed pavements, the gaze slides effortlessly from the golden crescents to the fringed hills beyond. We are staying in the hills outside the city, where the countryside has a late-winter uniformity, the fields echoing the seared brown of the trees.

Following our landlady's directions we set off, in the gloom of a dull afternoon, to climb Solsbury Hill. Down, across, round and up we go, staggering up a final, steep wooded stretch to the summit. We are thrilled to have ascended the hill that inspired Peter Gabriel's epiphany until we realise that we haven't. Solsbury Hill is opposite, its flat top unmistakeable against the grey sky. We set off once more, down, across and up until finally we really are there, circling with several other people a small plateau that overlooks the surrounding landscape.

The next day brings a change as sudden as the moment spring came to Narnia, and azure skies stretch from one horizon to the other. We take the canal path east, along the waterway that shadows the river Avon through a long, wide valley. Like a dog kept indoors too long, I can't help sniffing the air, which is full of smells released by the warmth, the distinctive scents of life near water. The canal is lined with narrowboats, and the weather has brought out their owners, who are busy sawing wood and making good the damage of winter. Some of the boats are clearly for weekends and holidays, with every rim and rail gaily painted and polished; others are permanent homes, possessions piled high on their roofs, their chimneys sending drifts of wood-scented smoke into our path. One deck is home to a brood of hens, on another waiting staff are preparing a tray of shiny champagne glasses. A whole lifeform has burst out of its winter dormancy. As the day lengthens, I have a growing sense of the circularity of the seasons and the connection between this place and its people.

By late afternoon, we've made it to Bradford-on-Avon. We've walked so far that we will never get back to the hillside cottage before nightfall; B's feet hurt and I can feel a familiar warning ache in my hips. We eat in a cafe in an eighteenth-century townhouse, and then take a taxi to a halfway point, where we will pick up the canal path again for the last couple of hours of light. The young taxi driver is full of praise for his place of birth. 'On a day like this, there's nowhere else I'd want to be,' he enthuses as the car weaves through the honeyed landscape. 'My children love it.' Briefly, I feel a twist of envy at this continuity of people and place, the uncomplicated identity expressed by his contentment.

But elsewhere in the world, Nature is presenting a far less benign face. It's the weekend of the Japanese tsunami and an earthquake has propelled an enormous wave over the north of the island, sweeping away everything in its path. Our golden day is bookended by the television news; we sit on our beds and watch, aghast, as more pictures of the disaster are released. One shows a huge black wave engulfing an entire town, tossing cars and boats carelessly aside. It's impossible to take in what's going on – in the aerial shots, the proportions seem wrong; even in disaster movies, I have never see anything like it. A reporter tells one of the human stories: a mother-of-two drives frantically ahead of the tsunami, stops in front of a cousin's house – which, being made of metal, is relatively protected – and jumps out to hand each child to a relative before being swept away by the water. Other reports show people returning to their former homes looking for mementoes. One woman stands, bemused, on the site of her former town. She has no idea where to look for the traces of her former life because no landmarks remain. Picking his way through a mound of rubble, a man finds a photo of a family, and tells the reporter: 'If those children have died, this will be precious for someone.'

As a well-travelled, twenty-first-century adult, I can't tell myself the consoling fiction that the scenes of suffering come from a distant land populated by strangers. There are too many connections, both global and personal, linking the now and the then, the here and the there, the us and the them. An old Gloucestershire friend now lives in Japan, and the breakfast news is presented by a boy who grew up in my village, turned famous and forty-something. It's impossible not to wonder how it feels if your place of belonging, with all its apparent permanency, is suddenly destroyed. Does it destroy your trust in the earth?

In the commentating that follows the disaster, experts say that the Japanese are well-used to cycles of destruction and reconstruction, the national psyche shaped by stoicism in the face of the indifference of nature. I am not so sure. What I do know is that my more delicate English psyche is incorrigibly attached to place, imprinted like ducklings with the first creature they see, by my formative landscapes.

It's always a bit of a wrench, leaving the familiar landscape of the west. I've done it so many times, by car or by train, as Sunday afternoon shifts into evening; the first half hour back in London is the only time I have a sense of dislocation, of being misplaced in this place of concrete. I spend the first half hour of the journey watching the world outside the window, waiting for that distinct point when the connection is lost, before reluctantly returning to the grey no-man's land and stale air that is the Country of Train.

This time, after the embrace of the hills around Bath, the feeling is accentuated. I know all is lost once we hit the flat land around Swindon. I watch the retreating view through the fishtank windows as long as I can: a solitary magpie sits in a tree, its white breast ablaze with the rose-gold of the setting sun.

A few weeks later, I'm back in the west unexpectedly, on a blazing April day. My mother, brother and I spend the afternoon in Cheltenham hospital. I'm pretty sure what the prognosis will be; the address on the letter on my mother's kitchen table detailing the urgent appointment is the same as that of the oncology unit where I went with my father four years earlier, despite it having been renamed the 'Thoracic Department'.

The evening before the appointment I meet up with my old friend Rich in a Gloucester pub. The chemotherapy for the cancer that has plagued him for the past two years has removed the dark eyelashes that entranced me in my teens, along with almost all his hair. But his mood is buoyant: sufferers from his condition have a ninety-five per cent recovery rate, and his consultant thinks he may now be in the clear. We sit by the fire, listening to a group of folk musicians from the Forest, and talk about what he will do with the rest of his life. He is fed up with being a professional musician; he fancies retraining as a forest ranger.

The following day in Cheltenham, the oncologist shows us X-rays of my mother's lungs. Despite being a non-smoker, she has lung cancer, the disease that killed my father. Euphemisms pass between us: 'inoperable', 'the best possible care', 'as comfortable as possible'.

Later, my brother drives us back east.

'When you're young you think you've got an eternity ahead of you,' he remarks, apropos of nothing, as the A40 slips away under the wheels. 'You don't get long on this earth.'

THE PAGAN PATH

Somewhere in the English psyche is a yen for a deeper relationship with the natural world than ordinary living can provide. The English arts are full of expressions of this Arcadian longing; a vision of paradise set against the backdrop of a chilly island. You find it in a certain period of children's literature: a rich seam of obliquely expressed Pantheism running from the Victorians to the mid-twentieth century. The secret garden lies, hidden and neglected, behind high walls until a robin leads Mary – who needs to return to English soil for the healing that will transform her – to the key. The land beyond the wardrobe is full of talking animals and trees that can walk. Remember that scene in *The Wind in the Willows* when Ratty and Mole paddle upstream one mid-summer morning and encounter the great god Pan on the island by the weir? When Mary Poppins goes to the zoo at full moon and dances with the animals? 'We are all made of the same stuff, remember, we of the Jungle, you of the City', says the hamadryad, making her a birthday gift of shed skin.[91]

Afterwards, in good platonic fashion, a forgetting takes place, a redrawing of the veil which protects the sources of transformation while leaving the seeker changed and ready to take her insights back to ordinary life. The secret garden's power to heal depends on its being apart from the cruel world that has done the damage: too many tramping feet and loud voices would destroy the magic. The children grow too old to return to Narnia. English children's literature is full of secrets, available in coded form to those ready to discover them. But twenty-first-century adults seeking spiritual experiences of nature in books have few places to turn. One exception, written a little over a hundred years ago, sounds so removed from the tenor of our age that it might as well come from another planet. *The Story of My Heart,* by Victorian nature writer Richard Jefferies, is a strange book, a kind of autobiography of the soul in which the author attempts to record the passionate relationship with the natural world that dominated his life. The few references to external events, daily pilgrimages to hills and brooks, an oak tree, are springboards for the experiences they inspire in his (Jefferies struggles to find the right word) psyche, soul or consciousness:

> I was utterly alone with the son and the earth. Lying down on the grass, I spoke in my soul to the earth, the sun, the air, and the distant sea far beyond sight. I thought of the earth's firmness—I felt it bear me up; through the grassy couch there came an influence as if I could feel the great earth speaking to me ... By all these I prayed, I felt an emotion of the soul beyond all definition; prayer is a puny thing to it, and the word is a rude sign to the feeling, I know no other.[92]

Being deprived of regular contact with nature is a form of torture. Working in an office – Jefferies was a journalist in the Swindon area – seems 'a waste of golden time while the rich sunlight streams on hill and plain'.[93] Yet what he longs for is not union with the divine in any traditional sense:

> There being nothing human in nature or the universe, and all things being ultra-human and without design, shape or purpose, I conclude that no deity has anything to do with nature. There is no god in nature, nor in any matter

anywhere, either in the clods on the earth or in the composition of the stars'. What he seeks is something 'higher, better and more perfect than deity.[94]

This is the other side of the receding sea of faith; what seems like a categorical rejection of organised religion turns out to be the birth-pangs of a new form of belief. It reminded me of my putative ancestor Claye's briefly indulged Pantheism: Nature is scrupulously fair to her children, giving to all in some way or another or at some time or another a chance; and that is why Nature may be better trusted than the clerics, who desire to so microscopically prescribe her aims and ends.[95]

But that was then. I needed to find how this yearning for a spiritual connection with nature was expressing itself in my own time, and the nature-based faiths were the obvious place to look.

I first came across Emma Restall Orr around the turn of the millennium. Her book was an unlikely choice for me but, recently freed of the constraints of academia, I was reading at will for the first time in years. Relishing my new freedom, I developed a habit of wandering the shelves of bookstores and putting my hand on a book as if delving into a lucky dip. One of these occasions turned up Restall Orr's *The Spirits of the Sacred Grove: The World of a Druid Priestess*.[96] I looked at it suspiciously. With its cartoonesque tree and cutesy owl, the cover looked decidedly New Age; not the kind of thing I would usually read. But, giving in to my instincts, I took it to the cash desk.

I read the book in almost a single sitting. It was New Year's Day, and for once I wasn't hung-over. Here was a clear mind and a block of unallocated time, spread out like a crisp new map, to spend on a mental adventure. But while I wanted a day in, I needed contact with the outside. I discovered that if I lay across the bed of my inner-city flat at a certain angle, I could get a proper view of the sky, one that almost cut out the blocks of flats that framed both sides. Throughout the day, whenever my eyes tired of print, I could glance up and rest them on the clouds sailing across the precious square of sky.

Recounting her life as a Druid priestess, the book took me into a world in which the physical and the visionary collided, melded and separated; a kaleidoscope of forms and voices, animal and human, present and past. Against a backdrop of English woods and meadows, it told of encounters with the spirits of place, conversations with departed ancestors, run-ins with malevolent sprites. At times, the author shape-shifted into a cat, luxuriating in the power of the feline form and relishing the efficient brutality of tooth and claw; or flew across the Ridgeway, made weightless by the wind. She took part in rituals to mark the eight points of the Druid year and aid changes of life: the step into womanhood for a thirteen-year-old, the rite of the elder for a mature woman. There was love-making in the leaf mould with the god of the wild wood who in ordinary reality seemed to be her husband of many years. The status of these transformations was never entirely clear: were they real or the result of an altered consciousness? Whatever the case, I was impressed by the courage and fortitude that allowed her to take her relationship with the natural world to such extremes.

After that, I heard London-born Restall Orr periodically on the radio, fluently expounding the role of Druidry in twenty-first-century Britain in dulcet, almost caressing tones. As joint chief of the British Druid Order she was fast becoming one of the world's best-known Druids, in demand to provide an alternative take on our relationship with nature. Images of her suggested glamour: a strong-featured and raven-haired thirty-something, she exuded an attractiveness allied to strength, a quality no doubt essential for all that stomping about the countryside and making love on damp forest floors. It was the ideal profile for a Druid priestess in a media age. For Druidry was undergoing a revival that was part of a wider resurgence of pagan spirituality in Britain: around ten thousand people were initiated into orders, with many more who had not formally signed up considering themselves pagan.[97]

Those wishing to revive an ancient British faith – arguably *the* ancient faith of the British Isles – had little to go on. The little evidence there was suggested that the Druids, a word possibly deriving from an Indo-European root '*dreo-vid*', meaning 'one who knows the truth' or 'very wise one', were a learned caste made up of teachers, judges, musicians and storytellers who also acted as spiritual leaders and healers. In a Hindu society, they would have been the Brahmin; in Plato's Republic, the philosopher-priests. But as part of an oral culture with no scriptural canon, the Druids had left almost nothing of their beliefs and practices. The difficulty was exacerbated by the fact that much of what was written about them came from the Romans, who were quick to jump to conclusions about the natives they were colonising. In a rare but influential first-hand account of Druid practice, Pliny describes them cutting mistletoe from a sacred oak, claiming authoritatively that Druids always worshipped in groves of oak.[98]

While Bardic traditions continued to flourish in Ireland, Scotland and Wales, the English Druids were largely forgotten until the seventeenth century, when the work of antiquarians such as John Aubrey put them on the cultural map. The following century, the eccentric vicar and self-proclaimed Druid William Stukely popularised the view that Stonehenge and Avebury were the work of sun-worshipping Druids. There was no evidence for such a claim but, after the religious turmoil of the sixteenth and seventeenth centuries, the idea of an indigenous religion practised by 'noble savages' who preceded Christianity must have been irresistible to many.

The twentieth century saw a further revival of Druidry with the founding of new orders, each pursuing a different version of a nature-based religion. The new movement was untroubled by the absence of proven historical foundations; as historian Peter Beresford Ellis puts it: 'one person's Druid is another person's fantasy'.[99] Ronald Hutton goes further, seeing contemporary forms of Druidry in terms of the function they serve for the modern psyche rather than as descendants of groups which existed objectively.[100] But regardless of how the relationship to the past was conceived, there was an appetite for a modern nature religion. In 1964, the academic and poet Ross Nichols founded the Order of Bards, Ovates and Druids, going on to introduce the annual cycle of eight festivals, which is now celebrated by most pagans. By the 1990s, as a nature-based spirituality with shamanic elements which played to the ecological spirit of the times, the new Druidry was flourishing, and Restall Orr was a leading figure.

Now, over a decade since I'd first come across her on the page, I was keen to meet her in person. She lived in south Warwickshire, a little over an hour's drive from Gloucestershire. She agreed readily enough to my request for an interview, while making it clear that it would have to fit around the demands of her business, a natural burial ground that was also being developed as a nature reserve.

The directions are precise. Along a ridge running parallel to a band of woodland, down into a dip and then a sharp right into a narrow lane. Of course, I miss the turning and find myself in the village centre, in a triangle of traditional Cotswold houses that ooze affluence. By the time I've turned round and corrected my mistake, I'm clearly in the poor end of the village, on a mini-estate of council houses tucked into the side of the valley. My interviewee lives in a red-brick terrace opposite, a new-build of tiny proportions.

She too is tiny, an olive-skinned face framed by lashings of dark hair. As I step across the threshold, I notice a folded wheelchair by the door; a stairlift covered with a funky zebra print waits at the bottom of the staircase. I follow her into the living room; her movements have an alive, animal-like quality. But there's something shrunken about her body, and her limp is pronounced.

I've caught her on the phone, in the middle of an involved consultation with a bereaved client. While she finishes the conversation, I look around the little sitting room. The furnishings are at odds with the ultra-modernity of the house: there's a wood burner, black sheepskins, a lot of red and green. A row of utilitarian office furniture is packed along one side. Although it is a cloudy day, the blinds are down, and the room is softly lit.

Then she's apologising and hugging me, folding herself into an armchair, her legs up under her. She's feeling relaxed today, having finished a chapter of her latest book that morning. What do I want to know? I'm intrigued by her path to paganism; it seems an unlikely choice for someone from London. She nods understandingly.

'My father was basically brought up on the streets in the war, without shoes, in the Blitz, and in a very broken Cockney family: I'm sure there were thousands of families with nowhere to go when the houses got flattened. He pretty much spent his time in the

Hackney marshes, and found his serenity there. There are beautiful havens of wildlife in the midst of that mess.'

Having made money in advertising, he retired early to indulge his first love as an ornithologist, travelling extensively. Her mother was a botanist. Most of her childhood was spent in wild places. 'So with my father looking at the skies, and my mother looking at the ground, I kind of meandered ... they taught me that nature was the source of peace, meaning, purpose: all unspoken, simply by nature being where I found them to be most harmonious, most comfortable in themselves. And the religion outside of that was angry, hypocritical; it didn't make sense to me; being in Spain or South America, in the middle of poverty, and going into church with gold on the altar. Even the dichotomy of being in the baking sunshine and going into the church, which was cool and shady, didn't feel like a haven out of the harsh world; it felt like decadence. I remember when I was very young watching a burial out in the fields in Spain, where nobody had any money and the church weren't really involved – I think it was suicide or a fight, a feud or something – so there was a burial in the fields, and people were singing. That seemed to me like real religion.

'When I wrote my first book in my early thirties, my parents – divorced by then – read it. Both of them said that I had described their religion in a way that they could never have described it. They had never spoken about paganism or Druidry at all, but both of them said, separately, that I had described their religion, and my father would now call himself pagan, as did my mother. I gave them a language which they didn't have, but they gave me the foundation.'

The other formative influence was physical, a hypersensitivity disorder inherited from her grandmother that left her in continual pain and sometimes unable to walk. The condition heightened the excesses of adolescence, and she became self-destructive. 'And then I decided in my late teens, early twenties that I needed to make a decision whether I live or die.' She pauses. 'I think that life is difficult for me: it's a challenge, every day, to keep going, and always has been. That required me to find a meaningful purpose, to be conscious of the values I have, of the value of life, in a way that made me a naturally religious person instead of just an environmentalist or an artist, because of a need for meaning rather than just the need to find ease, comfort or beauty. I needed to find something stronger, much more ecstatic, to make being alive worthwhile. So I sought out religion.'

It makes sense as a life story, but as a spiritual path it sounds rather consciously, laboriously constructed, I remark.

She laughs lightly. 'I think the self is a construction, but maybe that's because I have to do it consciously; I'm aware of living life much more consciously than people around me, so yes, I would say that I consciously sought out my religion. I wouldn't deny that my religion is a construction of what works for me.'

Her faith had been wrought of diverse sources: the Bible, Koran, Hindu scriptures, Buddhist and Zen texts, combined with travelling that brought her into contact with people of all religions. The Shintoism of Japan, so thoroughly embedded in ancestor worship, made the most sense, instilling in her a sense of peace and acceptance, while her encounters with people in the Amazon showed her that the world was filled with communication, and that relationship was the most important element of nature and religion. Then it was time to return to England to seek out something specifically British: the legacy of her own ancestors. She read voraciously, studying Arthurian and Welsh myths and legends, relishing the passionate engagement with the natural world expressed in English Romanticism. Texts about Druidry provided the basis for a kind of natural religion based on the country's ecology, along with a rich heritage of stories, art and songs that spanned Christianity and native shamanism.

'It makes perfect sense to talk about a natural British religion, because it is our heritage,' she explains. 'It's Britain understood with all the different colours and tones of its sanctity: the trees, the plants, the stones – all of that non-human. Human nature is a part of nature, and understanding how human nature is sacred allows us to gather our ancestry, our history, our heritage in its entirety – our language, our stories, our wars, our victories and our defeats, our love, the horror – everything in that is just as sacred, just as beautiful, just as brutal, as the flood and the drought.

'You're talking about specificity of place.'

'Exactly. I am. It's nothing to do with politics; there's no nationalism in Druidry. The British aren't special; it's just about us being here, and being in relationship with what is here and has always been here.'

'So why is blood, ancestry, so important? And what about people whose bloodlines are broken, through, say, adoption?'

'It's not that black and white; in the paradigm of the animist there is no black and white, fact or fiction,' she replies. 'It's all about perception, and stories, and relationship. So the adopted child is also connected to their birth mother and father, and those stories are important, but the stories they get from their community and their adopted parents are as important as the stories they get from the wind and the trees.'

'So you can make blood ties, just as you can create stories.'

'Exactly. And you don't have to go back that far before pretty much all of us with British blood are related. But it's not just the specificity of the blood that's important, it's the whole context. I'm relating to you as Emma, as a woman, as English, as a part of the eco-system of this valley: all of these things are a part of what we are, here and now. And my blood tie to my grandmother is a very small part of that; it's not more important than any other part of it.'

She pauses. 'I do think ancestry is important to me personally because I've been given a bad deal by my grandmother. We all have, in different ways, but mine is overt, and shrieks at me every day. That means I need to deal with it. I need to accept that my grandmother gave this disorder to my father, who rejected me because of it, because he saw his mother in me. So it's a process of healing the whole relationship. If I kicked off, and was resentful about the genes I've been given, I would not be living in a way that would make the rest of my ancestors proud.'

It's a funny thing, I tell her, that when I read her book over a decade before, I got no sense of disability or fragility, only of strength and vitality, putting the odd reference to pain or bodily collapse down to an excess of shamanic excitement.

She nods. 'Yes, I think in the early days of being known, I tried not to put it out there; it wasn't what I wanted people to see in me. Then, as I got worse, I started not being able to hide it, but also I needed to address it.'

Her involvement with the Druid community had come through motherhood. The pregnancy was accidental: childbearing could kill her, but she and her husband decided to consider it an adventure and go ahead. Feeling it would be unfair on a child to remain isolated, yet wary of mothers' and toddlers' groups, she joined the first Druid organisation she came across, the Order of Bards, Ovates and Druids. She did their correspondence course, and before long was deeply involved, becoming a tutor herself. Articulate and clean-living, she was an attractive figure for a movement that wanted to show the world that contemporary Druids were much more than dope-smoking hippies.

But the sense of belonging did not last long. 'I did the institutional journey until I became too' – she casts around for the right word – 'outlandish for OBOD, and they pretty much asked me to leave.' There's a pause as she considers how to explain what went wrong. 'I just went a bit too far into the deep, old Shamanic work. When you work with visions, in meditation and trance, and go through to the other side, exploring the subconscious and looking, as Jung did, at those edges between what is the subconscious and what is another reality, "what is madness?" becomes a question. Much Druidry is very cerebral, intellectual, very safe. And then there are edges which move into that deep journeying or exploration, whether it's in the way that Jung did it or the way the wild animist might do it, dancing around a fire in the middle of the night on magic mushrooms. But you get people, as you do in any religious or community, who aren't' – she lowers her voice tactfully – 'quite *safe*, who are mentally or emotionally unstable, who are going too deeply. For a while I was given the job of looking after those edge cases. For me it was, "this is interesting, how can it help you find stability?" but for many people those edge cases are dangerous and need to be brought back into the fold. So I probably worked in a way that was a bit too dangerous for them. But I have always worked with the dying, with mad folk, with people in those edge places. I live in pain; I'm not frightened of the edge. I was comfortable in that place. But I was a liability in the end.'

Effectively expelled from OBOD, she accepted an invitation to become co-chief of the British Druid Order. Disillusioned with institutional politics, she tried to use her position to foster a more cooperative, feminised form of Druidry that had a place for emotion and sensuality. Within a decade, she had moved on again, this time to create a complete alternative to a religious order. The Druid Network began with a handful of members, charging people a modest fee to cover the costs of the website that connected them: a loose, digitally based network, typical of the early twentieth century. Once the body had won charitable status, becoming the first pagan organisation to get official recognition as a religion in Britain, she withdrew from playing an active role there too. After twenty years as a priest-in-the-community, and with her health deteriorating, she decided to concentrate on writing. 'And now,' she concludes, 'I don't belong to anything.'

'You're a freelance pagan!'

'I am, I am completely,' she agrees. 'And that is I think an inevitable part of the journey. I was stupidly young to run an order through my thirties, but I had the energy then, the vibrant need, almost the religious insecurity that needed to be overcome. If you need to be loved, you've got the insecurity to be a big star! I had enough motivation in my soul to go out and do that work; by the time I hit forty, I didn't have any more of it.'

The period of her active involvement had seen a resurgence in British paganism, and Druidry was now an official part of the British religious scene: in the census of 2011 it had, for the first time, featured as a denomination in its own right and the Druid Network was recognised by the Charity Commission. Meanwhile, growing numbers were pursuing a pagan spirituality in their own way without joining orders in the way that pagans had thirty years before. The trend suggested the emergence of a broad nature-based spirituality which included people who considered themselves pagan without having ever attended a rite or met other pagans.

'I don't know what to think about that,' she says thoughtfully. 'I think, partly, it's wonderful that paganism is now so broadly – even if very superficially – understood. If an appreciation of the sanctity of nature which is not in conflict with a broad, integrated science or any other religion, that's a wonderful spirituality to be slowly seeping through our culture. It's better than having a spirituality seeping through the culture which says, "I've got the truth, and you don't", which paganism never says. It can't say it; it's too pluralistic.'

The interview is interrupted by a call from a colleague, and the businesslike tone of the conversation betrays the harsh realities of her burial business. 'No viewing,' she tells the other party. 'It's been twenty days. Not a pretty sight.'

'So why this emphasis on death?' I ask when she's finished the call.

'A lot of it is because I've almost died a number of times in my life,' she replies. 'I have a sense of death being very present, partly because of those experiences, and partly because of the way my body is. That puts a premium on my day: I'm not willing to do something that I'm not willing to die doing.'

There's so much I want to know about the Druid view of the dead, why it's so important to honour them, and in what sense the living can maintain a relationship with them. After two hours in her company, I am feeling safe enough to go off-piste and personal. I've been seeing a lot of the dead recently, I tell her, in dreams. Is that, according to the Druid way of thinking, how they communicate with the living?

'Yes, absolutely.' She is unsurprised by the question.

'The dead don't go away,' she goes on. 'Their stories continue in the mind, in the memories that continue in the community. We are still in relationship with them through our memories and our creativity. If we forget the dead, we don't learn from them.'

Elements of the past that are repressed go on working their subterranean influence through our lives, she adds: 'We call them the silent stories.'

It's the banality of dying that gets you. Hurriedly packing to go to my mother's deathbed two months before, I was suddenly struck by the grubbiness of the bedroom carpet and caught myself thinking: 'When I get back I'll give that a good clean. By then, she'll be dead.' It was only two weeks after the diagnosis and a few days since I had last seen my mother. And it was Easter, the time of my father's dying. The vicar had already been. 'Be prepared,' warned her neighbour over the phone.

For two days she lay in the house, calling for help every time the morphine loosened its grip. The house had been transformed into a home-hospice; the carers we'd hired to come in for a few hours at the beginning of the week were now round-the-clock. There were enough bedrooms for everyone, but no one was using them: my mother lay on a hastily constructed bed in the dining room, having become too weak to get back upstairs. My brother felt funny about sleeping in my father's old room and was camping on the sitting room floor. I felt the same way, so I bedded down on the narrow sofa in the study. We had left the spare room for the carer, but my mother's needs were so continual that the young nurse didn't get to use it. 'Help! Help!' she called as soon as she was left alone. I dragged myself up, as if responding to a crying baby; the carer was by the bedside.

Sitting by the bedside by day, I had a sense that a great vital process was taking place; we were all waiting for a specific, inevitable result, like the birth of a child. But nothing will soothe her anxiety. 'I can't believe it,' she cried again and again, calling our names in an appeal for us to stop this horrible experience. It's as if she is on a runaway train or fairground ride which is frightening her. 'Let me out!' she cried repeatedly. 'Let me out – just anywhere.' As time went on, our names gave way to those of people who had preceded us. My mother seemed to be seeing my father, talking to him. And then, in the voice of a very young, frightened child, came the cry: 'Mummy!'

In the quiet periods, we crept around the house. Outside, the blossom on the cherry tree was spread over one end of the garden, a carpet of delicate pink. On Easter Day I got three ready-meals out of the freezer, the kind delivered specifically for the elderly, and we sat down, the carer, my brother and I, for Easter Sunday lunch. In the afternoon, the vicar, a woman with an ultra-tactful manner who is new to my parents' parish, called again. In a whispered conversation in the kitchen, we agreed that this was a difficult death. 'You watch, thinking this is it – and then she takes another breath,' she said, recalling her visit to give the last rites a couple of days before. 'Are you Church of England? Would you like me to pray over her?' I muttered something about a loose affiliation and yes, I would like a prayer. We went into the dining room and the vicar prayed over the bed that tonight, Lord, Rosemary will be released.

That night was worse than the last. There was never enough morphine to 'make her comfortable', as the professionals put it. The doctors had prescribed a driver in addition to the slow-release patch, plus extra injections when necessary, but the only driver available was in the Forest of Dean. District nurses were summoned from the far end of the county; eventually they arrived, clumping about and shouting. From under her blanket of sedation, my mother groaned in protest. She surfaced again in the middle of the night, calling for help. I went to the bedside, but almost immediately fell back asleep at ninety degrees, my forehead pressed against the bedclothes. The carer sent me back upstairs.

Easter Monday. The cherry blossom was now brown, spread out below the tree like a singed carpet. Time slowed as I went downstairs and I wondered if, by the time I got to the bottom, I would be told she had gone. She was still here. My brother and I had a whispered meeting in the kitchen – his wife wanted him home – and there were decisions to be made. But when I put my head round the dining room door, it was clear that there was not much longer to wait. Her favourite carer was sitting next to her, the cat was on the bed. 'Have I got time to go to the loo?' shouted my brother from the hallway. Then we were all assembled, watching the slow tide of the breath. In. Out. In … Out. The gaps between the breaths lengthened; each time you thought it would be the last, and then came another. The three of us could not take our eyes off the prone figure. I watched as another breath was released and waited, with the pause, for its partner. But there was nothing; my mother's taut profile is still. After a few moments, the carer moved to the bed and closed her eyes. And then suddenly I had a strong feeling of being lifted up, as if the contents of my chest had been emptied upwards.

The physical feeling transmuted into inexplicable joy. Outside, it was a beautiful day. The carer and her manager gathered flowers from the garden to put on my mother's body: rosemary and some blooms of blue and white. There was a general feeling of congratulation as we waited for the undertaker: together, we did it.

The extraordinary feeling of being uplifted in mind and body lasted several hours, but had gone by the time the vicar called again.

The godmothers were out in force. Worcestershire Godmother, visiting the day before my mother began her dying, had been the last person to have a proper conversation with her. It made for a neat biographical symmetry: my mother had been the first person to see her, after her parents, when she was born. Dorset Godmother arrived on what had been a scheduled visit to my mother, and stayed for several days to help with the funeral arrangements. She stepped quietly into the role of secretary–housekeeper, preparing meals and fielding phone calls while I met with vicars. I was often in a meeting with a vicar, because two were to take the funeral: the former vicar of the former village who had known my parents for decades, and the current incumbent of the former parish. On meeting my godmother, the latter agreed that Dorset was indeed a nice county 'if you can't live in Gloucestershire.' At the door, he put his arm round me, saying comfortably: 'Now you're an orphan.' In the hours between visitors, my godmother exhibited a ruthless practicality uncharacteristic of her, insisting we sort through all my mother's clothes and personal possessions while she was there to help.

When we needed a break, we went on my favourite local walk, around a field bounded by a hill and the Severn, with a clear view of May Hill. The field was, this warm spring month, full of buttercups, and the willows on the river's edge were smothered with a cottony bloom that neither of us had ever seen before.

*

For reasons I won't labour, I wasn't that sad about my mother's going. But there's no doubt that, whatever the relationship, the change in one's universe after the death of a mother is seismic. There was Before and there was After, and while 'after' wasn't necessarily worse, it was unlike anywhere I had ever been. For the first few weeks I had a strong, physical sense that the ground under my feet was moving. I walked cautiously, uncertain that it would bear my weight.

'The absence of a person is unfathomable,' wrote a Greenwood cousin in her condolence letter. A few weeks after the funeral, I dreamed a dream. I was at a party, a sort of grown-up house party that spilled over into many rooms. Light refracted off the glasses; laughter bubbled out of mouths. My parents were there: we'd arrived separately, as if at some big family gathering: my father, genial and smiling; my mother, upright and faintly haughty. And then, suddenly, I was aware that they'd left. I went from person to person, room to room, a puzzled child-adult, asking repeatedly: 'Where are my PARENTS? Where have they GONE?' Increasingly incredulous – surely they wouldn't have gone without saying goodbye – I carried on approaching people with my question. But no one could tell me anything about my parents' whereabouts.

An answer of sorts came the following night. I was at the Big House, making sandwiches on the business side of the kitchen counter: my mother's usual place. My mother had just come in, and was standing on the other side only usually taken by the kitchen visitor. She was how I remembered her in her early forties, the mistress of a beautiful country house, strong-limbed, the almost-black hair pinned into an elegant French pleat, ever-busy, faintly glamorous. She was in a better mood than I had ever known her, radiating good humour, visibly excited. Somehow I asked her

– perhaps with a look rather than words – where she had been all this time. 'Oh, I've been on a boat in London,' she replied ebulliently. The image of a party boat, full of people and music, coursing merrily up and down the Thames, rose before me. 'I've been having a *great* time,' she added, somewhat unnecessarily.

The loss of my second parent engendered a need for familiar places. Back in London, I longed for Gloucestershire, the open skies and familiar lines of the county, the riveresque greeny-browns of its fields and the scent of the decomposing matter around its streams. The Welsh call it '*hiraeth*', a word that encompasses homesickness and a yearning for place and past that is experienced as a kind of inner call. It was a feeling that had sometimes assailed me in a London office, triggered by the cooing of pigeons or a burst of early spring sunshine. Now I had a house in Gloucestershire, one that would be free of criticism or rows, I could respond to that call. And after fifteen years of not owning a car, I had suddenly inherited one: my father's prized 'new' car, now over a decade old, that he hated anyone to drive.

But I won't use the motorway. My official explanation is that, after so long without a car, I am scared of them, with their unforgiving speed and enforced proximity to other vehicles. But my circuitous route-making is about more than that: I want the experience of a proper journey, marking out, mile by mile, the ground as it passes beneath me, the sense of being in the places I am passing through. It is said in Africa that you shouldn't move across the earth too quickly, because of 'the time it takes the soul to catch up'. As a modern air passenger, crossing continents in a few hours, I'd certainly suffered a sense of profound dislocation, as if I'd left a part of myself behind in the place I'd just been.

Driving from London to Gloucestershire the slow way allows me to mark out the space between city and country, my old life and the present one. If only I can get to it, the A417 will take me directly to Gloucester, a golden thread that runs all the way to my old village. Getting to the start of it is farcically long, and involves weaving through suburban streets, Surrey heathlands and endless roundabouts. Stopping for omelette and chips outside a cafe in the outskirts of Reading, I narrowly escape the advances of the man at the next table, who is wearing an ill-fitting suit of shiny grey and a hopeful smile. When he's finished his meal, he stops with his dog at the dumpster on the pavement corner and spends a good five minutes carefully disembowelling objects from its knotted contents. Each item is carefully inspected, the ones that pass muster carefully stowed in his rucksack. I have to stop myself from laughing openly when he swings round and surveys the street through the small pair of binoculars he has just acquired.

But while other people are busy acquiring possessions, I am trying to get rid of them. The most urgent thing is the cat, an impish, people-oriented creature barely out of kittenhood. In the two weeks following my mother's death, she followed me wherever I went, including the bathroom. But this cannot go on: I need to go back to London, and at some point will start travelling again. The neighbours have a friend who needs a cat, so one morning I lure her with coaxing tones and imprison her in a wire basket. I am already weeping at my betrayal as I drive across town; I continue to weep as the cat, with a mix of puzzlement and interest, explores her new home, which is mostly decorated in pink. Her new owner, who is a counsellor for the Samaritans, is patience itself. But when, at the moment of parting, I unleash a new wave of tears, she begs: 'Oh, don't start again.'

The house needs to be cleared, the infrastructure of two people's lives dismantled, the contents disposed of. When they moved from the Big House, my parents brought most of the antiques my father had acquired on his trawls through the auction rooms of the county along with them to their smaller, modern home. There are linen-press wardrobes, mahogany chests, a Regency sofa, bureau bookcases, a tallboy you could practically live in. ('Why did you keep all this big brown furniture?' asked a mystified neighbour. 'We *like* it,' replied my mother.) Everywhere, in drawers and cupboards, are edited versions of the larger household my parents used to run: tablecloths going back generations, enough glasses and crockery to wine and dine half a village. My father's collection of tools is still neatly laid out in the garage. What am I, a reputed minimalist living in a small flat, to do with it all? I open drawers and stare at the contents in despair: almost everything presents a problem.

For these objects, unwanted or not, are carriers of memory, portals to the past. There is the antique chair I had peed on as a toddler, the faded picture of my brother and me running up May Hill on a summer's day. Other things go back to a time before memory, to the lives of my ancestors: the silver-framed picture of Thomas Greenwood looking every inch the Victorian gentleman; the silver basket belonging to my great-grandmother, given 'on the occasion of her marriage as a token of esteem from the members and friends of Elstree Congregational Church'. The objects are testimony to an attitude to things of an earlier age when resources were so short that when people did manage to acquire things, they kept them for life and the generations after them. Looking at these new possessions, the political correctness of my own time that tries to counter materialism by saying such things are 'only objects' feels completely alien. It runs counter to the postwar ethic I had inherited which dictated that even a banal object was worthy of respect and care, by virtue of the fact that someone had made it, the owners had paid money for it and a nation had sacrificed some of its resources for its creation.

Maybe our animistic ancestors were onto something: reverence towards the objects that shape our world is one of the ways humans can render what matters into being, an admission of our inability to transcend the physical. Residues of this recognition permeate modern culture: we flock to museums to see objects from our shared past, and queue at the Antiques Roadshow to know the monetary value of the things that link us to our individual stories. Closet animists that we are, we know there is a certain sanctity to the material.

In the spirit of an honourable animism, there will be no house clearance.

So, a houseful of orphaned things, each requiring a home or appropriate burial. Some matches are easy: entering the kitchen, a relative looks longingly at the Kenwood Mixer, asks for it directly. My parents' former lodger at the Big House, dropping by on a pastoral visit, goes away with most of my mother's shoes after my godmother and I have brought down pair after pair in cardboard boxes, giggling at this great game of shoe shops. But I have to ask eight people before I find someone who wants the breadmaker. A and her partner are delighted; theirs has just broken.

Other things do not want to be disposed of, yet. They seem to give off a charge that says: 'No. Not yet. Leave me be.'

There is pressure, a deadline. The Inland Revenue require details of all assets within six months of death. I dream I am making my way across country in a horse-drawn wagon. The ground is rough and progress is slow. Then the cart is held up by men with pistols, demanding the contents. Are they highway men, or The Authorities? I protest that these are family heirlooms and I am their guardian. The scene fades, leaving the dispute unresolved. Other dreams take me on epic journeys through vast landscapes: I am walking barefoot across the country. Somehow sleep and waking have been reversed: I wake exhausted, longing for a break from all the action.

While I am staying in the house, I feel a strong need to re-arrange it, to fit it for its new life in my temporary ownership. The conservatory, a vessel of light jutting out into the garden, previously used only as a place to store garden furniture, becomes a room to receive my visitors. Gloucestershire is rallying round: neighbours pop in and out, friends and relatives come for lunch and tea. In the rare times I have for reading and writing, I do it there; in this outside-in room, my mind feels freer, lighter. Blackbirds, realising there's no longer a cat in residence, hop freely across the lawn.

It's the end of a long day but, like the girl in the story of The Red Shoes, I can't stop my feet from moving. Somehow, it is imperative to re-arrange the furniture in the dining room, left untouched since my mother died. There's a gap where the bed was, the mahogany dining table folded down and moved to one side; the piles of family photos my mother was in the middle of sorting. I move the table to the centre of the room, open its redwood leaves to form a welcoming circle. Then I go out to the garage to get the matching chairs. Now it needs something in the centre: perhaps a little silver vase – my christening vase, which I'd never quite managed to gain possession of until now. Too small. A crystal bowl from a kitchen cupboard, then. That's right.

DRUID DAYS

Summer. I decided to forget London and the pursuit of disappearing work and spend a month in the old country. In terms of my religious research, the timing was excellent: when I asked Emma Restall Orr to recommend something that would give me a taste of Druid life, she thought for a moment and said: 'Lammas'. One of eight key points in the Druid calendar, the festival traditionally marked the first harvest of the year, the time when the berries started to appear in the hedgerows and the first grain crops were brought in. Emma had helped to establish the five-day Druid Camp to celebrate Lammas some years ago, and it happened that it was held in a Gloucestershire field between the River Severn and the Forest of Dean.

So with July drawing to a close, I got my tent out of the cupboard, borrowed a camping stove from Jane and set off westwards along the A roads. After the long drive, my mother's house felt unwelcoming, the air heavy, sticky and stale. Gone was the light and joy it had acquired in the first days after her going. As I went from room to room, trying to set up my home for the next few weeks, the doubts started to crowd in: was spending a month bereaved and alone really such a good idea?

The next morning, I am jerked awake by a noise. I have the distinct impression that someone downstairs has called my name. Opening my eyes with difficulty, I stagger up: it must be the neighbour who often pops in, first thing, to see how I am. But everything is quiet as I peer down from the landing, and it's much earlier than I thought: the clock in the hall says five-thirty; far too early for a neighbourly call. Outside, a huge red sun straddles the horizon. This is no time to admire nature, so I get back into bed and fall back into a deep sleep.

'*ALEX.*'

It's my name again, this time spoken with the urgency my mother used to use when I was in danger of slumbering past the time for school or my Saturday job. I'm wide awake now: it's twenty to nine and yes, I need to get up and buy supplies although, I think grumpily, I wouldn't have overslept had I not been woken so early. As the morning stretches out, I realise that I am spinning out my preparations; the thought of camping with a bunch of strangers has suddenly become unappealing.

But as I drive through the narrow green lanes towards the campsite, relief starts to wash over me. This is a part of Gloucestershire I didn't even know existed, a pocket of farmland set in the bend of the river where you would never go unless some particular business took you there. And yet, as the crow flies, it is only seven miles from where I grew up.

Fluttering ribbons in the hedgerow mark the place where I need to turn off-road and drive though the fields to the higher ground where the camp is held. I park in the makeshift car park and walk slowly into the main field, taking in my surroundings. It's not like any campsite I have ever seen: a diverse mix of painted caravans, teepees and family-sized tents are loosely organised around some main tracks. Some have improvised gardens with boundaries of pots of flowers and herbs. Others have outside living rooms furnished with wooden chairs and rugs; there is even a wooden dresser. Chimneys of wood-burning stoves spout through the canvas, and through one open flap I glimpse a spinning wheel; these are the shelters of people accustomed to outdoor living.

Treading carefully around ropes and pegs, I make my way to the far side of the site. I want somewhere quiet; the choice of pitch will determine my quality of life for the next few days. Finally I find a clear space by the hedge that seems the right place to make my camp.

And there, through a gap in the hedge, is May Hill, viewed from a never-before-seen angle. Seams of trees break up its usually smooth sides, and its symmetrical outline looks uneven. But the distinctive caterpillar crown is still there. Carefully, I line up the tent with the gap in the hedge, so that the opening affords a view of the hill. The decision means turning my back on the rest of the camp, but the trade-off is worth it.

I light the stove, make a cup of tea, and lie down in the grass. A gentle heat steams up from the earth. Quiet reigns. Despite the fact I'm in a field with a large number of people, this is nothing like the camping I'm used to; the only sounds are the occasional voice of a child or the tap-tap of someone banging a tent peg into the ground. A bee muzzles some clover inches away from my head. This is what I wanted: a moment of repose in nature; a chance to enter into the indolence of mid-summer. There is, it's true, the hum of an engine a few fields away, but when I listen closely I realise it comes not from a car but a combine-harvester.

Then I take a stroll through the surrounding lanes. The fields are full of ripe wheat, and I'm suddenly remembering the particular mood of this time of year, long buried under an urban, adult perception of The Summer. As children, we'd wander the fields, plucking ears of grain and sucking out the untreated flour, spitting the husks back onto the dry earth. Now, the natural world around me is expressing the same blend of fulfilment and excitement; through the hedge I can see a herd of bullocks clustered together in the corner of a field, pushing each other and lowing in deep, bovine voices. One mounts another and humps him enthusiastically.

Attuning myself to the rhythms of life of Druid Camp is another matter. There's no paper programme to consult, and the list of the day's events on a chalk board outside the canvas cafe – 'Divinations', 'Oak management' and 'Reading Runes'– is opaque to me. When I do get an intimation that there's a talk or a workshop I might like to attend, it's hard to know where it will be held – none of the tents are marked; apparently everyone here can effortlessly distinguish the 'Big Yurt' from the 'Big Lodge', and knows the location of the Two-Pole Tent. People are friendly, greeting me as they pass, but this is clearly a family-oriented affair where most people know each other, and I wonder whether I've made a mistake in coming to such a gathering alone. I must at least make contact with the camp organiser, Mark Graham, whose details had been given to me by Emma. A woman in the queue outside the toilet huts gives me a description of him. 'He's li-th-e.' Her tongue stretches out the word onomatopoeically. 'No flesh on him.' She adds, even more helpfully: 'He's wearing red trousers. And he's usually without a top.'

I had seen the back-view of just such a creature earlier that afternoon; a cross between a panther and a Narnian faun loping across the camp, all red cotton and smooth brown skin. Others also seem taken with Mark's outfits; when I ask his whereabouts of a bearded man, he replies with a sartorial description: he went that way, and is apparently now wearing tight trousers, a fitted green jacket and buckled calf-length boots of soft brown suede.

I have, in the meantime, understood one thing from the chalkboard: at seven o'clock that evening, there is to be A Ritual. So, at a few minutes to the hour, I make my way towards to the circle of fluttering flags on the higher ground. About a hundred people are standing in a ring; at its centre a big man in black robes is moving about restively, spear in hand, stripes of paint on his cheekbones. Next to him is a black cauldron. 'To those behind us, our ancestors, who made us what we are, and what we want to be,' he declares. A horn full of cider is passed round the circle; each person is to drink to an ancestor or someone who has inspired them and then pour a splash, symbolising the contribution they and their forebears have made to the gathering, into the cauldron, which is being carried around the ring with the cup.

The horn is safely on the other side of the circle a good seventy mouths away; I have time to think who I will toast as I listen to other people's choices. Grandparents are a popular choice; only a few people mention a parent. Opposite, a black-robed man in his thirties drinks smilingly to his younger sister. 'She died a year and a bit ago. She taught me that life can end in the blink of an eye.' Next to him, a young woman raises the horn: 'To my daughter, who died too soon.'

The cup is moving closer, and is now only some ten people away. A middle-aged man with beaky features and long blond hair seems oblivious to those present as he takes the horn. 'FATHER!' he yells to the sky, using the over-loud tone folk use when addressing the deaf. 'THIS TOAST IS FOR YOU!' Somewhere behind the clouds, I can almost see an elderly man startled out of his nap. Further down-circle, a blond teenager drinks to her friends in Norway, gunned down by a lunatic the week before.

As the horn approaches my part of the curve, I fight a feeling that I want only to observe. But there is no question of not participating; the ritual won't let you. It's like being in the sea; when the wave hits you, you have to jump with it. So I drink to my grandmother, thanking her for her storytelling and love of nature, and to a second quasi-parental figure, a relation not of the blood but of the psyche, a healer of the soul with similar interests. The horn moves on, and the diminutive Caribbean-looking woman next to me gives thanks to 'the unknown ones' of her past. The phrase allays my worry about ancestor worship; how do you connect to your past if your bloodline is broken or sullied with bad blood?

When everyone has taken their turn, the lid is put on the cauldron and the spear placed across it. The act, says the ritual leader, seals the power of each person and those who have shaped them inside it for the duration of the camp.

'I liked your toast,' I tell my neighbour as we turn to go. Shadows of pain play across her face. She thanks me, touching me on the arm, lightly, twice.

The next morning, grey cloud hangs over the camp, emitting a steady drizzle, and the atmosphere is subdued. I stay in my sleeping bag, deep in a book and reluctant to engage with the outside world. When I finally crawl out of my canvas door, I see that a low green tent has appeared overnight, pitched a respectful few yards from mine. It looks big enough to shelter only one; it might not be the home of a self-contained couple nor, I think, staring at it hopefully, is it necessarily the sign of an unfriendly, maverick male.

'I'm Deborah. I'm your neighbour.'

The occupant of the tent is coming towards me. She's a little older than me, with olive skin, bright brown eyes and a smile that opens like a butterfly. She's wearing a blue poncho, cut at jaunty asymmetrical angles, the edges trimmed with bits of red braiding.

'Are you on your own?'

'Yes. I'm doing astrology. I've come as a worker, but I know people here. Do you?'

'Not a soul.'

'How brave!' She hugs me.

A friendship is forged, fast. I confess I've been at a loss as to how to fathom the workings of the camp, and she offers to help. 'I have access to a house not far from here,' I nod eastwards, across the fields towards the city. 'I was thinking of going back to have a bath.' I'm half-apologetic, not used to having more than one place to call my own, while quietly revelling in the luxury of camping just a few miles from home.

While I brew the coffee, Deborah squats down, rifling through the pages of a thick book densely packed with columns of data, numbers that track the positions of the planet at any given time. She wants to know the exact details of my birth. 'Sorry, I can't help this,' she apologises. 'I can look at people across the camp and say to another astrologer, "Oh, they're like *this*, that's the Cancer." It's a kind of shorthand.' She returns to her book. 'Sagittarius, Virgo rising.' Another glance at the data, and she gives me a sharp, appraising look: 'Oh, you like your treats.'

It's a fair cop. I've been outed as a closet hedonist within minutes of acquaintance. 'Yes, people don't usually realise that about me for a while,' I admit. 'They expect me to be more disciplined, self-denying.'

Scanning her columns of numbers, Deborah nods. 'That's why you want to go home for a bath.'

'Are you tidy?' She glances into my tent, taking in the food and utensils in their cardboard box. 'Oh yes, quite organised. That's the Virgo.'

'And given to catastrophic thinking, which is bad,' I add defensively, on the back foot at being seen through so quickly.

'Nothing is bad. Things just *are*.' Deborah corrects me, and I recognise a typical Druidic reproof.

Later, over the stove between our two tents, she tells me her life story. She had wanted to be an artist, but a talent for science had led her down a more respectable academic route. A PhD in biochemistry brought success: a mistake in the lab led to spectacular results, the visual proof of something her supervisor had been trying to demonstrate for years. But privately she felt she had been doing an art project rather than science, and she abandoned academia for travelling and motherhood. Eventually she fulfilled her long-held dream of going to art college, doing a correspondence course in psychological astrology along the way. She now made an intermittent living as an environmental artist, spending as much time as possible in nature, from which she gleaned materials for her art. 'I love ritual,' she smiles. 'And I'm good at improvising it: I find it really easy to do.'

She's a great communicator, fluent and engaging, her butterfly smile opening and closing as she talks. To make the life she wanted possible, she'd downsized, selling her flat and reducing her costs; at some point she planned to buy a plot of land. For the moment, she was living in a bender in her sister's garden so that she could visit her mother, who had dementia and was in a nearby nursing home, every day.

I find her ability to live so simply admirable, I tell her, but couldn't do likewise. I felt increasingly drawn towards a form of opt-out, a lifestyle involving not much more than writing, nature and people. But apart from the constant need for treats, my inner war-child conspired with the neo-peasant mentality I'd inherited from my father to rule out living in anything makeshift. 'You build a house with really thick walls, and a good roof to keep the rain out,' I explained. 'Then you stockpile tins of beans, in case there's a war.' In fatter times, the impulse translated into my mother's passion for housekeeping; nothing was so reassuring as a cupboard of shining glassware or a pile of folded linens. If feeling stressed in central London, I gravitated towards the household department of John Lewis, where I could remind myself of the outward and visible signs of domestic order.

Deborah looks amused. 'It's possible to go off-grid, even in a house,' she tells me. Briefly, we discuss the practicalities of urban self-sufficiency: you could fit photo-voltaic panels on the roof for electricity and have a wood-burning stove for heat which could also be used for cooking if necessary. The garden could be turned over entirely over to vegetable-growing. I can see this sort of approach working even in my wooded suburb; I could call it flat-steading.

The star speaker of this year's camp is Philip Carr-Gomm, author and leader of the Order of Bards, Ovates and Druids. He has been held up in his journey across the country and by the time he arrives, an expectant crowd has amassed in the three-pole tent.

Strikingly short, with a wide, handsome face and a deep, erudite voice, Carr-Gomm ranges comfortably about the floor of the tent, explicating the nature and history of pilgrimage. Humans have always gone to particular parts of the planet deemed sacred, he says, disregarding the time, cost and discomfort involved in making such gratuitous journeys: 'We can't help it; it's built into us: we've got to move.' Then he puts the issue into Druidic terms: 'The purpose of pilgrimage is to shake the Druid from the trance effects of ordinariness.' But these days, with air travel bringing the numbers taking part in pilgrimages such as the Hajj to unprecedented levels and the attendant damage to the planet, pilgrimage was looking rather unDruid-like. Was it then possible to replace at least some spiritual journeys with an eco-pilgrimage of the mind, he asks rhetorically, before suggesting the question must be made on a case-by-case basis. It's adept stuff, marrying an age-old impulse of the soul with a very practical contemporary issue.

The second part of the workshop involves doing some 'journeying'. We are each to go on an internal pilgrimage, imaginatively travelling to a place of our choice, which can be either somewhere we want to know well or a place we aspire to visit. I want to go to La Paz; I have just been reading about it and am entranced by the idea of this city-in-the-sky where the air is, quite literally, different. But I've never seen any pictures of the place and, without mental images, I struggle to imagine myself there. So, with time running out to accomplish my task, I hastily switch destination and pop back to Sinai. This is much more successful: I'm there in an instant, sitting in the fading, rose-tinged light in front of the table-top mountain. As the exercise ends, I experience the same sense of wrench that I felt when actually leaving the desert a few years before.

I'm still feeling uncomfortable when we are invited to share our experience with the person next to us. Leaning against one of the wooden tent poles beside me, Deborah has taken the opportunity to visit the standing stones of Calanis in the Hebrides for the first time.

'I felt how people would have felt looking up at the stars, before they knew anything about the cosmos, three or four thousand years ago,' she smiles. 'They would have watched the sun come up and go down, and put the stones there as a way of tracking it. I don't need to go there now.'

The ensuing discussion takes a critical view of what we've just been doing. Another Druid writer points out the danger inherent in trance: escapism. 'That's why Druids choose the Druid path,' she says. 'Unlike transcendent religions, we want to be in the here-and-now.' Someone else confesses to experimenting by driving while in trance, at the recommendation of her Shamanic teacher. The first trip had been just a short, local drive, but the second, albeit with a vigilant partner in the passenger seat, had taken her from southern England to Hadrian's wall.

'Hmm, don't try this at home.' The comment comes from the floor, the tone authoritative and disapproving. Carr-Gomm, visibly taken aback by the disclosure, jollies it off with a 'We won't tell the police'. Then he relaxes and confesses to his own shamanic misdemeanour. Once, while driving in heavy rain, he found that his windscreen wiper had broken. To rectify the problem, he had visualised a hawk on the roof of the car, its powerful wing keeping the windscreen clear. 'I should have pulled over,' he admitted ruefully. 'But it worked.'

Back at the tents, Deborah and I conduct our own discussion of the workshop. She is fast becoming my camp guide, the person most able to translate what I'm witnessing into a language I can understand. Fearless of questions, and able to make connections between very different disciplines, she's a natural interpreter. I have been intrigued by a workshop led by Druid writer Penny Billington on magic; not normally a Druidic practice. She had argued that Druids should consider practising magic, citing Cheltenham magician W. G. Gray's 1969 definition of magic as: … man's most determined effort to establish an actual working relationship through himself between his Inner and Outer states of being. By magic, he shows that he is not content to be simply a pawn in the Great Game, but wants to play on his own account. Man the meddler becomes Man the Magician, and so learns the rules the hard way, for magic is concerned with Doing, while Mysticism is concerned with Being.[101]

Deborah was becoming increasingly preoccupied with magic as a way of seeking to influence the course of events in her own life, and thought she detected it as a theme in Carr-Gomm's workshop.[102] 'He didn't mention magic, but that's what I'd call it. It's what happens when we forget the intellect and use our imaginations,' she enthuses, adding more reflectively: 'Magic's just common sense, really. We probably do it all the time.'

Success in magic, she continues, relies on setting your intention clearly. 'I did it, coming here, to get a lift. I just decided, on getting off the bus, that I didn't want to walk the two miles up the lanes. And straightaway, a lift appeared. I do it with parking places all the time.'

I'm half-intrigued, half-sceptical. 'So are there bigger things you want in your life? How come you can't get those?'

'Yes' she smiles. 'I'm working on the bigger things. It's all the same to the universe – it's us that gets in the way, with our lack of clarity. If you don't know exactly what you want, the universe doesn't know what to give you. There was a pair of shoes I really wanted, but they were expensive, and I wasn't going to pay £150. I found them on eBay for £50. The same happened with a stove: I wanted a very specific kind, something quite rare, and I found exactly what I wanted.'

'That's just what I call good shopping,' I laugh. 'I'm really good at it. I'm your typical thrifty, middle class consumer; I often find what I what. But I can't seem to do it with other stuff.'

'Maybe you're comfortable as a middle class consumer,' suggests Deborah, sagely. 'But maybe you're not so comfortable with other things.'

The camp has an uncanny way of bringing up personal matters that are secretly preoccupying me, smashing though my plan of staying comfortably in the role of observer. Waiting for Deborah to finish seeing someone in the Divinations tent, I am approached by a short, blond woman with periwinkle eyes and the kind of nose I've coveted since first encountering the strong female beauty of the Middle East. A complementary therapist who works with flower essences, she is touting for business: not that any money is involved; everything in the camp is free, once the entrance fee is paid. Despite the popularity of Bach's Rescue Remedy, it seems that few people appreciate the benefits of essences, and she isn't getting many takers. The blue eyes blink; she waits for the verdict. It would be churlish to refuse, so I follow her into the tent.

The session goes to the heart of a problem that has been frustrating me for some time. Writer's block is rather too grand a term for the malaise – it is rather that, amid depleted energy levels, worries about money and bereavement, I keep losing the thread of the book – it is like a signal, calling for attention, which I lack the resources to pick up consistently. Asking nothing of my circumstances, the essence-lady pinpoints the peculiar mixture of stuckness and impatience in which I am mired. 'It's about communication,' she pronounces in her Derbyshire accent. 'There's something that you need to say.' Then she lines up the bottles containing the essences that will help to remedy the malady: impatiens, wild oat, tomato, ready for mixing in a little blue bottle that I'm to take away. 'Oh, there's something else you need,' she adds, suddenly. 'I hate it when they do this. And she wants what?'

She pauses a few moments, as if awaiting instructions. 'Oh, turquoise.'

I can't suppress a faint snort. My birthstone.

As I rise to leave, she looks at me curiously. 'So what's it's about, then? This thing you need to say?'

Over the next few days, the lady of flower essences and I become friends, meeting up in the cafe with her husband and the friend who has accompanied them. I like her way of approaching life, which is simultaneously loving and no-nonsense; when she had discovered her children were dabbling in soft drugs, she had informed them that if they did so under her roof, the police would be called. When she learnt that I had recently lost my mother and, like her, belonged to the daughters-of-difficult-mothers club, she was empathy itself. 'Bless you,' she kept saying, looks of compassion shooting from the periwinkle eyes. Later, as we walk across the field to the ritual, with a further look of concern, she enquires sharply: 'She behaving herself, on the other side?'

'I'm not sure,' I admit. 'I've been woken up a couple of times.'

'If you're at all suspicious, do something in ritual to put a stop to it,' she says. 'It doesn't matter what you say: whatever comes to you will be fine. Just tell Spirit you don't want to hear anything from your mother that isn't positive. When you get to the house, light a candle or something. Put her with the ancestors.'

Later, in the cafe, I confess to her husband that I am, irrationally, uneasy being alone in the house, despite the fact that being in Gloucestershire makes me as happy as a spring lamb.

'Move some furniture around,' he advises, gently. 'That will shift things.'

I'm beginning to get the hang of Druid Camp; I like the playful spirit of the ceremonies and the fearlessness in the face of life's big issues. But I have to admit that in the camp a certain physical stereotype seems to be playing itself out: as I look about the camp, I notice that many of the men are big-bellied and bikerishly hairy and the women large, with raven tresses straight from the bottle.

There's a lot of black, and much of the white flesh on display is heavily patterned with tattoos. And how they like to dress up! Every ritual brings forth an array of capes and robes in rich colours and heavy fabrics, liberally accompanied by make-up and headgear. The first few minutes in the circle remind me of the church-going of times past, when part of the pleasure was noting who was sporting a new bonnet or waistcoat. It's a mystery how, given that Deborah's come by train carrying her camping gear on her back, she manages to produce so many outfits. Throughout the day, she appears in a rainbow of colours, changing according to the weather and event: vivid green is followed by egg-yolk yellow and, one evening, a satiny dress of various blues and patterns which, on closer examination, is made by the stitching together of wide ties.

I find that the evening rituals have a curious way of drawing me in. It seems to be something to do with the circle; at first it's chilly, standing on this hillside field, the evening breeze whipping the flags like sails. But as we join hands and begin the opening chant *Awen*, a feeling of warmth grows. I notice one mother-of-three, usually smiling and overtly maternal, give her skipping, attention-seeking offspring to understand firmly that this is Ritual, one time that we don't play up. It's never known in advance what form the ritual will take but, once underway, it makes sense. I watch as one person after another walks into the centre of the circle and, taking a seed from a pile and, making a pledge for the next year, throws it into the cauldron. There are appeals to ancestors, requests for support with creative projects and better living. An enormous young woman staggers into the circle and tearfully vows to do her best to keep on carrying her 'burden'. I have no intention, with a hundred people present, of walking onto this stage and making a public profession, but Deborah changes my mind. 'If you want to make something happen in the next year, this is a good way to do it,' she whispers. 'The circle is powerful.'

Then she's off to the cauldron, to make her own vow: 'I'm just beginning to realise that a lot of what I've been doing is magic. I vow to Ceridwen that I'm going to explore this further.'

I walk into the circle and, citing my ancestors, vow to finish my book.

Back at the tents, Deborah and I discuss the meaning of ritual. 'It's adult play, isn't it?' I say, the penny finally dropping.

'Yes,' she smiles. 'It's adult play. Adults *love* to play.'

It's Friday night, and there's a band on in the cafe-tent. They're called Shamus O'Blivion and their music is an anarchic folk-rock which blends the traditional and the contemporary, resulting in quirky adaptations such as a reggae version of 'Early One Morning'. 'We only do two kinds of songs – songs about dying, and songs about shagging,' roars the lead singer, a large man dressed in a shepherd's smock and sea-green leggings of shiny lycra revealing a substantial pair of buttocks. A black top hat with a price tag of 10/6 crowns his mop of grey curls. The band launches into a fast, post-punk version of the Raggle Taggle Gypsies. Then the lead singer tells us a joke.

A man approaches a well-heeled woman in a pub, and asks: 'Do you fancy a beer, and a shag?'

'Certainly not,' replies the woman, haughtily.

'Why, don't you drink?' responds her suitor.

I watch the crowd, plastic cup of wine in hand, bashing staves supplied by the band in time to a frenetic tune. 'These people are fun,' I say under my breath, and head off into the throng. But while the feet are willing, the lungs are weak, and at this pace I can't dance for long.

Back at the table, Mark alights on the seat beside me, his jacket zipped-down to reveal a smooth brown cleavage. What exactly am I writing about? he asks warily. He tells me he's pleased to succeeded in getting Druids represented on his local interfaith council where he finds dressing up in full Druid regalia, like the Anglican bishop, 'a bit of a hoot'. Like Emma, he feels that Druidry's official recognition as a religious denomination in the latest census is a step forward. Do most people here call themselves Druids? I ask as we survey the leaping figures on the dance floor, now enthusiastically crossing staves. 'No,' he shrugs. 'I don't think most people are bothered at all.' But before we can really start to talk, he's away into the dance crowd, leaving the conversation hanging.

'Normally, we dedicate the last song to the people who didn't dance,' roars the lead singer. 'But tonight, there's only that bloke over there.'

The next morning, Mark and Deborah are to give a workshop on the relation between astrology and ritual. My knowledge of astrology doesn't go beyond a superficial knowledge of the characteristics of a few signs, but I am interested in Deborah and Mark and the thinking that motivates them. So, as the sun climbs towards its zenith, I join a small group outside one of the teepees.

Mark begins with some definitions: astrology is the study of the relation between celestial bodies and terrestrial events; ritual a set of actions performed uniquely for their symbolic value. The main area of disagreement centres on the notion of 'as above, so below';

whether there is a relationship between the astronomical movements and life on earth. His manner is measured, almost academic, and I get a sense the explanation is pitched for me, as if to forestall the potential scepticism of the outsider. On the one hand, he continues carefully, there are some uncontroversial examples of the link between activity in the heavens and events in the sub-lunar world, such as the pull of the moon on the tides and – here Deborah interjects, pointing out that psychologists have long found the moon to have an effect on people's moods. On the other hand, Mark continues, astrology can be seen as just a language to help explain why things are the way they are. 'Most astrologers don't believe that planets have a direct physical effect on events here; they would talk about things like synchronicity. It's more to do with events that synchronise than one thing affecting another.'

I nod; I'm familiar with the Jungian notion of synchronicity, denoting a coincidence that is meaningful in terms of human experience, but with no causal basis.

'For the purpose of this workshop, we're going to believe in astrology,' Mark continues. 'If we're assuming some kind of link between those two things, we're assuming that a ritual that is astrological can have more potency. You're putting yourself in harmony with the cosmos by using a set of symbolic actions: for example, the expansive energy of the new moon is a good time to bring something into being, while the moon on the wax would be a good time to give up a bad habit such as smoking.'

'Is it more powerful when done as a group?' I ask.

'Yeah, I think it is.'

Over thousands of years, he goes on, ancient astrologers have observed repeated connections between the positioning of planets and seasonal changes; over time the twelve divisions of western astrology had emerged: 'For example, the sun is in Aries when you look at the sun and see the constellation of Aries behind. The constellations are entirely notional. You can look at them and see what the ancients were doing – they were using them as a clock, so that the ram, for example, is about spring, with all that flourishing and vibrant energy. They didn't have calendars; all they could do is look up at the skies. All the signs of the zodiac come from a division of the year into twelve sections, and those sections reflect what is happening in the year.'

I still don't understand how people can be divided into twelve astrological types, each sun sign sharing similar characteristics.

'It's got nothing to do with what newspaper astrologists predict,' reply two other members of the group in unison.

Deborah turns the full force of her radiance on me.

'You were born in Sagittarius, just approaching the coldest time of the year. Everyone born at that time of the year had to be held, and kept warm, otherwise you wouldn't survive.' Her arms make a cradling motion. 'That creates a similar imprint. What's happening in the first two years of a child's life affects their development; when you were a toddler, you were able to go out and explore, just at the time the weather was getting warmer. That's what Sagittarians do: explore!'

Smilingly, she returns to her favourite theme. 'Ritual is about bringing down that energy. That's what we are as human beings – lightning conductors. We're physical beings, and we need to make things physical.'

In the ritual that follows, each person takes the part of one of the key planetary players in the current skies. The golden-locked man who toasted his dead father is the sun, Venus is represented by a luscious young woman, and Mark becomes Uranus, the planet of change and upheaval. I choose to be the moon. This pause for reflection just before a bright new sliver waxes into being suits exactly where I am, newly orphaned, career disintegrating, but increasingly clear about what matters. Deborah has put foods representing the fruits of the season at the centre of the little circle: cherries, sunflower seeds and a mini-pack of oatcakes that she cadged off me earlier. We each ad-lib our contributions, me acknowledging the happy confluence of this lazy, ruminative time of year with my need for a pause, Mark paying homage to the uncertain weather of our island, where wind and rain can be often followed by sun. Then we nibble on the fruits of the season.

I push the remaining oatcakes towards Deborah; it's nearly lunchtime and I know she's eaten nothing so far today except a handful of fruit.

'That's very moon,' says Mark quietly, as he slips away to pay the band.

Ceridwen. I keep hearing the name of the mythical female figure who is the theme of this year's camp; the cauldron at the centre of the circle hers. But I know nothing about her, so when I learn that a professional storyteller has been hired to tell us her story, I make my way to one of the larger tents, which is full of people sitting expectantly on the grass. Ruddy-faced, tousle-haired and wearing a long patchwork coat, he has earned his living, brought up a family on storytelling for the past eighteen years, he tells us proudly. His stories are meticulously researched, but because they are part of an oral tradition he often finds that his listeners had their own ideas about the details, and interject with corrections. Cross-legged or hugging our knees, we listen as he roves around his grass stage, gesturing to the left and the right.

Ceridwen was the most feared and celebrated of all the women in the land. Some considered her a witch, others said she was a goddess. She lived in a castle surrounded by a village, which was itself surrounded by a mighty wood that extended up over a nearby mountain. The witch-goddess had many cauldrons simmering in the castle's many rooms, each containing a different remedy for the various maladies that beset the world. The greatest of them all burned eternally over a blue flame. Such was the greatness of Ceridwen that she had been given the privilege of stirring the cauldron of all souls or, as she thought of it, 'the pot of creation'.

Now, Ceridwen had two children. Her daughter was everything a mother could wish for: a beautiful, popular girl who slipped through life attracting universal admiration. But her son Avaggdu was the darkness to his sister's light and shunned by all who came across him. The boy had done no wrong; it was something to do with the look and feel of him.

As he grew towards manhood, Ceridwen realised with growing regret that the shadow was growing in every part of him. What to do? We find her, the mistress of cauldrons, stirring her potions, asking what change should she bring to her son. After a while, she decided to make an elixir for him to sip that would turn him into a wizard. In that way, he could become whatever he wanted to be.

She gathered all the necessary ingredients from the mighty wood – herbs grown in the shadiest patches, leaves from the highest branches, smells from the darkest hour – and put them into the cauldron. Then she added the one essential ingredient without which, the ancient stories tell us, no magic ever works. You could call it imagination or inspiration; it is that which makes wishes become reality and dreams come true.

The cauldron was too important to be entrusted to the servants of the castle. So Ceridwen ordered the guards to carry it, on poles, out into the village. As they progressed through the main street, eyes and noses appeared from behind every corner, and doors slammed shut, for Ceridwen's legendary power was feared. The soldiers carried the cauldron into the mighty wood, up to the top of the mountain where there lived a wise old man who answered the villagers' questions about crops and relationships. He alone was capable of stirring a potion able to turn her son into a wizard.

Ceridwen ordered her men to deposit the cauldron in front of him. 'I am Ceridwen,' she announced. 'I need you to stir this potion for a year and a day. Do not stop, even for a moment.' Then she left.

The old man stirred and stirred until his arm ached. Just as his strength was beginning to wane, a boy from the village put his head round the door of the cave. Gwion Bach was one of the old man's regular visitors, a kind of apprentice or magician's nephew. 'I'll help you stir your pot,' he said.

Together, the old man and the boy took it in turns to stir the cauldron. They stirred until the leaves turned crimson and gold and fell, withered and brown, to the forest floor. They stirred on through the autumn storms, the midwinter snows, and the late frosts. And they stirred as the thaw came, green shoots poked through the earth and the sweet songs of the birds filled the air. All summer long, the pair stirred and stirred, until finally the leaves began to turn crimson and gold.

'We think it's a year!' They said to each other. 'We're sure it's a year!'

One day to go. The old man fell asleep, relieved and exhausted, and Gwion Bach started to think of all the things he could do once his duty was done: climb trees, roam rivers, skim stones with his friends. And, for a moment, he stopped stirring.

BANG! In that moment, everyone in the castle and everyone in the village knew that something had happened. The cauldron split, and the elixir burst out and flowed into the ground. Drops flew into the air, and three landed on Gwion Bach's arm. Without thinking, he did what he always did when scalded by some soup or stew. He bent and sucked the burning liquid off his skin.

In that moment – although he didn't understand how – Gwion Bach knew everything.

But before he could relish his new powers, he saw Ceridwen flying towards the mountain in pursuit of whoever had ruined her elixir. As she neared the cave, all the trees bowed. For Ceridwen had become the wind.

Gwion Bach ran and jumped, sliding down the mountainside, tripping over tree roots and stumbling in burrow-holes, as Ceridwen howled after him. At one point he fell and, on getting up, found he had four legs and a coat of fur. As a hare, he coursed easily down the mountain, his powerful hind quarters carrying him easily over obstacles.

Suddenly, he was brought up short by the dark river that flowed at the bottom of the mountain. He felt Ceridwen's breath on his back: she had become a hunting hound. Her claws were on his back, her teeth on his neck. The two struggled by the water's edge until they fell in. And Gwion Bach found that, where there had been fur, there was now scale.

Upstream swam the salmon, his silvery-red scales glinting as he leapt over dams and fallen trees, diving back into the sanctuary of the water. But of course, after a while he felt the force of Ceridwen swimming behind him, now in the form of an otter. Gwion Bach took an extra-high jump and leapt into the air. As a dove, he could leave both hill and water, and allow himself to be propelled upwards by the currents. Before long, he felt Ceridwen's breath on his back once more. The strong claws of a hawk sank into his neck. Feathers flew. Bones snapped.

But a kernel of him slipped out of her grasp and fell to earth. As a grain of corn, he buried himself in a farmer's field.

Almost straightaway, it was pecked out of the ground and swallowed by a black-feathered hen. At last, Ceridwen had caught the boy who had ruined her elixir. But she was bitter: her son would now never become what he could have been.

Nine months later, she gave birth to a third child. As she looked into the eyes of her baby boy, she saw those of the hare, the salmon, the dove. Gwion Bach had used his new-found magical powers to turn himself into her child. Ceridwen wanted to destroy him, but found she could not.

What to do?

After some deliberation, she put the baby into a basket and took him to the river. But before she left him, she put an enchantment on her son to prevent him from growing hungry, sick or lonely until he was found.

The basket sailed along the river, eventually arriving in the kingdom of Gwyddno Garanhir. The king's son Elfin was fishing when he saw a shining light among the rushes. He dropped his fishing rod and waded into the water. The light came from the basket, from the forehead of the baby who lay there. Elfin took him home to the palace and named him Taliesin, meaning 'the one with the radiant brow' or 'enlightened one'.

And so began the story of Taliesin, the first poet of the Welsh language and the Chief of the Bards. According to some, he is also one of the few shining souls who knows the resting place of King Arthur.[103]

It is the night before Lammas, and the birth of a new moon. 'Enlightenment is available on Saturday night, for those who are brave enough to go on the journey,' Mark announces in the morning meeting with a broad grin. Then a new addition to the camp's infrastructure is opened as a willowy woman steps forward and cuts the pink ribbon around a cardboard toilet seat. The compost toilet is open.

That evening, the usual circle re-forms beneath the fluttering flags. The part of Ceridwen is played by the other camp organiser, a sizeable woman clad in purple and black. She spins round, glaring at us, all-too-convincing as she roars in fury: '*WHAT DID YOU DO TO MY SON?*' This culminating ritual is on a grand scale, and requires a lot of personnel to manage the flows of people through its various stages. Earlier, I had zipped Deborah into a black velvet cocktail dress, and now she stands a way down-circle, ready to shepherd people in the right direction, her outfit completed with a pair of natty red horns.

The circle crouches. A woman-hare is coursing around the ring, her legs in tights, face framed by a lollopy pair of ears, crayoned whiskers streaked across her cheeks. Section by section, the circle is disappearing, as little groups spring up and follow her. There's a tap on my shoulder. *Follow the hare!* someone whispers urgently. Then I am part of a line running across the field, haring after the hare. Up and round we run, and then through a canvas door. One of the tents has been transformed into a narrow tunnel, with sheets of plastic serving as internal walls. Ahead I can see blueness – water? – a series of paddling pools that will have to be waded through. I look at my feet; the only pair of robust shoes I have with me. The man in front of me is taking off his. *Hurry! Hurry!* whisper disembodied voices.

Back outside, a line re-forms, giggling as it dries its feet, and puts its shoes back on. A figure in sky-blue robes stands at the entrance of a second tent, daubing the fingers of each person with the contents of a bright azure pot. Inside, exquisite creatures flutter around us: woman-sized birds, glorious in gauze, satin, with wings of silver and gold. *Fly! Fly!* they urge us. But there's no time to stop and look; we must hurry on.

Out in the field, we squat, our faces close to the earth. We're the grain now, pecked, ever so gently, from above, by black figures with long black beaks. Then comes the signal and we're off, heading towards a tent whose entrance has been turned into a giant green woman. Her wicker head inclines quizzically to the left, towering above two orbs of greenery culled from the surrounding hedges. Two cherry-nipples protrude delectably from their centre.

We cram into the tent and sit; some of us, lots of us, more of us. Is it possible to fit more people into such a small space? It's warm, so warm, inside the womb of the goddess, but I'm quite happy; the atmosphere is safe rather than claustrophobic, and no one is too close. But one or two participants are clearly not enjoying themselves. 'I want my mummy!' shouts a little girl, louder and louder until she's lifted over the heads, into her mother's arms and out into the fresh air. Opposite me is the obese young woman who had spoken of her burden during one of the rituals. She is crying, the women beside her are holding her, looking at her, talking to her. Meanwhile, a song has begun to rise gently out of the seated crowd, a circular chant whose beginning is impossible to separate from its end: *We all come from the goddess/And to her we shall return/Like a drop of rain/Flowing to the ocean/We all come from the goddess.* Gradually, as it repeats and repeats, the warmth and sound seem to become one ...

Some time later, I find myself back outside in the circle, the cool of an English evening on my face. Someone dabs something sparkly on my forehead with a smile and a remark about a 'shining brow'. Grinning broadly, Mark declares us reborn.

Sunday dawns bright and fresh, the humidity of the previous days banished. A light breeze flutters across the camp, setting the flags and tent flaps a-dance, and there's a feeling of festivity as I make my way across the field, nodding at various acquaintances. It is the first of August, fully Lammas now, and many of the figures walking about the camp sport the season's colours of orange and yellow. The festival was originally a Celtic feast called Lughnasa in which the Sun God puts his power in the grain, and dies when the grain is harvested. In Anglo-Saxon times, it was marked by the baking of a 'loaf-mass' from the first crop which was then taken to church. It is hard, in this tale of sacrifice and renewal, to separate the pagan elements from the Christian, but I'm starting to feel that since stories are always evolving, it doesn't really matter.

Hoping to hear more indigenous stories, I attend a session on British goddesses in the small yurt, joining a small group of women sitting cross-legged on the floor around a pentangle of apples, their glossy red skins blazing like a fire at the heart of the tent. Pictures adorn the creamy walls, each depicting a primitivist female who embodies a different point of the Druid year, dark blues and reds in winter, yellowy-greens in spring. I can't take my eyes off the one for Lammas: a blaze of orange and yellow on a canvas on which a sheela-na-gig figure is giving birth within a giant apple.

Their creator, Somerset-based artist Dechen, talks softly about Madron: the goddess of grain, fulfilment, the mother of life; the springs and wells that can be found all over the British Isles are a reminder of her presence. She has, she says, spent a lot of time exploring the spiritual traditions of other cultures, but now feels the need to know more about those particular to Britain. Because so much of our native knowledge and so many of our practices have been lost, the process of rediscovering them is an exciting one. And the varied, changing seasons in this country are very helpful in teaching us, she goes on, providing points for marking the rhythms of life. The important thing is to find ways of being in a relationship with nature. We pause to admire the tiny spiders industriously climbing the sides of the yurt, one spinning itself up and down from the centre. Then Dechen reads a passage from a book by Kathy Jones which makes womanly connections between land and psyche.[104] As she reads, a tiny spider settles on the pages. She concludes with a prayer of thanks for the abundant gifts of the season. 'We give thanks, Madron,' she says softly.

This is the kind of New Age atmosphere I would normally steer clear of, but it is so comfortable in this apple-scented tent, the morning light illuminating the white canvas as we talk about the weather. All of us have noticed that everything is much earlier than usual; apples, sloes and plums catching people unawares for picking, storing and jam-making. There is, someone points out, talk in the scientific community of the shifting of the earth's axis brought about by the Japanese earthquake and causing changes in the seasons. If this is so, people will have to re-adjust, to plant what is needed for the winter earlier.

The short visualisation that follows involves travelling up to the stars and then down into the centre of the earth. I find it impossible to do either and, for once, it's not because I'm distracted or resistant. It's more that I want to be right here, right now, in this sunny field in Gloucestershire, savouring the details of this new–old world. So I give up trying to go anywhere, and my inner eye floods with orange and yellow, kaleidoscopic shapes that merge and separate. Right at the end, an ear of white-gold wheat appears, filling the entire screen. I can see it in minute detail; it is perfectly formed, the ear curled round on its stalk, each grain full and plump. Like the woman in the picture behind me, it is framed in an apple. Now I know what I will do to bring new life to my dead mother's house, or my mother's dead house. I will gather a few stalks of wheat from the edge of a nearby field and fill a vase, bring the fecundity of the outside in.

The session draws to a close. We cut up the apples into halves, horizontally, to reveal little stars at the centre, put them into dishes and offer them around the camp. No one refuses.

I stand next to Deborah in the circle for the closing ritual. A few times, in passing over the camp stove, she had professed an interest in fairies. I didn't know what she meant and let the idea pass, along with the half-formed thought that she was a bit away with them.

Robes and capes feature prominently at this final gathering, their rich colours and thick fabrics making for a formal dressiness. Deborah is delighted with her new hat, a felt affair in blue with a high point that can be folded down allowing it, as she points out, to be worn in the street. About sixty degrees down-circle, a young woman is wearing her felt hat with the point extended to its fullest length. It is an exquisite creation in cream, adorned with pale pink flowers and green fronds that accords perfectly with her blond locks and outfit: a close-fitting dress in dark olive-green, with matching tights.

'She looks like a flower fairy,' whispers Deborah.

She does. She could be straight out of my childhood book *Flower Fairies of the Spring*, perhaps Wood Sorrel or Larch, sitting sweetly on their branches, dressed in delicate pinks and greens.

So which seasonal fairy is Deborah? I scrutinise her brown skin, dark eyes, feel her warm, ripe energy; there is no doubt that she is an autumn sprite. Mentally, I scan my childhood copy of *Flower Fairies of the Autumn*.

I muse out loud. 'A berry fairy ... Mmm ... Something red.'

'Poisonous?' she sounds a little alarmed.

'No ... Something like rosehip ...' I'm thinking hard, sifting through my limited knowledge of autumn fruits.

'Hawthorn?' suggests Deborah.

The hedge sheltering our part of the camp was full of hawthorn. For days, my view of the world had been framed by dangles of compact red berries, set against the distinctive backdrop of May Hill.

'Yes, that's it. Hawthorn.'

The ritual gets underway, and each person picks a piece of mistletoe from the cauldron, and chooses a word or a phrase that summarises the camp for them. We sing *Awen*, turn east, south, west, north: hail and farewell to the spirits of the quarters. Then, hands looping through and over, the circle dances and, all too soon, it's over.

*

The final thing I want to do before leaving is sit down and talk to Mark about how he saw the camp. The interview, agreed during our first meeting, had been postponed and re-arranged several times during the course of the camp and now, finally, he tells me to wait for him in the cafe. But he never comes, and gradually, as the field starts to empty, I realise that all the re-arrangements have been an indirect way of saying that he doesn't want to talk. So I pack up the car, and prepare myself for the return to the house. I figure it might ease the transition back to inside-living if I take some of the outside in, so I gather hawthorn – traditionally used for protection – from the branches behind the tent. Out in the narrow green lane, I stop the car and gather some golden wheat ears from an adjoining field.

Back at the house, I put the berried branches into a jug, and the wheat into a vase. A sudden inspiration sends me to the drawer where the Christmas decorations are kept, to fetch some corn dollies. Deck the halls with boughs of Lammas. This had always been a special time in Gloucestershire, and now it had a name.

THE END OF THE BEGINNING

Were my experiences at Druid Camp real, or merely the result of projection? I remembered Emma Restall Orr's lack of concern about whether her experiences were a matter of fact or fiction. I was increasingly wondering whether such distinctions had much to contribute to the business of living meaningfully. In any case, it seemed to me that, as a gentle, optimistic faith founded on the desire to live in harmony with nature, Druidry had a lot going for it. With its appreciation of the past, awareness of the future and celebration of the present, it offered a workable way of relating to one's own place and history. It had stories and rituals to deal with the dark side of life and found a place for the contradictions and conflicts of human desires, balancing them against the different interests of the natural world. The more I thought about it, the more it struck me as a very British faith. Perhaps it also provided a way out of the literalism of the age, a way of countering sterility and disconnectedness by reconnecting with imagination and meaning. In this light, practices such as astrology could be seen as symbolic ways of forging this connection.

I decide I will, without signing up to any particular group, quietly begin to integrate some seasonal patterns into my life, to take notice of times other than the official highpoints of the Christian and academic year. Why shouldn't I mark Lammas, a time I'd always experienced as special, yet never named? And

Imbolc, that liminal moment in early February when, while still some way of winter to go, there's a change in the air as palpable as if someone has thrown a switch. Now that I'm in Gloucestershire, it's easy to track the minutiae of the season, to absorb its detail and nuance. I can step out into the lanes at any time, into the golden glory of an afternoon or the gathering peace of early evening, watch the fall of the light, take in the acrid smell of water and willow. Even the odour of muck-spreading in the nearby fields is welcome, and I inhale deeply. The field near the house has been shorn like an old Lammas meadow and is empty of sheep. It's now bordered, hill-wise, by fruiting hawthorns, their berries and leaves a glossy red and green.

As summer slips into autumn, I monitor the hawthorns as they progress into winter. Most of the berries have wizened and turned the colour of dried blood; some branches are already bare, while others in shadier spots are still laden with smooth red baubles heavy with juice. The chilly August that followed the early, dry summer has meant that everything has gone to fruit early. Apples are already bowing the branches and the hedges are full of sloes and wild plums and berries. In my new-found role as amateur phenologist, I have become berry-aware.

It's an excellent year for blackberries, and the brambles hang heavy with jewelled drupes in almost-black, begging to be made into crumbles and tarts. It's easy to oblige; I'm re-learning to bake after a long period of abstinence, making full use of the kitchen my mother has left me. Large, newly fitted and well-equipped, it's the opposite of the one I have in London. The easy-gliding drawers are stocked with pans, spatulas and baking tins of all shapes and sizes. There are enough aprons to shield an army of cooks. I recognise old friends from decades ago: the curious hand-turned meat-mincer, and the rolling pin that has smoothed hundreds of miles of pastry.

My baking times are snatched hours, set-asides ring-fenced from other tasks. There's so much to do, with the endless paperwork of death, and the careful, little-by-little clearing of the house. I also have a busy social life: A lives in a tiny village half an hour away; other friends dot different parts of the county. With people regularly coming to stay or eat, meal times turn up more quickly than I can deal with them. But there is a well-stocked larder and two freezers full of parcels of food, sometimes entire meals, sometimes portions of fruit and veg. There are bags of homemade croutons and little foil envelopes of mint. They are all labelled explanatorily in my mother's neat hand, some accompanied by strict instructions: *SMOKED HADDOCK – Thaw – DO NOT COOK FROM FROZEN*.

One evening, A comes over to eat. I haven't had time to shop and I'm assembling the makings of a fish dish from various sources, concocting a meal in the haphazard style of a cookery competition. She and I belong to the generation of women with culinary half-knowledge: learning to cook had to defer to the higher claims of education and pleasure-seeking; I was nearly twenty before I produced my first meal for guests. 'Can you freeze tomatoes?' she asks curiously, as I whip a plastic container labelled '*TOMS*' out of the freezer. 'Oh, sure, as long as you only want to cook with them,' I reply confidently. I didn't know this before; it's as if my mother is teaching me from the grave.

My first car boot sale. Dutifully, A gets up at 5.30 on a Sunday and drives across the county to help me run a stall in a field down the road. My ostensible purpose is to get a bit of cash for all my sorting efforts, but really there's a deeper impulse at work: the desire to be fully engaged with the disposal of the objects, to get a sense of their new homes. After a slow start, the good people of Gloucester oblige, volunteering stories about why they want a particular thing. A white-haired woman lights up at the sight of my mother's old-fashioned iron – just a hot plate attached to an electric cord – she wants it for her own mother. 'She's ninety and comes to stay with me for two months every year. But she won't use my steam iron,' she tells me. Another woman fingers a set of ramekins with a strange, happy look in her eyes. 'They're for lunches for the Rotary Club,' she explains. 'I need some exactly the same as what we've already got: they complain if they think anyone's got more than them.' I'm brisk with dealers, and discourage anyone who doesn't know what beryl is as being unworthy of inheriting my grandmother's green china, however many pounds they offer. My uncommercial approach is vindicated by a woman who lovingly handles a wooden doll in crinoline and bonnet which had been handsewn by my mother in case there should be a child in need of a doll. It will be perfect for some of her six grandchildren to play with, she says, fingering the lacy longjohns beneath the velvet skirt: 'We've been doing the Victorians.'

I do car boot sales myself,' she adds. 'And sometimes, if I don't like the person, I won't sell, for any price.'

I agree enthusiastically.

The woman takes a tin of brightly coloured fridge magnets in the shape of ladybirds from the trestle table and holds it up. 'How much is this?'

'Fifty p,' I tell her. She looks pleased.

Our friend Rich's cancer has taken off again, and he has returned to Gloucester to live with his parents while he gets treatment at Cheltenham. His prognosis seems to be getting more certain by the week, although no one will say so explicitly. A phone conversation with A behind the Divinations tent at Druid Camp takes a turn for the theological. Rich is worried about what is to become of him, and we share some of his apprehension; once you know one of your tribe is leaving, you want to know about the destination. I can hear the anxiety in her voice; despite her churchy background, she's really not sure about what comes next, and won't be fobbed off with some idle consolation. 'It's a win–win,' I hear myself telling her. 'It's either fine or, if there's nothing, you don't know about it anyway.'

A couple of weeks later, we take Rich out. We've privately agreed that going out with him is a two-woman job: he is a big man and his damaged spine means he can no longer walk without help. The Cotswold manor is a good choice: his Zimmer frame can just about cope with the shallow steps, and the bar overlooks lush grounds. As we sip deliciously expensive wine, he texts compulsively. He needs to be in touch with Everyone, All The Time, even through the night; I've taken to leaving my phone downstairs. 'Life is great', he generally says, or 'I will beat this'. While A is in the loo, he looks up from the little keyboard and turns to me, his eyes wide with alarm. 'I've never thought about death,' he says. 'I can't imagine it: the end of everything, and then just nothing.'

Another couple of weeks, and his denial is fracturing. Suddenly, after a meeting with his consultant, he summons a group of us to a favourite pub. It's an odd gathering, this living wake around a sick-looking man, a reunion of a tribe formed by place and circumstance that has long since scattered: some of us haven't seen each other in twenty-five years. There's an embarrassed moment like a cough as everyone picks up the menu. Then laughter peals out as several pairs of hands rummage simultaneously for reading glasses.

As he is helped into his girlfriend's car at the end of the evening, I give Rich a tub containing my latest baking efforts. It's hard to go wrong with him on gastric matters, especially now; his enthusiasm for food is greater than ever. When we speak on the phone the next day, he praises my pastry. I am gratified.

In the autumn, I return to London. On my wrist is an uncomplicated part of my legacy: a pearl-studded bracelet, the gold-plate rubbing off in places, that I remember since girlhood. The catch is loose, but I ignore the inner promptings telling me to get it fixed until, one day, having just left the station, I find my wrist bare. For the rest of the day, I try to tell myself that the loss of a bracelet doesn't matter: it's only a thing, after all. But that night, drifting off to sleep, I miss its presence so powerfully I can almost feel it on my wrist, see the tiny golden claws clutching the pearls. The next day, I go back to the station, and tentatively describe it to the Polish woman who sits dourly in the ticket kiosk. 'Moment,' she says, and disappears into the gloom. Seconds later, she's back, dangling the bracelet a foot away from my face on the other side of the glass. I'm nearly hysterical with gratitude. The woman manages a small smile.

I've also brought my blackberrying habit back to the city. The bushes grow differently here, spreading low over the rough ground in the park at the end of my road. I have learnt there are many different species of blackberry. This year, two seem to be predominant: a tight-knit, small berry and a larger fruit composed of loose, juicy drupelets. Once one sort is over, the other comes into its own, with the result that the blackberry season lasts a good two months. In Gloucestershire freezer and cupboards are stocked with berries and jam, but in south London I am fruitless and in urgent need of seasonal fruit for a tart. I head for the far side of the park with a plastic container; there are wild patches that are bramble-full. As I move further into the undergrowth, a teenage boy pauses on his run along the path, his brown sculpted flesh nicely set off by a white vest top.

'Scuse me, are those nai-ce?' I straighten up. I recognise the nasal tones of south London, but am puzzled by the question. No one would ask that where I come from. 'They're blackberries. Now's the time.' The nod is polite, but the look is blank, uncomprehending. I try to be more explanatory, to furnish my temporary pupil with an example. 'You know blackberry and apple crumble, pie?'

The youth nods, but I can tell by his face that he still doesn't get it. Now on the back foot, I fall back on the ruthlessly commercial logic of the times: 'They're two quid in the supermarket.' The light of understanding dawns on the boy's face. 'Ah, so you thought you'd come here and get some.'

That evening, I take my blackberry and apple tart round to a friend's house, where we are to mark the autumn equinox in our little patch of suburbia. There are five of us around a metal table on a patio overlooking an upward-sloping garden. Nobody has any experience of such seasonally inspired gatherings, and I don't mention the word Druid. But I have done a bit of research. The autumn equinox – equinox means equal night – is one of the two times in the year when day and night are of the same length, the point at which the northern hemisphere enters the dark, resting half of the year; it's almost certainly the origins of the Christian harvest festival. But I can find little about what to do, now, on this particular pagan festival; even in Druid circles it seems to be little-celebrated. So I gather whatever strikes me as autumnal from the woodland at the end of the road – some acorns, bright leaves and berried sprigs – and put everything into a basket with some orange candles.

Others have bought apples, pears, quinces. The fruits of the season tumble onto the table in no particular order, but somehow a study of abundance emerges out of the mess, asymmetrical and glowing with colour. It's a visual feast; like a still life, but better. 'Oh, I feel quite moved,' says a friend as she stares at it, entranced. 'I could do that for the table at home.'

Then we attempt a casual ceremony, a loose concoction of poem, song and thought. I have rejected my first idea – a reading of Keat's 'Ode to Autumn' – as too safe, for me anyway. I have chosen, instead, something riskier: a New Agey poem about the inevitable passing of Mabon, when the dying sun god returns to the arms of the goddess of fertility. It's a bit soupy, but it gives us a story, with pictures, with which to understand the draining away of light and warmth and attendant feelings of loss. Someone sings the English folk song 'The Trees They Grow So High', a young widow's lament for the boy-husband beneath the grass. Someone else says it's sad, oh so sad, but the singer and I don't think so, really: seen from the perspective we're cultivating this evening, it's all part of the cycle of life. There's talk of reversing the traditional dualism of light and dark, and of the need to embrace the latter. Mine is heartfelt: I'm uneasy about the coming season, anticipating the disablingly low energy levels winter always brings. Someone else describes how, at this time of year, she loves to make chutney because it reminds her of her dad. Our hostess, who is recovering from a disappointing relationship, expresses thankfulness for the sociable atmosphere that has arrived on her patio. I am surprised at how easily this kind of talk comes to us, a clutch of twenty-first century women living in London.

As the darkness gathers around us, we eat supermarket quiche, homegrown tomatoes and blackberry tart. Whatever we have been doing, it confirms the possibility of an instinctive, celebratory spirituality. Deborah was right. Ritual is easy.

From our respective parts of the country, A, B and I communicate regularly about Rich as if fussing over a child. We relay information and concerns via text, email, phone. We're a satellite back-up team led by B, whose skills as a hospice matron are much in demand now that we are in the second half of life. At eighty, Rich's mother is struggling to cope with the son on whom she dotes: Rich is on a roller-coaster, swinging wildly between joy and rage, self-pity and determination to live, and everyone around him is being lashed with his extreme emotions. I'm familiar with the denial that can accompany cancer; in the months between his diagnosis and death, my father returned from hospital appointments with garbled, optimistic accounts which gave us no real idea of how he was until, finally, I overrode his protests and accompanied him. The child of Nazi Austria was fighting his cancer with charm, kissing the nurse's hand and telling the consultant his best jokes, terrified that if he stepped out of line, the NHS would refuse to treat him. As the session ended, the oncologist rolled his eyes and asked: 'Can you come with him next time?' When it became clear there was to be no treatment, my father fantasised about buying an untested drug via the internet that could reportedly extend life. There was a plan for him to take a last trip to Vienna to see friends and family; I would go with him, and we would pace ourselves. But every time it came to setting a date, my father backtracked; he would rather go 'in the summer', when he was feeling better. My mother, well aware that he had no such summer before him, became so exasperated that she accidentally paid me two compliments: 'Why don't you just go and show off your beautiful daughter?' she half-shouted. 'She's very efficient, you know: she can easily organise it.' Muttering something about going to the loo, my father staggered from the room. 'Is he crying?' whispers my mother in amazement.

On the way back from a weekend in Gloucestershire, I go to see Rich in the hospice where he has gone for respite care. His uncle is sitting mournfully by the bedside. We exchange bereavements – he lost his wife not long ago – and find that both of us have lost the taste for travel. When he leaves, Rich and I are left alone. He has everything he needs, he says, tapping the CDs and bottle of red wine by the bed. It's not the easiest of visits: he is tearful and angry about a family matter. Then he is screaming in pain from his en-suite bathroom: 'Alex! Help me!' I'm not up to this: I run for the nurses.

On the way out, just as I'm about to descend the stately wooden staircase, I'm stopped by the resident counsellor. 'Have you been visiting Rich?' he asks. 'Can I borrow you for five minutes?' He draws me into his consulting room. 'Are you surprised by the way he is?'

I tell him what I know. He shrugs and sighs.

'You don't always get epiphanies,' he says as we part. 'Life's a bitch, and then you die.'

Rich's funeral coincides with an autumn heatwave that brings, according to the weather folk, the highest recorded temperatures October has ever seen. Day follows cloudless day, bar the odd wisp streaking decoratively across the sky, and the low autumn sun bathes everything in a golden glow. The constant ambient heat is accompanied by a light, caressing breeze, creating an animalistic sense of well-being I'm unused to in Britain. Oh, I could live in this country.

The funeral is a two-day affair, with an Anglican service on the Sunday to allow Rich's musician friends to play, to be followed by a short ceremony at the crematorium on the Monday. B comes to stay and drives us up to the yellow-stoned village above the city. The church is packed with friends and relations from all over the country; by the pulpit stands Rich, looking out from a giant photo on an easel. He is surrounded by his favourite things – a climbing rope, his cycling helmet, a rugby shirt – and is smiling crinkily. I am sitting right in his line of vision; it seems as if he is looking straight at me. Looking back at him, I feel a piercing sense of puzzlement. Where *are* you? I ask him silently. I go out to compose myself and stand awhile beneath the cool of the yew tree.

Afterwards, at the village cricket club, the old crowd is drinking enthusiastically, trading banter and jokes. It's like slipping into a warm bath. Time passes; the sun's rays lengthen, radiating ever more widely across the grass. There's the usual argument about where the drinking should continue, but eventually I persuade A, B and her daughter to come home with me.

The next day, as we ready ourselves for the service at the crematorium, there is a flurry of calls; B's father-in-law, long ill with cancer, has finally died. She embarks on a new round of death-related communications before we drive to the crem, a simple stone building set in the middle of the city. I've been here before but, transformed by the bright light and caressing breeze, it's almost like being in the Lebanese mountains. We're early, so we josh about with some old mates outside. There's plenty to work with: 'Chinese section', remarks a gnomic little white sign from a bed of lavender, while a larger sign announces sternly: 'Any chippings found in this section will be removed by the Sexton'.

Half an hour later, in the cool of the building, all high spirits are gone. I feel empty, numb. It was the vicar saying calmly: 'And now it's time to say goodbye to Rich,' and the Yes track that played out the coffin. The crowd, as it files back out into the light, is almost silent. I go and greet the uncle I met at the hospice bed, but neither of us has much to say and, after a minute, I murmur a politeness and rejoin B. She is talking to one of the idols of our rock-chick youth in whose band Rich had latterly played. The rock star is short, and looks sad as he stands tightly clasping his wife's hand. All the things I might have had to say to him about the music that enchanted my youth are as nothing. We shuffle our feet and make funeral smalltalk.

The giant photo of Rich follows us around like a portable shrine, reappearing prominently at the pub where we had gathered with him weeks before. Photo albums circulate with images of past revelry; R points out that hers and mine are so similar that they could belong to the same person. We're still going strong as the family packs itself into cars. One of Rich's mates manfully shoulders the giant photo. 'It's not the first time I've carried him,' he says cheerfully in parting.

300

The same week, I decide to take advantage of The Glorious Weather and pay that visit to May Hill. Although I've seen its caterpillar outline from so many directions uncountable times, I have not been to the top since childhood. Seen from afar, the hill is necessarily flat, one-dimensional; I want the bodily experience of being among the pines. The summit has become a place of the past, the stuff of distant childhoods and storybooks, part of that confused mental space where you're not sure whether you dreamt something or actually experienced it. The sense that the place I knew as an eight-year-old has disappeared has been confirmed by a couple of failed attempts to revisit the hill while my parents were still alive. Each time, I'd drive towards the Forest and follow the sign pointing up to May Hill. But somehow, among the many little roads encircling the summit, I never found the right turning and would end up in ever-narrowing lanes until, terrified of scratching the car and incurring my father's wrath, I turned tail and retreated to the A40.

But now, nobody except me cares if the car takes a knock. And so, jettisoning my plans for a more utilitarian Wednesday, I set out to catch the day.

Round and round the narrow lanes we go, me and my car, circling the lower reaches of the peak until we reach a sandy layby. A wooden signpost indicates a footpath covering the last leg of the ascent, towards the stand of trees. The little parking place is already half-occupied by a scruffy camper van; outside stands a half-dressed, leggy man, thinning blond hair trickling down over a smooth brown back. (*Oh*, grumbles an inner voice, *I come here for the first time in nearly forty years and the first thing I see is a hippy.*) As I lock the car, I notice that he's cradling a baby clad in just a nappy, its tiny, pudgy limbs exposed to the sun. The child is squawking in the bird-like way of the recently born and, with the utmost tenderness, the man bends to kiss it.

I set off up the footpath. The lower slopes are a mix of woodland and meadow, with ferny glades between the trees. Slender white birches mingle with oaks; little apple trees shed their crop on the woodland floor and ponies graze tranquilly on the vegetation. There are mushrooms everywhere: rubbery forms sprawling out of tree trunks like the dissolving features of a vanquished sci-fi enemy. Little caps pop out of the undergrowth, poison-red and white-speckled. Beyond the trees, the open field leading up to the summit is dotted with beige: erect, knob-headed fungi and neat parasol mushrooms. Some of them are so furniture-like that it's easy to imagine a Rackhamesque world of faery folk to go with them, sheltering under them or using them as tables.

One more stretch of field and I enter the pines. It is clear there are two, distinct stands of generations: the clump of Victorian veterans and an outer ring planted to mark the Queen's Silver Jubilee. This is not the peaceful hilltop it appeared from the distance, but a place of movement and elemental energy. The wind rushes through the branches, creating a circle of sound that shuts out everything else, roaring and rising like a tide. Every so often, it dies down completely, uncovering the other sounds of the world: a burst of birdsong or the drone of a distant plane.

The quietness, now, belongs to the distant horizons, all three hundred and sixty degrees of them. On a clear day, you are supposed to be able to see twelve counties from this summit. I don't know about that, but as I walk round the circle of trees, I can certainly see the wide silver loop of the Severn meandering around the promontory where Druid Camp had taken place two months before. To the north and west, the fields fall away in a patchwork of colours which fades into the charcoal outlines of the Malvern and Black Mountains. But the best view of all is skyward. Lying down, head on rucksack, I can see nothing except vertical trunks and green against blue. If I slow everything down and look, really look, I see that each needle is perfectly varnished, its honed point catching the sun.

On my way down an hour or so later, I cross paths with the hippy and his partner coming up. The man's upper body is swathed in a sling, but it is the woman who is carrying the baby, her arms forming a cradle, holding the child almost ceremonially up to the sun. If early imprinting works, one of their child's formative experiences will be of a softly warming light and a gentle, dancing breeze.

Back in the London hills, I was newly conscious of the influence of place on people. Upper Norwood tended to inspire a passionate loyalty which, long-standing residents speculated, was at least partly due to its distinctive geographical location above the surrounding districts. The top of the highest hill, while no longer home to a Victorian pleasure dome, provided a natural site for a town centre whose independent shops and cafes exerted a powerful gravitational pull. Local loyalty also generated a place-based protest culture whose affiliates would spring into action whenever there was a cause that needed espousing: the rebuilding of the palace, the movement against the rebuilding of the palace, the campaign for the creation of a local cinema; I had even heard of a crusade to save a single tree. Once one came to an end, a new campaign tended to form in its place, while others went on for years, gently colliding and overlapping with each other, generating a seemingly infinite variety of ways in which the people of the palace could express their commitment to the place where they lived.

The local library, the country's only independent library and an integral part of the high street since the late nineteenth century, is under threat from funding cuts. A campaign rolls into action and, as a lifelong library user, I join. I am a reluctant campaigner, but I am feeling the pull of the past in the place of my present: a framed certificate recognising Thomas Greenwood's contribution to the public library movement hangs in the hall; I pass it every time I go to a library meeting. We organise public meetings, lobby councillors and flash mob a council meeting with a rendition of 'Books, glorious books'. In the pub after one particularly boisterous meeting with council officials, the library campaigners are drinking with the Transition Town crowd. Among them is a Brazilian anthropology student who is doing his thesis on the community in Crystal Palace. 'How are we?' I ask curiously. 'Unusually empowered,' smiles the anthropologist.

There was another reason why I felt particularly protective of my local area. In the wake of my mother's death, I discovered it held some ancestral connections. The news came via an email from one Francis Eames, who calculated that we were fourth cousins. A keen family historian, he had only recently become aware of my side of the family, having met my mother's closest cousin a couple of months before. He was sorry that he was getting in touch too late to meet my mother, he wrote, but would like to visit me. My great-great-grandfather had lived in the street next to mine, and his children had gone on to live in houses nearby; he would happily come and show me their various addresses. The new connection promised to throw light onto the dark side of my maternal line, the story that had gone silent with the suicide of my grandfather.

And so it was that one Saturday afternoon in May I found myself haring around south London with a party of new relatives in pursuit of some dead ones. Just after midday, Cousin Francis stands on the doorstep, a big, smiley man in his fifties carrying a large holdall. He is closely followed by Cousin Brian, a man in his sixties who reminds me of an animal character in a children's story, perhaps Ratty or Mole. He, too, has a large bag. They are joined by Cousin Andrew and his wife, whom I've known all my life, and the party is complete.

The new cousins disgorge their ancestral booty onto my living room floor. There are endless papers and documents testifying to births, deaths and weddings, and I learn that my great-grandparents married in the church at the end of my road. There is silverware engraved with lengthy inscriptions of gratitude to former Eameses for their contributions to company and community, photos, wills, diaries documenting life in London more than a century before.

After lunch, we pile into Francis' car to do a tour of the ancestral homes. Most were bombed during the war, but we identify the site of the Victorian villa where my great-great-grandfather lived on Belvedere Road. Number 57 must have been on the stretch of lawn between houses which is now home to several cherry trees and a night time playground for fox cubs. It's a road I tramp up and down most days. By dint of rough calculations of house numbers versus the space between the buildings, we pinpoint the site as more or less opposite the Victorian postbox. We take photos of each other standing by it, grinning broadly.

Then we get back into the car and go in search of more ancestral homes. The house on the incline of Anerley Hill was also bombed and the gap filled by a more modern construction, while the Central Hill residence was knocked down in the sixties to make way for a housing estate. We have to drive a couple of miles north before we finally stand before an actual house: a handsome, detached Victorian villa in Dulwich. Francis and I survey it with undisguised envy, trying to put a current value on it before reminding ourselves that our forebears probably just rented it. I have another reason for harbouring negative feelings: here lived the snotty Anglican in-laws who derided my sweet-natured grandmother and, after their son's suicide, left her alone with her grief.

Our last stop is Nunhead Cemetery, where Brian has some graves to visit. As we walk up the tree-lined avenue, an exquisite smell piques my nostrils. Combining the sweetness of honey with the freshness of citrus, the scent is intoxicating. Lime blossom, says Andrew, a horticulturist: a rare smell in Britain, because it needs consistent warmth to bloom. We are now in the heart of the cemetery, in front of the derelict Anglican chapel. Brian veers off suddenly, almost sniffing as he follows his ancestral trail. He darts into overgrown corners to examine various tombfaces and then, rounding a corner, stops suddenly and climbs onto a flat-topped grave, his enthusiasm visibly mounting. Clearing the vegetation from the face of the stone, he reads aloud a lengthy inscription about one of his ancestors.

Francis and I watch from ground level.

'He's a tomb-chaser,' I tease.

'Once he gets a sniff of a cemetery, there's no stopping him,' agrees Francis.

Later, I go to the local library to consult early twentieth-century directories about my ancestors' movements. The librarian responsible for keeping them smiles knowingly when I explain what I'm after. He's convinced, after thirty-four years in the job, that there is such a thing as genetic memory. He's known many cases of people moving to the area and subsequently discovering that a grandfather or an uncle used to live round the corner or kept a shop in the next street.

The Gloucester house is for sale. Men tramp in and out, making assessments. What helps is that I tend to know everyone I'm dealing with or, if I don't, I know someone who did. The estate agent's face breaks into a broad grin when he realises who my father was. *Otto? Such a character.* As he walks into the living room, he recognises the furniture: three or four decades ago, he had sold some of it to my father when working as an auctioneer. 'He used to tell me everything was rubbish, and then come and buy it,' he recalls with a laugh. But these days, big brown antiques are out of fashion. The auctioneer will take the best stuff, but there are plenty of things that are not worth his while. I show him, with some pride, the enormous dinner service of hand-painted Royal Worcester that my mother had always said was 'worth something'. Not so, says the auctioneer: people don't want that kind of thing because you can't put it in a dishwasher. His removal man comes to take the best stuff, and I recognise in the large-framed man of sixty the young man who had lived on a farm a mile down our road in the 1970s. 'You probably remember my van, don't you?' he says, pointing to the scruffy grey vehicle outside.

Now that he mentions it, I do. In that instant I am back in the garden of the Big House, looking up from my play among the bushes as he hurtles, far too fast, the roller-shutter door rattling, down the lane.

Gradually, the family possessions are finding new homes. A takes the 1960s coffee table that my brother and I used to walk on when playing touch-off-ground around the sitting room; R wants the Elko-sofa for her conservatory overlooking the Stroud valley; B loves the big clock that my father bought at a church sale, with 'MANNS: GLOUCESTER' running across its broad face. I find it comforting that in this redistributive reincarnation, I will see these things in the houses of my oldest friends.

One week I drive into Wiltshire to visit a Greenwood cousin. She has been looking into the family history, and we are to spend a couple of days pooling knowledge. We spread our boxes of photos and papers out on her dining room table and sit down after breakfast to work through them, pairing pieces of information, putting names to photos. A scrap of paper detaches itself; on it, in the delicate hand of an earlier age, are some lines of verse, signed by my great-grandmother. I reach for her biography of Thomas Greenwood which is lying beside me on the table and open it at random; the poem is there on the page in front of us. 'It's as if we're watching her write,' says my cousin. Browsing the internet, we discover that Greenwood's *Free Public Libraries* has been resurrected by the digital age. Scanned and bound because its new publishers believe it to be 'culturally important', it is now available from online retailers.

The book, when it arrives at my London flat, is a weighty tome, nearly five hundred pages of detailed advice on the practicalities of setting up libraries combined with a passionate argument for the provision of a publicly funded library for every town and rural community of any size. It includes some jokes. Greenwood reports on a public meeting of the ratepayers in Widnes, Lancashire, to consider a resolution to found a free library: 'The Chairman then invited anybody who wished to speak against the resolution to step on the platform, but for a time no one offered to do so. (A Voice: "I think they are all Quakers.")'[105]

The details resonate with the debates of my own time: the library should be housed in a purpose-built building at the heart of the community and be staffed by a professional librarian. Others sound quaintly anachronistic: Greenwood dismisses fears that open-access shelving encourages theft, and reports on the different systems for the 'vexed' subject of classifying books. The new library committee, advises my great-great grandfather, 'have little or no idea of the work they have before them'. In twenty-first-century Upper Norwood, as one of the trustees of the new charitable trust set up to save the local library, I can't suppress a knowing smile.

In midwinter, I do the final clear of my parents' house. Clearing the little drawers in the recesses of the secretaire bookcase, my hand curls round something soft: a roll of brown hair in a time-weathered plastic bag. When I was nine, I had given in to my mother's urging to have my waist-length hair cut, and my father had kept the pony tail. I have no idea how to deal with this micro-corpse from my childhood; I feel vaguely repulsed, but I can't just throw it away. I stuff the bag of hair into the box of photos as another thing to be dealt with later. Right to the end, things keep surfacing: the pastry board that has slipped under a drawer, the pieces of Cotswold stone from the drive of the Big House: an ammonite set in a golden pebble and a grey fossil in the shape of a gnarled toenail.

On the last day, I'm still surrounded by piles of dusters and stationery, desperately tired, uncertain whether I'll make it back to London to chair a library meeting, or indeed ever. Then I discover I've forgotten to give the auctioneer the last few antiques stored in the sideboard. He drives halfway across the county at a moment's notice to pick them up and makes a point of coming in to admire my work, the emptiness of the house.

More men turn up with vans and take stuff away. Sometimes, when I think about all these things being dispersed over the world, I feel physical pain.

'*Don't grieve. Everything you lose comes around again in another form*', advises Rumi.[106]

IN THE GARDEN

Back in my London garden, I'm going about my autumn tasks when a robin appears on the fence, head cocked to one side. He drops to the ground where I'm planting some bulbs, and hops towards me until he's a yard or so away. He stares. I stare. In a flash, his head turns and a passing insect ends its life in his beak.

The next time he visits, I scatter some sunflower seed on the ground in front of him; he hops to it and investigates. But apparently he's after the juicer things I'm turning up with the soil. Or nothing. He sits on the rake head and regards me.

The robin returns regularly throughout the winter. I see him looking up at me through the kitchen window as I put on the kettle. When I go out, he appears on the fence, bobbing. After a while, I realise that it's possible to whistle him up; if I make my fractured, wispy imitation of a bird-call, I am usually rewarded by the whirr of wings. He goes to the low-branched tree where he sings, and I sit on the bench and listen. I'm close enough to see his throat working furiously; it's hard to believe that such a tiny frame could produce a sound of this volume. Sometimes we take it in turns; although my whistling is nothing to his melodic fluency, in conversational terms, it seems to work. I'm feeling my way in this relationship with a creature so different; I've only ever known domesticated mammals who appreciate tone and touch. But how do you have a relationship with a bird? Human voices alarm, and you cannot touch them unless they are captive. Even the way they see the world, with their eyes placed laterally on both sides of the head, is different. Someone on Twitter tells me that robins are highly territorial, 'alpha violent' birds who will fight to the death. I feel a momentary stab of disappointment, but it soon passes. I don't feel humans are in position to feel superior.

At Christmas, Rich's parents send me a gardening token. When it slides from the envelope, I'm puzzled, even a little embarrassed. I'm too old to be sent such things. But when I read the note – 'Please buy something for the garden in memory of Rich' – understanding dawns. It is obvious what to get for the man who loved mountaineering, for the spot by the bare fence that needs cover. I go to the local gardening centre and buy a climbing rose. It isn't until a week or so later that I get round to planting it, hurrying outside just as the light is beginning to ebb. I am kneeling, piling up the earth, discarding the rubble that any movement of the soil turns up, when the sound comes from the branches behind. The robin is singing his evening song, liquid notes cascading out of his breast.

Better than Tavener, Rutter, this requiem mass, flowing powerfully on, rising above the sounds of the rush-hour traffic a couple of streets away and the coarser calls of the bigger birds in the surrounding trees. Here, closer to the ground, it's just me and the robin, linked by a golden thread of song. The evensong continues as I pack the good, brown earth securely in around the roots of the rose, the garden darkening around me.

Spring at last. I'm exchanging regards with the robin when I notice another bright-breasted bird hovering in the branches behind him. The second robin is a longer-faced, slim-torsoed bird who eyes me cautiously. A couple of days later, the pair are flying in and out of a gap in the ivy that covers the post at the bottom of the kitchen steps, bits of vegetation in their beaks. The spot they have chosen for their nest is very close to us humans, in full view of both flats' sets of windows. I will have to pass it every time I go down into the garden.

I don't like to disturb my new neighbours, so it's a while before I lift the ivy screen that conceals the nest and see the clutch of blue eggs. The next time I look there are some speckled feathers; after a moment, a head turns casually and a bright eye looks at me as if to say *Yes?* So she's sitting; I'll bother them no more. She cannot leave the eggs for any length of time; it is dangerous for them to cool beneath a certain point. For the next few days the male robin stays nearby, hovering watchfully in the branches near the nest. He hardly sings now, stopping, as if exhausted, after a bar or two.

A week or so later, the parents are flying in and out of the ivy, their beaks crammed with bugs. It's a cold spring of endless rain, and I know from the one further peek I allow myself that only a single survivor remains from the clutch. As I lift the leaves which conceal the nest, its upturned yellow beak opens in expectation of food. For the next few evenings, while the parents are busy with the pre-night feed, I rake up the nearby ground to bring worms to the surface.

Despite all this effort, there is peril for the newly hatched. Putting on the kettle one morning, I see a squirrel is crouched on the steps, level with the nest, his gaze focused, haunches poised to spring; the male robin is sounding the alarm from the nearby branches. I fling open the kitchen door and make a fuss; the squirrel scarpers. It is partly my fault. When I first saw the nest, I scattered some birdseed on the ground nearby. Intended to help the robins, it has only alerted a predator.

I abandon my work and concoct a plan of defence. I cover half the ivy post – the side facing squirrel-wise – with garden netting, taking care to leave the leafy path to the nest unobstructed. Then I sprinkle the whole post liberally with chilli powder, a substance loathed by squirrels but ignored by birds. From the branches a yard or so away, the two robins watch in silence. I stand back and wait. The male robin flies towards the door in the ivy, gets caught in the netting and flaps around in panic. I shake him free, adjust the netting, and watch a few successful entries and exits through the ivy. Conscience salved, I return to my computer.

Rich's girlfriend comes to stay before returning to her native Germany. She hasn't had the best experience of Britain since moving to be with her new love two years ago. Apart from the boyfriend dying of cancer, her work in the public sector, so nicely organised in Germany, is badly paid and subject to repeated reorganisation; in Britain, she can't afford to rent her own flat. She has spent the past two months exploring the north of the country, and is now heading home to resume her old job. After a day's sightseeing in central London, we sit in the garden with a glass of wine. The robins fly around our heads, swooping like swallows across the space between us and the nest.

A few evenings later, the garden is empty. After weeks of hyperactivity, the air is still, and no one is hunting on the ground outside the kitchen. That morning, both robins had been flying around busily as usual. But, unusually, I had seen the female take a bath in the bowl on top of the shed, submerging herself and splashing, and then shaking her feathers dry. Then she'd taken a second bath. I go down into the garden; it is eerily quiet. I go to the ivy post and part the leaves. The nest is clean, tidy and completely bare. Has the squirrel finally got the chick, or has he fledged?

I pace around the garden, whistling loudly. I pace and whistle; the minutes lengthen. Then, suddenly, the male robin shoots out of the tree that towers over the garden next door. He flies into the sycamore tree above mine, descending branch by branch until he finally arrives on the fence. He's singing all the while, with a strength I haven't heard for some time. Reassured, I stand and listen.

He's still singing when, the sky darkening, I go inside and look up the next stage of robins' reproductive cycle. It seems that once the chick has fledged, the mother's job is done until the next time. It falls to the father to spend a couple of weeks teaching his offspring how to survive. Then the two generations part ways so that each can establish his own territory.

The next day is a sunny Saturday. I'm having lunch outside when I feel the need to look round. A tiny brown bird is standing on a post nearby, gazing about, a green caterpillar held firmly in his beak. After a while, he turns his whole body to survey the scene sideways, and I clearly see the squat shape of a newly fledged robin. Then he takes off, flying low and straight, almost grazing my head as he makes for the bushes where he hatched.

It's a mad spring. The garden is full of fledglings, cheeping excitedly as they experiment with short, low flights from branch to fence and back again. There must be nests all around, in the trees and shrubs of the neighbouring gardens. Young greenfinches hog the birdfeeder, fighting amongst themselves. The fledglings seem fearless. Five tiny blackbirds dive around a squirrel who is crouched defensively in the branches of a shrub, cheeping loudly, dive-bombing him. The squirrel seems cowed, almost paralysed. I give up trying to read and watch as two fledglings sit side-by-side on the fence: one has something in his beak; the other grabs it and flies off. The victim takes off in pursuit.

Then I have empty-nest syndrome, quite literally. Most of the birds have gone; the garden is quiet.

In a sense, garden birds are a cultural construct, a product of the suburban sprawl which has drawn birds from the surrounding woodlands to human homes for only a hundred and fifty years. Add the British desire for a garden, no matter how small and urban, and the national habit of birdfeeding – the RSPB estimate that over half the adults in Britain feed birds – and you have the perfect environment for what naturalists call 'adaptive behaviour'.[107] As modern Britons, we go out of our way to bring birds into our lives, to have them close enough to watch their behaviour, to be awoken by their song.

Why do we crave their company so? Birder and writer Simon Barnes suggests the reasons go back to humanity's earliest experiences. The Aves were here with the dinosaurs before they evolved into songbirds; the world into which humans later came had an avian soundtrack. While the human sensitivity to rhythm probably derives from our mammalian heartbeat, our sense of melody may well have come from their song, which we imitated with voice and flutes, the first instruments. Birds, says Barnes, 'gave us the chants of our oldest ancestors; birds gave us folk songs; birds, ultimately, gave us Bach'.[108]

One evening in late spring, I look up from the stove to see a small fox sitting at the bottom of the kitchen steps, front paws neatly together. He is looking up at me with that serene blink that some say expresses a mammalian smile. I blink back, and carry on cooking.

The next weekend, I come down into the garden to find him sniffing the fleece I left on the sunlounger. He responds immediately when I tell him to leave it alone, retiring to the corner where he sits and chews some grass. He reappears regularly over the next few days, slipping under the fence in the corner and sniffing his way along the border to the kitchen steps. One day, he is accompanied by a tiny toddling cub who almost falls over as he tries to plough his way through the long grass that I have left uncut, Lammas-style. They approach the steps: Little Fox hunting something in the wood pile, while Toddling Cub is sniffing at the compost heap. I can see his ribs.

The butchers tease me rotten when I tentatively enquire about cheap cuts of chicken suitable for foxes. 'Arf! Arf! They got you! You'll never stop if you start,' says one. 'Lots round here do it,' says another: 'One feeds them jam sandwiches. Another won't leave 'em to go on 'oliday.' In vain I protest that I am not that kind of woman; I believe these foxes have been orphaned and intend to feed them for a short time while they are finding their feet. Handing me over a huge pack of chicken for ninety-nine pence, the butcher is having none of it: 'Shall we put aside two packs for you next week?'

I don't see the tiny cub again, but the older one is always in the garden, slipping in through the gaps in the fence that I had tried so hard, a few years before, to block with boards. I now consider the corner the fox's rightful home, his daytime living quarters, and put chicken and kitchen scraps there, along with a bowl of water. I am careful not to feed too much: the fox has probably adopted me because he is orphaned; if is going to survive, he needs to learn to scavenge effectively.

Soon it is difficult to go into the garden without drawing him out of his daytime bed on the other side of the fence. If I go out into the garden in the morning he appears, blinking sleepily, his fur crumpled. Then, paws neatly together, he sits down a few yards behind me and watches as I hang out the washing or cut back some ivy. I follow his gaze: he's fascinated by the drops of water and the sunlight bouncing off the glossy leaves. Things start to move around the garden overnight. First a sponge disappears from the shed and reappears at the other end of the garden. Then a brush is transported into the long grass. The cream umbrella I use as a sunshade is turned upside down and covered in pawprints. One afternoon, I look out to see the fox lying in a pool of sun, entirely absorbed in play with something. An hour later, he's still there. When he's gone, I go out to investigate. His new toy is a blue woollen mouse, with pink stripes and a chewsome tail. Over the following few days, the mouse moves around the garden until finally it is abandoned, having been separated from its tail.

As the spring turns to summer, a clear routine emerges. The fox sleeps through the morning unless he hears something interesting. He surfaces at lunchtime to spend the afternoon in the garden, playing or curling up in a patch of sunlight for a nap. Sometimes I throw his latest toy – an orange he has foraged or a frisbee I found in the shed – and he fetches it, taking it into his corner. I am careful not to touch him: he must retain his wildness and I must keep my caution. He retires again in the late afternoon for another rest, getting up in the early evening to wander slowly around the immediate area. The night times are the most active, patrolling and hunting in the farther woods and streets.

The fox often joins me for lunch, shooting into the garden at the sound of cutlery on plate, skidding to a halt and looking round as if to say, *Am I late? Have I missed anything?* One day he appears with a knotted carrier bag, heavy with some mushy foodstuff that had appeared on the grass overnight. While I eat food, he carries the bag from spot to spot, putting it down and eating from it every few minutes. In between times, he has a scratch or sits and watches me. I am pleased: he is learning to find food and bring it home for later.

One lunchtime, after I've thrown him several chips from my plate, the fox does a dance in the middle of the lawn. He leaps into the air, spinning his little frame around to land in a completely different place. A cursory lick of the sponge that is lying nearby and he's off again, jumping and whirling into a reverse pirouette. Then he hunkers down a few yards away and, ever so slowly, starts creeping towards me. Our eyes lock as he approaches the sunlounger where I am sitting, legs outstretched. His eyes hold a mix of fear and desire. I keep completely still as, ever so gently, he puts his mouth around the toe of my boot, enclosing it affectionately with his long snout. Then he's off again, hurling himself backwards through the air towards the border, where he bites the head off a giant daisy.

I know this is animal magic, a rare opportunity to get to know a wild creature who, for reasons to do with his history and my garden, is temporarily willing to trust a human. Foxes are famously secretive animals: perhaps centuries of being hunted has registered in their genes or collective memory, making them adept at hiding. In the 1970s, the zoologist David MacDonald went to extraordinary lengths to learn more about foxes, trapping them to attach radio-tracking devices and then following them, night after night, on their journeys across rural Oxfordshire. He hand-reared a cub so that she would cooperate with being observed once returned to the wild, a project which involved five months of sleeping with a small snout snuggled into his ear. Once she was old enough, the pair would go tracking together. 'I was rapturously immersed under Niff's tutelage', he recalls. 'She taught me to pause as we rounded a bend or topped a rise, to see before being seen; to cross slack ground below the icy wind; to circle downwind of anything unfamiliar'.[109] The experiment was successful, and several generations of hand-reared foxes, released back into the wild, yielded unprecedented observations of vulpine courtship, breeding habits and family dynamics.

Not for most of us, this super-human attempt to get to know the animal Other. Despite the presence of urban foxes in English towns and cities since the mid-twentieth century, we know little about their behaviour. Close encounters characterise them as vermin, child-maulers, a threat to the suburban order. And yet for some, contact with a non-domesticated mammal provides a glimpse of a world not shaped by human hand, with what remains of the wild on our doorstep, and we want to form some sort of relationship. But on what basis? I don't speak avian or vulpine; I only speak human. Yet I am beginning to feel that it's possible to have an understanding with a wild creature based on the sharing of place and the mutual experience of fear, enjoyment and curiosity.

As the summer goes on, the fox becomes increasingly curious to see how the human half lives, and makes repeated attempts to get into the flat. I am not keen on this venture: I know his love of footwear and textiles, and don't want to see prized items of my wardrobe disappear behind the fence. While I'm reading in the garden, he tries to sneak past me, making for the steps that lead up to the open kitchen door. I get up and follow him; he's halfway up the steps. When I call him back, he stops and makes as if to come down. Then, with another glance at the kitchen door, he mounts another step. 'No,' I tell him firmly, 'Come down.' Reluctantly, he obeys.

I have to laugh when later that day, as I'm stirring something on the stove, two furry ears appear over the top of the kitchen steps.

I am off to Gloucestershire, and will be away for some time. Concerned about Little Fox's nutritional needs – he is still quite small – I persuade my downstairs neighbour to put some dog biscuits over the fence every day that I am away. The pair are introduced. 'This is Uncle Matt,' I say brightly as the fox stares, ears up, from the far corner of the garden. ''Lo,' says Uncle Matt, weakly. The next task is to establish the new feeding place so that all my neighbour has to do is throw the food over the fence. I put biscuits out in the new place, and spend a couple of afternoons repeatedly pointing out the new picnic ground. Initially, the fox is reluctant: the new site means running past me and eating closer to the house. But I continue the training and, within a week, he has changed his habits and is happily crunching by the fence.

It is six weeks before I return, loaded with local ale for my long-suffering neighbour. The garden bears the signs of vulpine life: the washing line has been nipped in two, and the section of line with the pegs is lying in the middle of the grass. A few flowers have been decapitated. An empty pot of vanilla yoghurt lies by the fence: clearly the biscuits have been followed by a self-sourced pudding. I have brought Little Fox a stuffed mouse that used to belong to my mother's cat; I hope he will enjoy biting its tail off.

But apart from glimpses of a small vulpine form trotting down the pavement, I don't see the fox again. The mouse lies ignored by the sunlounger, its tail firmly on. Little Fox has grown and gone into wild independence, leaving me just memories and a few holes in the garden.

It's been enough. And there has been a teaching. I now see the value of things I previously wanted to expunge: the prolific, soil-sapping cypress next door is, from an avian point of view, excellent for perching and hiding. The creatures of my suburban garden have shown me how to come into the peace of wild things, as the poet Wendell Berry puts it.[110]

I don't think my experience is unusual. The BBC's Springwatch is one of the nation's most popular programmes, its hidden cameras bringing the secret life of the natural world into Britain's living rooms for a marathon outside broadcast each year. It's one of the myriad ways in which contemporary Britons demonstrate their biophilia, a trait so pronounced that it's tempting to say that the love of nature is emerging as the nation's secular religion, as British spirituality goes through another major shift.[111] Perhaps our feeding of wild creatures is our version of the sacrifices our ancestors used to make, a way of making a gift to the Other. Like the institutional religion it replaces, the new naturalism is a broad church, encompassing the scientism of the naturalists, the political passion of the eco-warriors and the overt spirituality of neo-paganism. Perhaps most importantly, it captures the quiet relationship with nature that people all over the land enjoy in their parks and gardens.

When I started out on this journey, I thought I would probably end up as I began, in the garden. I was pretty sure that faith in Britain was alive and well but, like any traveller who has only read about a place, I lacked a real sense of its sights, sounds and smells. It's been profoundly rooting, this tracing of the threads of meaning that bind people to their place and past, and it's clear to me now that authentic faith is shaped not so much by doctrine and creed as by birth and biography. So I'll go no more a-roving in the spiritual byways of my native land. This is enough for me, for now; this is as good a place to stop as any.

And, in any case, no one has the last word about God.[112]

NOTES

1   Alex Klaushofer, *Paradise Divided: A portrait of Lebanon*, Signal Books, 2007, p. 155.

2   See *The Spirit of Things Unseen: Belief in Post-Religious Britain*, published by the think-tank Theos in 2013. The research found that three-quarters of adults (seventy-seven per cent) believe that 'there are things in life that we simply cannot explain through science or any other means', and that over half the British public (fifty-four per cent) hold a spiritual belief such as the existence of a soul or life after death. Online at: http://www.theosthinktank.co.uk/files/files/Reports/Spirit%20of %20Things%20-%20Digital%20(update).pdf

3   This is what appears on the dust jacket of my edition; the book is listed as Grace Carlton, *Spade-work: The Story of Thomas Greenwood*, Hutchinson & Co, 1949.

4   Ibid. p. 44.

5   Thomas Greenwood, *Free Public Libraries: Their Organisation, Uses and Management*, Simpkin, Marshall & Co, 1886, vii.

6   Stephen Claye, *The Gospel of Common Sense*, Simpkin, Marshall, Hamilton Kent & Co, 1898.

7   Carlton, p. 138.

8   Ibid. p. 5.

9   Ibid. p. 27.

10 Ibid. p. 30.

11 Ibid. pp. 62–63.

12 The website ChartistAncestors at http://www.chartists.net. At the time of publication, the website was being rebuilt, so the original link cannot be provided.

13 Carlton, p. 18.

14   Ibid. p. 13.

15   Online at: self.gutenberg.org/article/whebn0000190007/john %20greenwood%20(divine)

16   Joyce Reason, *Barrowe and Greenwood: A Heritage Biography*, The Independent Press, 1961 and Leland H. Carlson (ed), *The Writings of John Greenwood 1587-1590*, published for the Sir Halley Stewart Trust by George Allen & Unwin, 1962.

17   Online at: http://www.royal.gov.uk/historyofthemonarchy/kingsandqueensofe ngland/thetudors/elizabethi.aspx

18   Online at: https://archive.org/details/byqueenproclamat00eliz

19   'Greenwood's Examination', quoted in Carlson, pp. 22–26 (some sections omitted). The examination is not dated but Carlson calculates it as taking place on 24 March 1588/9.

20   Quoted in Carlson, p. 18.

21   Ibid. p. 14.

22   *An Apology for the Nonconformists, shewing their reasons, both for their not conforming, and for their preaching publickly, though forbidden by law*, by John Troughton the Younger of Bicester, T. Parkhurst, 1681; *The Non-Conformist: an answer to the inquiry Why are you a Dissenter? Or Twenty reasons for dissenting from the Church of England* by Primitivus, Tebbutt, 1840; *A discourse of Secret Prayer. Together with two essays on prayer*, Henry Grove [Publisher not known], 1752; *The Nonconformist Conscience, considered as a social evil and a mischief-monger. By one who has had it*, Eveleigh Nash, 1903.

23   *The Rule of St Benedict in English*, The Liturgical Press, 1982, p. 29.

24   Ibid. p. 90.

25   Peter Levi, *The Frontiers of Paradise: A Study of Monks and Monasteries*, Athena, 1990, p. 15.

26   James A. Mohler, *The Heresy of Monasticism: The Christian*

Monks, Types and Anti-Types: An Historical Survey, Alba House, 1971, xvi.

27 'What matters is not the sacrifice, but the music', *The New Statesman*, 24 January 2008.

28 *The Rule of St Benedict*, p. 23.

29 'Introversion: Part 1: Recollection and quiet' in Eveline Underhill, *Mysticism: The Nature and Development of Spiritual Consciousness*, Oneworld, 1993.

30 St John of the Cross, *Dark Night of the Soul*, Dover, 2003, p. 61.

31 Ibid. p. 110.

32 Ibid. p. 88.

33 Ibid. p. 87 ff.

34 Ibid. pp. 99–102.

35 Online at: http://www.iep.utm.edu/eckhart/

36 Online at: http://www.newadvent.org/cathen/05274a.htm

37 This extract from *The Cloud of Unknowing* is published in Gordon L. Miller, *The Way of the English Mystics: An Anthology and Guide for Pilgrims*, Burns and Oates, 1996, p. 73.

38 Ibid. p. 73.

39 Mother Teresa, *Come Be My Light*, edited by Brian Kolodiejchuk, Rider, 2008, p. 233.

40 Ibid. pp. 187–188. I am unable to include the brief citation included in the original manuscript as The Mother Teresa Center refused permission to use it. This followed a correspondence in which MTC requested approval of this chapter to ensure that Mother Teresa was 'accurately' represented.

41 Levi, p. 183.

42 St Teresa, *The Life of Saint Teresa of Avila by Herself*, Penguin, 1957, p. 279.

43 Karen Armstrong, *The Spiral Staircase*, Harper Perennial, 2005.

44   See Susan Shields, *Mother Teresa's House of Illusions: How She Harmed her Helpers As Well As Those They 'Helped'*, published by the Council for Secular Humanism. Online at: http://www.secularhumanism.org/library/fi/shields_18_1.html

45   'The squalid truth behind the legacy of Mother Teresa', *New Statesman*, 22 August, 2005.

46   'Vicar is shocked by raids on holy tabernacles in village churches in East Challow and West Hanney', *The Oxford Times*, 3 March, 2009.

47   No record of that broadcast is available, but details of the Stanbrook move to Yorkshire can be found in *The Guardian*, 30 October, 2009.

48   The Northumbria Community Trust, *A Way for Living: Introducing the Rule of the Northumbria Community*, Collins, 2004, p. 8.

49   The Northumbria Community website. Online at: http://www.northumbriacommunity.org/who-we-are/introducing-the-community/the-nether-springs/

50   Esther de Waal, *Celtic Light: A Tradition Rediscovered*, HarperCollins, 1991, p. 82.

51   John O'Donohue, *Eternal Echoes: Exploring our Hunger to Belong*, Bantam, 1998, pp. 164–165.

52   Quoted in De Waal's *Celtic Light*, p. 53.

53   Verses five and six of 'Expressions of faith' of the Evening Prayer, in *Celtic Daily Prayer: Inspirational Prayers and Readings from the Northumbria Community*, Collins, 2005, pp 22–23.

54   Dietrich Bonhoeffer, *Life Together*, SCM Press, 1954, p. 16.

55   Ibid. p. 16.

56   See the chapter 'The solitary life' in Thomas Merton's *The Monastic Journey*, Sheldon Press, 1977.

57   Miller, p. 18.

58   Ibid. p. 28.

59   Ibid. p. 28.

60 Ibid. p. 101.

61 Sara Maitland, *A Book of Silence,* Granta, 2008.

62 See: 'I am a hermit' in *The Guardian,* 20 June 2009. Online at: http://www.theguardian.com/lifeandstyle/2009/jun/20/experience -hermit and 'Alone in a crowd', published in *The Tablet,* 17 October 2009.

63 'The Solitary Way of Life' at the Fellowship of Solitaries website. Online at: http://www.solitaries.org.uk/solitary-way-of-life.html.

64 Eve Baker, *Paths in Solitude,* St Paul's, 1995, p 100.

65 Duffy, Eamon, *The Stripping of the Altars: Traditional Religion in England 1400–1580,* Yale University Press, 2005.

66 Martin Palmer, *The Sacred History of Britain. Landscape, Myth and Power: The Forces That Have Shaped Britain's Spirituality,* Piatkus, 2002, pp. 174–177.

67 English Bible History. Online at: http://www.greatsite.com/timeline-english-bible-history/john-rogers.html.

68 John, 18:18

69 Martha Gellhorn, *Travels with Myself and Another,* Eland, 1983.

70 The Confraternity of St James. Online at: http://www.csj.org.uk/the-present-day-pilgrimage/pilgrim-numbers/

71 Laurie Dennett, 'Spirit Of The pilgrimage', The Confraternity of St James. Online at: http://www.csj.org.uk/the-present-day-pilgrimage/thoughts-and-essays/spirit-of-the-pilgrimage/

72 Ibid.

73 Reza Aslan, *No God but God: The Origins, Evolution and Future of Islam,* Arrow Books, 2006, p. 204.

74 Idries Shah, *The Sufis,* Octagon, 1977, p. 16.

75 Ibid. p. 25.

76   Aslan, p. 199.

77   Rumi, 'A great wagon', in *Selected Poems*, Penguin, 1999, p. 36.

78   Ibid. 'Unmarked boxes', p. 272.

79   Aslan, p. 199.

80   See 'The Labour WAGs: The Blair Babes who became the Women Against Gordon' in Mail Online, 5 June 2009. Online at: http://www.dailymail.co.uk/debate/article-1190711/The-Labour-WAGs-The-Women-Against-Gordon.html

81   See 'Minister backs new Muslim group', BBC Online, 9 July 2006. Online at: http://news.bbc.co.uk/1/hi/uk/5193402.stm

82   Sufi Zikr & Meditation. Online at: http://sufizikrmeditation.blogspot.co.uk/2009/12/sufi-zikr-meditation-live-webcast-maida.html.

83   See 'Muslim parents "banning children from music lessons"'. 1 July 2013, BBC Online. Online at: http://news.bbc.co.uk/local/london/hi/people_and_places/religion_and_ethics/newsid_8780000/8780567.stm.

84   Robert Macfarlane, *The Wild Places*, Granta, 2008.

85   Warwick, Alan R., *The Phoenix Suburb: A South London Social History*, The Blue Boar Press, 1973, p. 17.

86   Richard Mabey, *Gilbert White: A Biography of the Author of The Natural History of Selborne*, Profile, 2006, p. 5.

87   Ibid. p. 135.

88   Gilbert White, *The Natural History of Selborne*, Penguin, 1977.p. 33.

89   Ibid. pp. 15–16.

90   Professor Faraday is quoted in *The Story of Norwood* by J. B. Wilson and prepared by H. A. Wilson, The Norwood Society, 1990, p. 46.

91   P. L. Travers, *Mary Poppins*, Lovat Dickson, 1938, pp. 172–173.

92   Richard Jefferies, *The Story of my Heart: My Autobiography*, Green Books, 2002, pp. 18–19.

93   Ibid. p. 29.

94   Ibid. pp. 53–55.

95   Claye, p. 77.

96   Restall Orr, Emma, *Spirits of the Sacred Grove: The World of a Druid Priestess*, Thorsons, 1998.

97   According to the 2011 UK census, around 57,000 people identify themselves as pagan. The Order of Bards, Ovates and Druids interprets the data on the religion category of the census here: http://www.druidry.org/community/blog/2012/12/17/uk-2011-census-publishes-figures-druids.

98   Pliny, cited by Peter Beresford Ellis in *A Brief History of the Druids*, Robinson, 2002, p 61: 'The Druids – for so they call their magic – hold nothing more sacred than the mistletoe and the tree on which it grows provided it is an oak. They choose the oak to form groves, and they do not perform any religious rites without its foliage'.

99   Ibid. p. 11.

100 See Ronald Hutton, *The Druids*, Continuum, 2007.

101 William G. Gray, *Magical Ritual Methods*, Helios, 1969, pp. 7–8.

102 See Philip Carr-Gomm and Richard Heygate, *The Book of English Magic*, John Murray, 2009.

103 The basis for this version of the Ceridwen story comes from storyteller Adrian Beckingham, as told at Druid Camp. My notes were supplemented by internet research and – in the great tradition of oral storytelling – further adapted by me.

104 Kathy Jones, *Priestess of Avalon, Priestess of the Goddess: A Renewed Spiritual Path for the 21st Century*, Ariadne, 2006.

105 Greenwood, p. 117.

106 Rumi, 'Unmarked boxes', p. 272.

107 RSPB website. Online at: http://www.rspb.org.uk/makeahomeforwildlife/advice/helpingbirds

/feeding/

108 Simon Barnes, *Birdwatching with Your Eyes Closed*: An Introduction to Bird Song, Short Books, 2012, p. 72.

109 David Macdonald, *Running with the Fox*, Unwin Hyman, 1989, p. 61.

110 Wendell Berry, 'The peace of wild things', from *The Selected Poems of Wendell Berry*, Counterpoint, 1999.

111 Edward Wilson's influential biophilia thesis holds that there is an instinctive bond between humans and other living organisms. Edward O. Wilson, *Biophilia: The Human Bond with Other Species*, Harvard University Press, 1984.

112 I'm indebted to Karen Armstrong for this formulation, which was made during a talk at the Quaker Meeting House on 9 June 2010.

ACKNOWLEDGEMENTS

For a book about hidden forms of faith and those living on the edges of organised religion, it seems right to acknowledge that the influences for this project came from myriad sources, past and present, conscious and unconscious, from books and people. The subject matter meant that I kept an intensified form of the silence that writers tend to keep about work-in-progress, with the result that relatively few people were involved during its creation. Nonetheless, I've derived much support from friends who provided sources of encouragement and good counsel. The feedback provided by my beta-readers Sarah Chatwin, Jenny Pearson and Liz Porter has been invaluable.

Thanks, in addition to all the interviewees named in the book, go to Unitarian minister Andy Pakula.

At the time of my mother's death, the good people of Gloucestershire rallied round to an extent that was beyond the call of duty, notably the staff of Nightingale's Care. When, in that long slog that follows the death of a parent, I needed a neighbour, Di and Pete Canning were there. Julie Bowman – a traditional healer for our times – stepped in to provide support for my faltering health.

Ongoing thanks are due to libraries and librarians past and present – how would I have lived my life without them? I couldn't have done the research for this book without the British Library and the free access it provides to even the most obscure texts, nor could I have lived comfortably without Upper Norwood Library. It has continued to provide a wonderful service for the community in Crystal Palace during the most difficult of times.

Strange to say in a book about religion in a post-institutional age, but I remain thankful to the Church of England for being there.

I am grateful to Felicity Knight and Jack Wheatley for their gifts with proofreading and graphics. In coming to my aid with formatting, John Harvey and Rory O'Farrell of the OpenOffice community demonstrated that there is indeed altruism on the internet.

BIBLIOGRAPHY

Armstrong, Karen, *Through the Narrow Gate*, St Martins, 1981.

Armstrong, Karen, *The Spiral Staircase*, Harper Perennial, 2005.

Armstrong, Karen, *A History of God*, Vintage, 1999.

Armstrong, Karen, *Islam: A Short History*, Phoenix, 2001.

Armstrong, Karen, *The Battle for God: Fundamentalism in Judaism, Christianity and Islam*, HarperCollins, 2000.

Aslan, Reza, *No God but God: The Origins, Evolution and Future of Islam*, Arrow Books, 2006.

Baker, Eve, *Paths in Solitude*, St Paul's, 1995.

Barnes, Simon, *Birdwatching With Your Eyes Closed: An Introduction to Bird Song*, Short Books, 2012.

Bloomfield, Edward H., *The Opposition to the English Separatists 1570-1625, A Survey of the Polemical Literature Written by the Opponents to Separatism*, University Press of America, 1981.

Bolam, Gordon, Goring, Jeremy, Short H. L. and Thomas, Roger, *The English Presbyterians from Elizabethan puritanism to modern unitarianism, Beacon Press, 1968*.

Bonhoeffer, Dietrich, *Life Together*, SCM Press, 1954.

Bradley, Ian, *The Celtic Way*, Darton, Longman & Todd, 1993.

Bradley, Ian, *Believing in Britain: The Spiritual Identity of Britishness*, I. B. Tauris, 2007.

Brown, Mick, *The Spiritual Tourist*, Bloomsbury, 1998.

Brunton, Paul, *A Search in Secret India*, Rider, second edition, 1970. Carlson, Leland H. (ed) *The Writings of John Greenwood 1587-1590*, published for the Sir Halley Stewart Trust by George Allen & Unwin, 1962.

Carlton, Grace, *Spade-work: The Story of Thomas Greenwood*, Hutchinson & Co, 1949.

Carr-Gomm, Philip and Heygate, Richard, *The Book of English Magic*, John Murray, 2009.

Chittick, William C. *Sufism*, Oneworld, 2000.

Claye, Stephen, *The Gospel of Common Sense*, Simpkin, Marshall, Hamilton Kent & Co, 1898.

Colegate, Isabel, *A Pelican in the Wilderness: hermits, solitaries and recluses*, HarperCollins, 2002.

Chryssides, George, *The elements of Unitarianism*, Element, 1998.

Davie, Grace, *Religion in Britain since 1945: Believing without belonging*, Blackwell, 1994.

De Waal, Esther, *Seeking God: The Way of St Benedict*, Fount, 1984.

De Waal, Esther, *Celtic Light: A Tradition Rediscovered*, HarperCollins, 1991.

De Waal, Esther, *The Celtic Way of Prayer: The Recovery of the Religious Imagination*, Hodder & Stoughton, 1996.

Dicken, A. G., *The English Reformation*, B. T. Batsford, 1989.

Duffy, Eamon, *The Stripping of the Altars: Traditional Religion in England 1400-1580*, Yale University Press, 2005.

Ellis, Peter Berresford, *The Druids*, Robinson, 1994.

Ellis, Peter Berresford, *A Brief History of the Druids*, Robinson, 2002.

Ellis, Peter Berresford, *A Brief History of the Celts*, Robinson, 2003.

Evangelisti, Silvia, *Nuns: A History of Convent Life 1450-1700*, Oxford University Press, 2007.

Evans, G. R., *A Brief History of Heresy*, Blackwell, 2003.

Furlong, Monica, *C of E: The State It's In*, Hodder and Stoughton, 2000.

Greenwood, Thomas, *Free Public Libraries: Their Organisation, Uses and Management*, Simpkin, Marshall & Co, 1886, vii.

Greaves, Ron, *The Sufis of Britain: An Exploration of Muslim Identity*, Cardiff Academic Press, 2000.

James, William, *The Varieties of Religious Experience: A study in human nature*, Longmans, Green and Co, 1928.

Jefferies, Richard, *The Story of my Heart: My Autobiography*, Green Books, 2002.

Johnson, Dale A., *The changing shape of English nonconformity, 1825-1925*, Oxford University Press, 1999.

Kavanagh, Jennifer, *The World is our Cloister: A guide to the modern religious life*, O Books, 2007.

King, Ursula, *Christian Mystics: Their lives and legacies through the ages*, Routledge, 2004.

Harvey, Andrew, *The Direct Path*, Rider, 2000.

Hostler, John, *Unitarianism*, The Hibbert Trust, 1981.

Hutton, Ronald, *Stations of the Sun: A History of the Ritual Year in Britain*, Oxford University Press, 1996.

Hutton, Ronald, *The Druids*, Continuum, 2007.

Levi, Peter, *The Frontiers of Paradise: A Study of Monks and Monasteries*, Athena, 1990.

Mabey, Richard, *Gilbert White: A biography of the author of The Natural History of Selborne*, Profile, 2006.

Macdonald, David, *Running with the Fox*, Unwin Hyman, 1989.

Maitland, Sara, *A Book of Silence*, Granta, 2008.

Merton, Thomas, *Contemplation in a World of Action*, University of Notre Dame Press, 1948.

Merton, Thomas, (ed) Patrick Hart, *The Monastic Journey*, Sheldon Press, 1977.

Miller, Gordon, L., *The Way of the English Mystics: An Anthology and Guide for Pilgrims,* Burns and Oates, 1996.

James A. Mohler, *The Heresy of Monasticism: The Christian Monks, Types and Anti-Types: An Historical Survey*, Alba House, 1971.

The Northumbria Community Trust, *Celtic Daily Prayer, Inspirational prayers and readings from the Northumbria Community,* Collins, 2005.

O'Donohue, *Eternal Echoes: Exploring Our Hunger To Belong,* Bantam, 1998.

Palmer, Martin, *The Sacred History of Britain. Landscape, myth and power: The forces that have shaped Britain's spirituality,* Piatkus, 2002.

Ramadan, Tariq, *Western Muslims and the Future of Islam,* Oxford University Press, 2004.

Reason, Joyce, *Barrowe and Greenwood: A Heritage biography,* The Independent Press, 1961.

Restall Orr, Emma, *Spirits of the Sacred Grove: The World of a Druid Priestess,* Thorsons, 1998.

Restall Orr, Emma, *Living with Honour: A Pagan Ethics,* O Books, 2007.

Rogerson, Barnaby, *The Heirs of the Prophet Muhammad And the Roots of the Sunni-Shia Schism,* Abacus, 2006.

Rumi, *Selected Poems*, Penguin, 1999.

Sardar, Ziauddin, *Desperately Seeking Paradise: Journeys of a sceptical Muslim*, Granta, 2005.

Shah, Idries, *The Sufis*, Octagon Press, 1977.

St Benedict of Nursia, *The Rule of St Benedict in English*, The Liturgical Press, 1982.

St John of the Cross, *Dark Night of the Soul,* Dover, 2003.

St Teresa, *The Life of Saint Teresa of Avila by Herself,* Penguin, 1957.

Stuart, Jim, *Manifesto for Silence: Confronting the politics and culture of noise*, Edinburgh University Press, 2007.

Tacey, David, *The Spirituality Revolution: the emergence of contemporary spirituality*, HarperCollins, 2003.

Teresa, Mother, *Come Be My Light,* (ed) Brian Kolodiejchuk, Rider, 2007.

Thompson, David M., *Nonconformity in the Nineteenth Century,* Routledge, 1972.

Underhill, Evelyn, *The Essentials of Mysticism and Other Essays,* Dent, 1920.

Underhill, Evelyn, *Mysticism: The Nature and Development of Spiritual Consciousness,* Oneworld, 1993.

Ward, Keith, *God: A Guide for the Perplexed*, Oneworld, 2002.

Watts, Michael R., 'The dissenters', Vol 1, *From the Reformation to the French Revolution*, Clarendon Press, 1978.

Warwick, Alan R., *The Phoenix Suburb: A South London Social History*, The Blue Boar Press, 1973.

Watts, Michael R., 'The dissenters', Vol 1, *From the Reformation to the French Revolution*, Clarendon Press, 1978.

Watts, Michael R., 'The expansion of evangelical nonconformity', Vol 2, *From the Reformation to the French Revolution*, Clarendon Press, 1978.

White, Gilbert, *The Natural History of Selborne*, Penguin, 1977.

Wilson, A. N., *God's Funeral*, Abacus, 2000.

Wilson J. B. and prepared by H. A. Wilson, *The Story of Norwood,* The Norwood Society, 1990, p. 46.

Alex Klaushofer is a journalist writing on social affairs and religion. Her work on Britain and the Middle East has appeared in a variety of publications such as the *Guardian, Observer* and *Daily Telegraph.* She is the author of *Paradise Divided,* a book of travel writing about Lebanon. In a previous life she gained a PhD in philosophy and taught the subject for several years.

You can visit her website at www.alexklaushofer.com and find her blog on subjects relating to the book – our relationship to place, nature and contemporary forms of faith and meaning – at www.thesecretlifeofgod.net. She tweets under @alexklaushofer.

In Search of Glastonbury, a short travelogue and companion piece to *The Secret Life of God,* is available as an ebook.

CPSIA information can be obtained at www.ICGtesting.com
Printed in the USA
LVOW07s0407281015

459962LV00004B/435/P